Bulgarian Verbs

Antoaneta Getova
Penka Novakova

Bulgarian Verbs

Antoaneta Getova
Penka Novakova

2009

Bulgarian Verbs

All inquiries should be directed to:

Dunwoody Press

6525 Belcrest Rd., Suite 460

Hyattsville, MD 20782, U.S.A.

ISBN: 978-1-931546-65-2

Library of Congress Control Number: 2009930353

Printed and bound in the United States of America

Table of Contents

Preface

Bulgarian like most Indo-European languages has a complex verb system which is characterized by two aspects, nine tenses, four moods and two voices. Although the Bulgarian verb has a rather complicated paradigm, many of the forms are rarely used. The purpose of this book is to provide a practical guide to Bulgarian verb conjugations by omitting the forms that are not frequently used and hence simplifying the verb paradigm.

The book contains 250 of the most commonly used verbs translated into English and conjugated in seven tenses and three moods. Each verb's paradigm is presented on a separate page in a table. The conjugated verbs are in alphabetical order. In addition to this, the book provides an overview of the Bulgarian verb system and an index with 500 less frequently used verbs with a reference to the appropriate conjugation pattern.

This book will be beneficial for anyone who studies the Bulgarian language at the novice, intermediate or advanced level. The handbook on Bulgarian verbal conjugation is self-explanatory, easy to navigate and targets a self-studying audience. It will be extremely useful for all who teach Bulgarian since there are no other practical guides for Bulgarian conjugations available. And last but not least the book will be valuable for all Bulgarians who are looking for precision in mastering their mother tongue.

The authors would like to thank Dunwoody Press for publishing this book and especially Thomas Creamer, Director of the Language Research Center at McNeil Technologies, Inc., for his continuous support and invaluable linguistic comments and suggestions.

Abbreviations

f	feminine
m	masculine
n	neuter
imperf	imperfective (aspect)
perf	perfective (aspect)
pl	plural
reflex	reflexive
sg	singular

Bulgarian Verb System Overview

In this book, we present the most frequently used grammatical forms: 7 verb tenses (out of 9), 3 moods (out of 4), as well as the past active and the past passive participles.

The main grammatical characteristics of the Bulgarian verb are **person, number, tense, aspect, mood,** and **voice.**

Person and Number

Bulgarian verbs have different endings for the first, second, and third person, singular and plural. There is no infinitive in Bulgarian so the form for **first person, singular, present tense** is considered the base form.

Singular				
1st person	**аз**	обича**м**	*I*	*like/love*
2nd person	**ти**	обича**ш**	*you*	
3rd person	**той**		*he*	
	тя	обича	*she*	*likes/loves*
	то		*it*	
Plural				
1st person	**ние**	обича**ме**	*we*	*like/love*
2nd person	**вие**	обича**те**	*you*	
3rd person	**те**	обича**т**	*they*	

In Bulgarian, the use of personal pronouns along with verbs is not mandatory since the grammatical information for person and number is indicated by the verb ending.

Обича**м** шоколад. — Обича**ш** ли шоколад?
I *like chocolate.* — *Do* ***you*** *like chocolate?*

In a formal setting, the second person plural form of the verb (обича**те**) is often used to address a single person. This is to express politeness when talking to strangers, to people whom we don't know very well, or in a business setting.

Обича**те** ли шоколад? (polite question to one person)
Do you like chocolate?

Aspect of the Verb

Aspect is a difficult concept to understand because it is frequently identified with the concept of tense.

There are two aspects in Bulgarian - **imperfective** and **perfective**. The two aspects add nuances of duration and completion to the verb. **Imperfective aspect** shows incomplete, continuous, or repetitive action. **Perfective aspect**, on the other hand, shows that the action is performed only once and is completed.

Imperfective	вземам	*take, borrow*
Perfective	взема	*take, borrow*

Many verbs in Bulgarian have both imperfective and perfective forms. The two aspects differ in their usage. The imperfective aspect is often used in the **present** and **past continuous tenses** (see also section 2.3.2).

Вземам такси.	*I am taking a taxi.* (incomplete, continuous action)
Вземам такси всеки ден.	*I take a taxi every day.* (incomplete, repetitive action)
Вземах такси.	*I was taking a taxi.* (repetitive action in the past)

The perfective aspect is used more often in the **past simple** and **future tenses.**

Взех такси.	*I took a taxi.*
Ще взема такси.	*I will take a taxi.*

Tenses

There are nine verb tenses in Bulgarian: present, **past simple, past continuous, present perfect, past perfect, future, future in the past, future perfect, and future perfect in the past.**

Present Tense

According to the ending of the verb in the **third person singular present tense**, we recognize three conjugations: **E-conjugation, И-conjugation, and А/Я-conjugation.**

		E-conjugation	И-conjugation	А/Я-conjugation	
аз	*(I)*	чета *read*	вървя *walk*	обичам *like*	донасям *bring*
ти	*(you)*	четеш	вървиш	обичаш	донасяш
той, тя, то	*(he, she, it)*	чете	върви	обича	донася
ние	*(we)*	четем	вървим	обичаме	донасяме
вие	*(you)*	четете	вървите	обичате	донасяте
те	*(they)*	четат	вървят	обичат	донасят

About 70% of Bulgarian verbs belong to the А/Я-conjugation; most of them are imperfective verbs.

Past Simple and Past Continuous

The **past simple** and the **past continuous tenses** can be formed from both the perfective and imperfective forms of the verbs. However when the verb has both imperfective and perfective aspects the perfective form is more frequently used in the past simple wherein the imperfective is used in the **past continuous tense**.

Endings for the past simple tense: Endings for the past continuous tense:

аз	*(I)*	-х	-х
ти	*(you)*	-	-ше
той, тя, то	*(he, she, it)*	-	-ше
ние	*(we)*	-хме	-хме
вие	*(you)*	-хте	-хте
те	*(they)*	-ха	-ха

There are different models for forming the **past simple tense** according to the **vowel** preceding the **endings –х/-хме/-хте/-ха**.

a) verbs from **E-conjugation** take **endings -ах, -ях, -ех, -ох,** and **–ух.**

Verbs (Present tense)		разбера *understand*	успея *succeed*	приема *accept*	чета *read*	чуя *hear*
Endings		**-ах**	**-ях**	**-ех**	**-ох**	**-ух**
аз	*(I)*	разбр**ах**	усп**ях**	при**ех**	чет**ох**	чу**х**
ти	*(you)*	разбра	успя	прие	чете	чу
той, тя, то	*(he, she, it)*	разбра	успя	прие	чете	чу
ние	*(we)*	разбр**ахме**	усп**яхме**	при**ехме**	чет**охме**	чу**хме**
вие	*(you)*	разбр**ахте**	усп**яхте**	при**ехте**	чет**охте**	чу**хте**
те	*(they)*	разбр**аха**	усп**яха**	при**еха**	чет**оха**	чу**ха**

Note the following phonetic changes:

- verbs with suffix **–ера** in present tense elide the vowel **–е** in past simple tense (разбера – разбр**ах**).

- verbs with suffix **–ея** in present tense elide the vowel **–е** in past simple tense (успея – усп**ях**).

- verbs with suffix **–ма** in present tense omit **-ма** in past simple tense (прие**ма** – при**ех**).

- the **-ох** ending changes to **–е** in second and third person singular.

b) verbs from **И-conjugation** take **endings –их and –ях.**

Verbs (Present tense)		намаля *decrease*	вървя *walk*
Endings		**-их**	**-ях**
аз	*(I)*	намал**их**	върв**ях**
ти	*(you)*	намал**и**	върв**я**
той, тя, то	*(he, she, it)*	намал**и**	върв**я**
ние	*(we)*	намал**ихме**	върв**яхме**
вие	*(you)*	намал**ихте**	върв**яхте**
те	*(they)*	намал**иха**	върв**яха**

c) verbs from **А/Я-conjugation** take **endings –ах** and **-ях.**

Verbs (Present tense)		използвам *use*	вечерям *dine*
Endings		**-ах**	**-ях**
аз	*(I)*	използв**ах**	вечер**ях**
ти	*(you)*	използва	всчеря
той, тя, то	*(he, she, it)*	използва	вечеря
ние	*(we)*	използв**ахме**	вечер**яхме**
вие	*(you)*	използв**ахте**	вечер**яхте**
те	*(they)*	използв**аха**	вечер**яха**

Present Perfect and Past Perfect

The **present perfect** tense is formed by the **present tense** of the auxiliary verb **съм** (*be*) and the **past active participle** of the **verb** (see section 2.5.2). The **past perfect** tense is formed by the **past forms** of the auxiliary verb **съм** and the **past active participle** of the verb.

		Present Perfect	Past Perfect
аз	(*I*)	**съм** чел/чела/чело *have read*	**бях** чел/чела/чело *had read*
ти	(*you*)	**си** чел/чела/чело	**беше** чел/чела/чело
той	(*he*)	**е** чел	**беше** чел
тя	(*she*)	**е** чела	**беше** чела
то	(*it*)	**е** чело	**беше** чело
ние	(*we*)	**сме** чели	**бяхме** чели
вие	(*you*)	**сте** чели	**бяхте** чели
те	(*they*)	**са** чели	**бяха** чели

When used as part of the complex tenses (present perfect, past perfect, future perfect, and future perfect in the past) the participle agrees in gender and number with the subject. Note that there are different forms for **masculine, feminine** and **neuter singular**. The forms for the **masculine, feminine,** and **neuter plural** are the same (**чели**).

Future and Future in the Past

The **future** tense is formed by adding the particle **ще** (for positive forms) or **няма да** (for negative forms) in front of the **present forms** of the verb.

Positive	Negative
Ще чета.	Няма да чета.
I will read.	*I will not read.*

The **future in the past** is formed by adding **щях/щеше/щяхме/щяхте/щяха да** (*would*, for positive forms) and **нямаше да** (*would not*, for negative forms) in front of the **present tense** of the verb.

		Future in the Past Positive	Future in the Past Negative
аз	(*I*)	щях да чета *would read*	нямаше да чета *would not read*
ти	(*you*)	щеше да четеш	нямаше да четеш
той, тя, то	(*he, she, it*)	щеше да чете	нямаше да чете
ние	(*we*)	щяхме да четем	нямаше да четем
вие	(*you*)	щяхте да четете	нямаше да четете
те	(*they*)	щяха да четат	нямаше да четат

The future in the past tense often appears in conditional sentences.

Ако имах време, щях да чета повече.
If I had time I would read more.

Future Perfect and Future Perfect in the Past

The **future perfect** tense is formed by the particle **ще** (for future tense) and the forms for the present perfect tense of the verb (**съм чел, си чел**). The **future perfect in the past** is formed by adding **щях/щеше/щяхме/щяхте/щяха да** to the forms of the **present perfect tense** of the verb (**съм чел, си чел**).

		Future Perfect	**Future Perfect in the Past**
аз	(*I*)	ще съм чел/чела/чело *would have read*	щях да съм чел/чела/чело *would have had read*
ти	(*you*)	ще си чел/чела/чело	щеше да си чел/чела/чело
той	(*he*)	ще е чел	щеше да е чел
тя	(*she*)	ще е чела	щеше да е чела
то	(*it*)	ще е чело	щеше да е чело
ние	(*we*)	ще сме чели	щяхме да сме чели
вие	(*you*)	ще сте чели	щяхте да сте чели
те	(*they*)	ще са чели	щяха да са чели

These two verb tenses are difficult to form and are not frequently used so they are not presented in the verb conjugations.

Mood

There are 4 moods in Bulgarian: **indicative, conditional, imperative,** and **non-witness.**

The indicative mood presents actions as actual facts (i.e. something that happened, is happening, or will happen).

The conditional mood expresses unreal and hypothetical actions and events which could happen only if certain conditions are met.

> Бих чел повече, ако имах време.
> *I would read more if I had time.*

The conditional mood is formed by **conditional forms** of the verb **съм (бих/би/бихме/бихте/биха** *would***)** and the **past active participle** of the main verb.

аз	бих чел/чела/чело	*I would read*
ти	би чел/чела/чело	*you would read*
той	би чел	*he would read*
тя	би чела	*she would read*
то	би чело	*it would read*
ние	бихме чели	*we would read*
вие	бихте чели	*you would read*
те	биха чели	*they would read*

Apart from their conditional meaning, these forms are often used in Bulgarian to express a polite request.

> Бихте ли изпратили писмото?
> *Could you send the letter?*

The imperative mood presents an action as a command or request. Forms are only in the 2nd person singular and plural. Singular endings are **-и** after a consonant, and **-й** after a vowel. Plural endings are **-ете** after a consonant and **-йте** after a vowel.

	Perfective	Imperfective	
Sg	взем**и**	взема**й**	*take*
Pl	взем**ете**	взема**йте**	*take*

There are a few exceptions to this rule.

	Sg	Pl	
дойда	ела	елате	*come*
ям	яж	яжте	*eat*
държа	дръж	дръжте	*hold*

Perfective verbs do not have negative imperative forms. The negative is formed only from imperfective verbs.

	Positive (Imperfective/Perfective)		Negative (only Imperfective)	
Sg	вземай/вземи	*take*	не вземай	*do not take*
Pl	вземайте/вземете	*take*	не вземайте	*do not take*

The non-witness mood shows that the speaker has not witnessed the action he is talking about or has doubts about its authenticity. Its forms are the **past active participle** in the **third person singular** or **plural**. It is often used by speakers/writers telling stories which they have not witnessed.

Той ходил.	*He has (allegedly) gone.*
Те ходили.	*They have (allegedly) gone.*

Voice

Active and Passive Voice

A verb is in the **active voice** when the subject is the agent or actor of the verb. When the subject is the patient or the target of the action, it is said to be in the **passive voice**.

Архитектът завърши проекта.
The architect completed the project.

The verb **завърши** (*completed*) exemplifies the active voice, whereas in

Проектът е завършен от архитекта.
The project has been completed by the architect.

The verbal phrase **е завършен** (*has been completed*) is passive.

The past passive participle is used to form the passive voice (see section 2.5.2).

Past Active and Past Passive Participles

The past active participle of the verb is formed by replacing the ending –**х** of the **first person singular past simple tense** form with the suffix –**л**. Past active participles have different forms for gender and number (see section 2.3.3).

Past Simple Tense	M	F	N	Pl	
ходих	ходил	ходил**а**	ходил**о**	ходил**и**	*gone*

The past passive participle is formed by replacing the ending **-х** of the form for the **first person singular past simple tense** with the suffixes **-н, -ен,** or **-т.**

Past Simple Tense	M	F	N	Pl	
опитах	опита**н**	опита**на**	опита**но**	опита**ни**	*tasted*
внесох	внесе**н**	внесе**на**	внесе**но**	внесе**ни**	*imported*
взех	взе**т**	взе**та**	взе**то**	взе**ти**	*taken*

Only transitive verbs have past passive participles. The past passive participle has gender and number similar to the grammatical characteristics of adjectives. It is used to form the passive voice or it functions as a modifier.

Reflexivity

Reflexivity in Bulgarian is a lexical and grammatical category. Reflexive particles **се** and **си** added to the verb can change the meaning of the verb (**lexical** function) or the subject-object relations in the sentence (**grammatical** function).

Some reflexive verbs such as **усмихвам се** (*smile*), **страхувам се** (*be afraid),* and **въобразявам си** *(imagine)* are always used with reflexive particles. They usually express emotions or feelings. In other cases, the reflexive particles, when added to the verbs, change their meanings completely (**lexical** function).

отивам *(go)*	отивам си *(go home)*
връщам *(return, give back)*	връщам се *(go back, go home)*
смея *(have the courage, dare)*	смея се *(laugh)*

The **grammatical** function of the reflexive particles most often is **reflexive**, i.e. the **subject** and the **object** of the action are the same.

Active		Reflexive	
мия **го**	*I wash him.*	мия **се**	*I wash (myself).*
обличам **го**	*I dress him.*	обличам **се**	*I get dressed.*
говоря **му**	*I talk to him.*	говоря **си**	*I talk to myself.*

Word order is very important when using reflexive verbs. The reflexive particles **се** and **си** cannot be placed at the beginning of the sentence.

Връщам **се** довечера.	*(I) am coming back tonight.*
Спомням **си** всичко.	*(I) remember everything.*

When the sentence starts with another word, **се** or **си** are in front of the verb.

Той **се** връща довечера	*He is coming back tonight.*
Тя **си** спомня всичко.	*She remembers everything.*

The forms for the present perfect tense of reflexive verbs are of particular challenge. Usually the particles **се** or **си** are after the auxiliary verb **съм** (*be*), but in the 3rd person singular they are placed before the forms of the auxiliary verb.

Аз **съм се** чудил.	Чудил **съм се**.	*I have wondered.*
Той **се е** чудил.	Чудил **се е.**	*He has wondered.*

How the Verbs Are Presented

The verbs are translated into English on every page. If there are more than one meanings of the verb which are synonymous they will be separated by comma.

лизам/вляза	*enter, come in*

If the meanings are not synonymous then they will be separated by semicolons.

включвам/включа	*turn on; include*

Verbs with two aspects

The two aspects of the verb differ in their usage mostly in the present, past simple and past continuous tenses. The verbs that have two aspects like **включвам/включа** (*turn on; include*) are particularly difficult to conjugate because of the vast variety of forms (two forms for each person). We attempt to simplify the conjugation of the verbs with two aspects by omitting the rarely used (or completely unused) forms. The imperfective aspect is always used in the present tense (**включвам**) and used most often in the past continuous tense (**включвах**). In contrast to this the perfective verbs are more often used in the past simple tense (**включих**). That is why we chose to present the forms for present and past continuous of the imperfective verb and the forms for past simple of the perfective verb. The forms for both aspects, imperfective and perfective, will be conjugated in the future, future in the past, present perfect, past perfect tenses, the conditional and imperative moods. The past active participles when used as part of the complex tenses (present perfect and past perfect) and the conditional mood agree in gender and number with the subject of the action.

Аз съм че**л**. (M)	*I (male) have read.*
Аз съм чел**а**. (F)	*I (female) have read.*
Ние сме чел**и** (Pl)	*We (male and/or female) have read.*

We do not present the forms for feminine and neuter of the complex tenses and the conditional mood in the conjugations since the forms of the past active participles are shown right above the tenses and can be replaced when needed.

Below is the paradigm of the verb with two aspects (**включвам/включа** *turn on; include*) as it will be presented in the book.

включвам/включа; turn on, plug in; include

	Present	**Past Simple**	**Past Continuous**
аз	включвам	включих	включвах
ти	включваш	включи	включваше
той	включва	включи	включваше
ние	включваме	включихме	включвахме
вие	включвате	включихте	включвахте
те	включват	включиха	включваха

	Future	**Future in the Past**
	(For negative, replace **ще** with **няма да**)	(For negative, replace **щях/щеше/щяхме/щяхте/щяха** with **нямаше**)
аз	ще включвам/включа	щях да включвам/включа
ти	ще включваш/включиш	щеше да включваш/включиш
той	ще включва/включи	щеше да включва/включи
ние	ще включваме/включим	щяхме да включваме/включим
вие	ще включвате/включите	щяхте да включвате/включите
те	ще включват/включат	щяха да включват/включат

Past Active Participles

M	**F**	**N**	**Pl**
включвал/ включил	включвала/включила	включвало/включило	включвали/ включили

	Present Perfect	**Past Perfect**
аз	съм включвал/включил	бях включвал/включил
ти	си включвал/включил	беше включвал/включил
той	е включвал/включил	беше включвал/включил
ние	сме включвали/включили	бяхме включвали/включили
вие	сте включвали/включили	бяхте включвали/включили
те	са включвали/включили	бяха включвали/включили

	Conditional Mood	**Imperative Mood**	
аз	бих включвал/включил	**Positive**	**Negative**
ти	би включвал/включил	включвай/включи	не включвай
той	би включвал/включил		
ние	бихме включвали/включили		
вие	бихте включвали/включили	включвайте/включете	не включвайте
те	биха включвали/включили		

Past Passive Participles

M	**F**	**N**	**Pl**
включван/ включен	включвана/включена	включвано/включено	включвани/ включени

Verbs with one aspect

Verbs like **ходя** (*go, walk, hike*) that have forms for only one aspect will be presented in all seven tenses and three moods as shown below.

ходя; go, walk, hike

	Present	**Past Simple**	**Past Continuous**
аз	ходя	ходих	ходех
ти	ходиш	ходи	ходеше
той	ходи	ходи	ходеше
ние	ходим	ходихме	ходехме
вие	ходите	ходихте	ходехте
те	ходят	ходиха	ходеха

	Future	**Future in the Past**
	(For negative, replace **ще** with **няма да**)	(For negative, replace **щях/щеше/щяхме/щяхте/щяха** with **нямаше**)
аз	ще ходя	щях да ходя
ти	ще ходиш	щеше да ходиш
той	ще ходи	щеше да ходи
ние	ще ходим	щяхме да ходим
вие	ще ходите	щяхте да ходите
те	ще ходят	щяха да ходят

Past Active Participles

M	**F**	**N**	**Pl**
ходил	ходила	ходило	ходили

	Present Perfect	**Past Perfect**
аз	съм ходил	бях ходил
ти	си ходил	беше ходил
той	е ходил	беше ходил
ние	сме ходили	бяхме ходили
вие	сте ходили	бяхте ходили
те	са ходили	бяха ходили

	Conditional Mood	**Imperative Mood**	
аз	бих ходил	**Positive**	**Negative**
ти	би ходил	ходи	не ходи
той	би ходил		
ние	бихме ходили		
вие	бихте ходили	ходете	не ходете
те	биха ходили		

Past Passive Participles

M	**F**	**N**	**Pl**
N/A	N/A	N/A	N/A

A few verbs like **зная** (*know*) have forms for past simple tense that sound rather strange and are not used in contemporary Bulgarian. These verbs will be presented only with their forms for past continuous tense that is used for both past simple and past continuous meanings.

зная; *know*

	Present	**Past Simple = Past Continuous**
аз	зная	знаех
ти	знаеш	знаеше
той	знае	знаеше
ние	знаем	знаехме
вие	знаете	знаехте
те	знаят	знаеха

	Future	**Future in the Past**
	(For negative, replace **ще** with **няма да**)	(For negative, replace **щях/щеше/щяхме/щяхте/щяха** with **нямаше**)
аз	ще зная	щях да зная
ти	ще знаеш	щеше да знаеш
той	ще знае	щеше да знае
ние	ще знаем	щяхме да знаем
вие	ще знаете	щяхте да знаете
те	ще знаят	щяха да знаят

Past Active Participles

M	**F**	**N**	**Pl**
Знаел	знаела	знаело	знаели

	Present Perfect	**Past Perfect**
аз	съм знаел	бях знаел
ти	си знаел	беше знаел
той	е знаел	беше знаел
ние	сме знаели	бяхме знаели
вие	сте знаели	бяхте знаели
те	са знаели	бяха знаели

	Conditional Mood	**Imperative Mood**	
		Positive	**Negative**
аз	бих знаел		
ти	би знаел	знай	не знай
той	би знаел		
ние	бихме знаели		
вие	бихте знаели	знайте	не знайте
те	биха знаели		

Past Passive Participles

M	**F**	**N**	**Pl**
N/A	N/A	N/A	N/A

Reflexive verbs

We present two groups of reflexive verbs with particle **се** or **си** in the book:

1) verbs that can be used both as reflexive and non-reflexive

Глезя детето.	*I spoil the child.*
Глезя се.	*I behave badly.*

In these cases, **се** and **си** are placed in parentheses after the verb.

глезя (се)

2) verbs that are only reflexive

усмихвам/усмихна се	*smile*
влюбвам/влюбя се	*fall in love*

Note that the reflexive particles **се** and **си** are omitted in the forms for the past active and past passive participles.

Below is the paradigm of the verb усмихвам се (smile) as it is presented in the book

усмихвам се/усмихна се; *smile*

	Present	**Past Simple**	**Past Continuous**
аз	се усмихвам	се усмихнах	се усмихвах
ти	се усмихваш	се усмихна	се усмихваше
той	се усмихва	се усмихна	се усмихваше
ние	се усмихваме	се усмихнахме	се усмихвахме
вие	се усмихвате	се усмихнахте	се усмихвахте
те	се усмихват	се усмихнаха	се усмихваха

	Future	**Future in the Past**
	(For negative, replace **ще** with **няма да**)	(For negative, replace **щях/щеше/щяхме/щяхте/щяха** with **нямаше**)
аз	ще се усмихвам/усмихна	щях да се усмихвам/усмихна
ти	ще се усмихваш/усмихнеш	щеше да се усмихваш/усмихнеш
той	ще се усмихва/усмихне	щеше да се усмихва/усмихне
ние	ще се усмихваме/усмихнем	щяхме да се усмихваме/усмихнем
вие	ще се усмихвате/усмихнете	щяхте да се усмихвате/усмихнете
те	ще се усмихват/усмихнат	щяха да се усмихват/усмихнат

Past Active Participles

M	**F**	**N**	**Pl**
усмихвал/ усмихнал	усмихвала/усмихнала	усмихвало/усмихнало	усмихвали/ усмихнали

	Present Perfect	**Past Perfect**
аз	съм се усмихвал/усмихнал	бях се усмихвал/усмихнал
ти	си се усмихвал/усмихнал	беше се усмихвал/усмихнал
той	се е усмихвал/усмихнал	беше се усмихвал/усмихнал
ние	сме се усмихвали/усмихнали	бяхме се усмихвали/усмихнали
вие	сте се усмихвали/усмихнали	бяхте се усмихвали/усмихнали
те	са се усмихвали/усмихнали	бяха се усмихвали/усмихнали

	Conditional Mood	**Imperative Mood**	
аз	бих се усмихвал/усмихнал	**Positive**	**Negative**
ти	би се усмихвал/усмихнал	усмихвай/усмихни се	не се усмихвай
той	би се усмихвал/усмихнал		
ние	бихме се усмихвали/усмихнали		
вие	бихте се усмихвали/усмихнали	усмихвайте/усмихнете се	не се усмихвайте
те	биха се усмихвали/усмихнали		

Past Passive Participles

M	**F**	**N**	**Pl**
N/A	N/A	N/A	N/A

Bulgarian Verbs

Bulgarian Verbs

1) **атакувам**; *attack*

	Present	**Past Simple**	**Past Continuous**
аз	атакувам	атакувах	атакувах
ти	атакуваш	атакува	атакуваше
той	атакува	атакува	атакуваше
ние	атакуваме	атакувахме	атакувахме
вие	атакувате	атакувахте	атакувахте
те	атакуват	атакуваха	атакуваха

	Future	**Future in the Past**
	(For negative, replace **ще** with **няма да**)	(For negative, replace **щях/щеше/щяхме/щяхте/щяха** with **нямаше**)
аз	ще атакувам	щях да атакувам
ти	ще атакуваш	щеше да атакуваш
той	ще атакува	щеше да атакува
ние	ще атакуваме	щяхме да атакуваме
вие	ще атакувате	щяхте да атакувате
те	ще атакуват	щяха да атакуват

Past Active Participles

M	**F**	**N**	**Pl**
атакувал	атакувала	атакувало	атакували

	Present Perfect	**Past Perfect**
аз	съм атакувал	бях атакувала
ти	си атакувал	беше атакувал
той	е атакувал	беше атакувал
ние	сме атакували	бяхме атакували
вие	сте атакували	бяхте атакували
те	са атакували	бяха атакували

	Conditional Mood	**Imperative Mood**	
аз	бих атакувал	**Positive**	**Negative**
ти	би атакувал	атакувай	не атакувай
той	би атакувал		
ние	бихме атакували		
вие	бихте атакували	атакувайте	не атакувайте
те	биха атакували		

Past Passive Participles

M	**F**	**N**	**Pl**
атакуван	атакувана	атакувано	атакувани

2) **балансирам**; *balance, equalize*

	Present	**Past Simple**	**Past Continuous**
аз	балансирам	балансирах	балансирах
ти	балансираш	балансира	балансираше
той	балансира	балансира	балансираше
ние	балансираме	балансирахме	балансирахме
вие	балансирате	балансирахте	балансирахте
те	балансират	балансираха	балансираха

	Future	**Future in the Past**
	(For negative, replace **ще** with **няма да**)	(For negative, replace **щях/щеше/щяхме/щяхте/щяха** with **нямаше**)
аз	ще балансирам	щях да балансирам
ти	ще балансираш	щеше да балансираш
той	ще балансира	щеше да балансира
ние	ще балансираме	щяхме да балансираме
вие	ще балансирате	щяхте да балансирате
те	ще балансират	щяха да балансират

Past Active Participles

M	**F**	**N**	**Pl**
балансирал	балансирала	балансирало	балансирали

	Present Perfect	**Past Perfect**
аз	съм балансирал	бях балансирал
ти	си балансирал	беше балансирал
той	е балансирал	беше балансирал
ние	сме балансирали	бяхме балансирали
вие	сте балансирали	бяхте балансирали
те	са балансирали	бяха балансирали

	Conditional Mood	**Imperative Mood**	
аз	бих балансирал	**Positive**	**Negative**
ти	би балансирал	балансирай	не балансирай
той	би балансирал		
ние	бихме балансирали		
вие	бихте балансирали	балансирайте	не балансирайте
те	биха балансирали		

Past Passive Participles

M	**F**	**N**	**Pl**
балансиран	балансирана	балансирано	балансирани

3) **безпокоя;** *bother, disturb* **безпокоя се;** *worry, be concerned*

	Present	Past Simple	Past Continuous
аз	безпокоя	безпокоих	безпокоях
ти	безпокоиш	безпокои	безпокоеше
той	безпокои	безпокои	безпокоеше
ние	безпокоим	безпокоихме	безпокояхме
вие	безпокоите	безпокоихте	безпокояхте
те	безпокоят	безпокоиха	безпокояха

	Future	Future in the Past
	(For negative, replace **ще** with **няма да**)	(For negative, replace **щях/щеше/щяхме/щяхте/щяха** with **нямаше**)
аз	ще безпокоя	щях да безпокоя
ти	ще безпокоиш	щеше да безпокоиш
той	ще безпокои	щеше да безпокои
ние	ще безпокоим	щяхме да безпокоим
вие	ще безпокоите	щяхте да безпокоите
те	ще безпокоят	щяха да безпокоят

Past Active Participles

M	F	N	Pl
безпокоил	безпокоила	безпокоило	безпокоили

	Present Perfect	Past Perfect
аз	съм безпокоил	бях безпокоил
ти	си безпокоил	беше безпокоил
той	е безпокоил	беше безпокоил
ние	сме безпокоили	бяхме безпокоили
вие	сте безпокоили	бяхте безпокоили
те	са безпокоили	бяха безпокоили

	Conditional Mood	Imperative Mood	
		Positive	**Negative**
аз	бих безпокоил	безпокой	не безпокой
ти	би безпокоил		
той	би безпокоил		
ние	бихме безпокоили		
вие	бихте безпокоили	безпокойте	не безпокойте
те	биха безпокоили		

Past Passive Participles

M	F	N	Pl
безпокоен	безпокоена	безпокоено	безпокоени

4) **благодаря;** *thank, express gratitude*

	Present	**Past Simple**	**Past Continuous**
аз	благодаря	благодарих	благодарях
ти	благодариш	благодари	благодареше
той	благодари	благодари	благодареше
ние	благодарим	благодарихме	благодаряхме
вие	благодарите	благодарихте	благодаряхте
те	благодарят	благодариха	благодаряха

	Future	**Future in the Past**
	(For negative, replace **ще** with **няма да**)	(For negative, replace **щях/щеше/щяхме/щяхте/щяха** with **нямаше**)
аз	ще благодаря	щях да благодаря
ти	ще благодариш	щеше да благодариш
той	ще благодари	щеше да благодари
ние	ще благодарим	щяхме да благодарим
вие	ще благодарите	щяхте да благодарите
те	ще благодарят	щяха да благодарят

Past Active Participles

M	**F**	**N**	**Pl**
благодарил	благодарила	благодарило	благодарили

	Present Perfect	**Past Perfect**
аз	съм благодарил	бях благодарил
ти	си благодарил	беше благодарил
той	е благодарил	беше благодарил
ние	сме благодарили	бяхме благодарили
вие	сте благодарили	бяхте благодарили
те	са благодарили	бяха благодарили

	Conditional Mood	**Imperative Mood**	
аз	бих благодарил	**Positive**	**Negative**
ти	би благодарил	благодари	не благодари
той	би благодарил		
ние	бихме благодарили		
вие	бихте благодарили	благодарете	не благодарете
те	биха благодарили		

Past Passive Participles

M	**F**	**N**	**PL**
N/A	N/A	N/A	N/A

5) **блестя;** *shine*

	Present	**Past Simple**	**Past Continuous**
аз	блестя	блестях	блестях
ти	блестиш	блестя	блестеше
той	блести	блестя	блестеше
ние	блестим	блестяхме	блестяхме
вие	блестите	блестяхте	блестяхте
те	блестят	блестяха	блестяха

	Future	**Future in the Past**
	(For negative, replace **ще** with **няма да**)	(For negative, replace **щях/щеше/щяхме/щяхте/щяха** with **нямаше**)
аз	ще блестя	щях да блестя
ти	ще блестиш	щеше да блестиш
той	ще блести	щеше да блести
ние	ще блестим	щяхме да блестим
вие	ще блестите	щяхте да блестите
те	ще блестят	щяха да блестят

Past Active Participles

M	**F**	**N**	**Pl**
блестял	блестяла	блестяло	блестели

	Present Perfect	**Past Perfect**
аз	съм блестял	бях блестял
ти	си блестял	беше блестял
той	е блестял	беше блестял
ние	сме блестели	бяхме блестели
вие	сте блестели	бяхте блестели
те	са блестели	бяха блестели

	Conditional Mood	**Imperative Mood**	
аз	бих блестял	**Positive**	**Negative**
ти	би блестял	блести	не блести
той	би блестял		
ние	бихме блестели		
вие	бихте блестели	блестете	не блестете
те	биха блестели		

Past Passive Participles

M	**F**	**N**	**Pl**
N/A	N/A	N/A	N/A

6) **боледувам;** *be ill, suffer*

	Present	**Past Simple**	**Past Continuous**
аз	боледувам	боледувах	боледувах
ти	боледуваш	боледува	боледуваше
той	боледува	боледува	боледуваше
ние	боледуваме	боледувахме	боледувахме
вие	боледувате	боледувахте	боледувахте
те	боледуват	боледуваха	боледуваха

	Future	**Future in the Past**
	(For negative, replace **ще** with **няма да**)	(For negative, replace **щях/щеше/щяхме/щяхте/щяха** with **нямаше**)
аз	ще боледувам	щях да боледувам
ти	ще боледуваш	щеше да боледуваш
той	ще боледува	щеше да боледува
ние	ще боледуваме	щяхме да боледуваме
вие	ще боледувате	щяхте да боледувате
те	ще боледуват	щяха да боледуват

Past Active Participles

M	**F**	**N**	**Pl**
боледувал	боледувала	боледувало	боледували

	Present Perfect	**Past Perfect**
аз	съм боледувал	бях боледувал
ти	си боледувал	беше боледувал
той	е боледувал	беше боледувал
ние	сме боледували	бяхме боледували
вие	сте боледували	бяхте боледували
те	са боледували	бяха боледували

	Conditional Mood	**Imperative Mood**	
		Positive	**Negative**
аз	бих боледувал		
ти	би боледувал	боледувай	не боледувай
той	би боледувал		
ние	бихме боледували		
вие	бихте боледували	боледувайте	не боледувайте
те	биха боледували		

Past Passive Participles

M	**F**	**N**	**Pl**
N/A	N/A	N/A	N/A

7) **боря се;** *fight, battle*

	Present	**Past Simple**	**Past Continuous**
аз	се боря	се борих	се борех
ти	се бориш	се бори	се бореше
той	се бори	се бори	се бореше
ние	се борим	се борихме	се борехме
вие	се борите	се борихте	се борехте
те	се борят	се бориха	се бореха

	Future	**Future in the Past**
	(For negative, replace **ще** with **няма да**)	(For negative, replace **щях/щеше/щяхме/щяхте/щяха** with **нямаше**)
аз	ще се боря	щях да се боря
ти	ще се бориш	щеше да се бориш
той	ще се бори	щеше да се бори
ние	ще се борим	щяхме да се борим
вие	ще се борите	щяхте да се борите
те	ще се борят	щяха да се борят

Past Active Participles

M	**F**	**N**	**Pl**
борил	борила	борило	борили

	Present Perfect	**Past Perfect**
аз	съм се борил	бях се борил
ти	си се борил	беше се борил
той	се е борил	беше се борил
ние	сме се борили	бяхме се борили
вие	сте се борили	бяхте се борили
те	са се борили	бяха се борили

	Conditional Mood	**Imperative Mood**	
		Positive	**Negative**
аз	бих се борил		
ти	би се борил	бори се	не се бори
той	би се борил		
ние	бихме се борили		
вие	бихте се борили	борете се	не се борете
те	биха се борили		

Past Passive Participles

M	**F**	**N**	**Pl**
N/A	N/A	N/A	N/A

8) **бръсна се;** *shave*

	Present	Past Simple	Past Continuous
аз	се бръсна	се бръснах	се бръснех
ти	се бръснеш	се бръсна	се бръснеше
той	се бръсне	се бръсна	се бръснеше
ние	се бръснем	се бръснахме	се бръснехме
вие	се бръснете	се бръснахте	се бръснехте
те	се бръснат	се бръснаха	се бръснеха

	Future	Future in the Past
	(For negative, replace **ще** with **няма да**)	(For negative, replace **щях/щеше/щяхме/щяхте/щяха** with **нямаше**)
аз	ще се бръсна	щях да се бръсна
ти	ще се бръснеш	щеше да се бръснеш
той	ще се бръсне	щеше да се бръсне
ние	ще се бръснем	щяхме да се бръснем
вие	ще се бръснете	щяхте да се бръснете
те	ще се бръснат	щяха да се бръснат

Past Active Participles

M	F	N	Pl
бръснал	бръснала	бръснало	бръснали

	Present Perfect	Past Perfect
аз	съм се бръснал	бях се бръснал
ти	си се бръснал	беше се бръснал
той	се е бръснал	беше се бръснал
ние	сме се бръснали	бяхме се бръснали
вие	сте се бръснали	бяхте се бръснали
те	са се бръснали	бяха се бръснали

	Conditional Mood	Imperative Mood	
аз	бих се бръснал	**Positive**	**Negative**
ти	би се бръснал	бръсни се	не се бръсни
той	би се бръснал		
ние	бихме се бръснали		
вие	бихте се бръснали	бръснете се	не се бръснете
те	биха се бръснали		

Past Passive Participles

M	F	N	Pl
бръснат	бръсната	бръснато	бръснати

9) **бързам;** *rush, hurry*

	Present	**Past Simple**	**Past Continuous**
аз	бързам	бързах	бързах
ти	бързаш	бърза	бързаше
той	бърза	бърза	бързаше
ние	бързаме	бързахме	бързахме
вие	бързате	бързахте	бързахте
те	бързат	бързаха	бързаха

	Future	**Future in the Past**
	(For negative, replace **ще** with **няма да**)	(For negative, replace **щях/щеше/щяхме/щяхте/щяха** with **нямаше**)
аз	ще бързам	щях да бързам
ти	ще бързаш	щеше да бързаш
той	ще бърза	щеше да бърза
ние	ще бързаме	щяхме да бързаме
вие	ще бързате	щяхте да бързате
те	ще бързат	щяха да бързат

Past Active Participles

M	**F**	**N**	**Pl**
бързал	бързала	бързало	бързали

	Present Perfect	**Past Perfect**
аз	съм бързал	бях бързал
ти	си бързал	беше бързал
той	е бързал	беше бързал
ние	сме бързали	бяхме бързали
вие	сте бързали	бяхте бързали
те	са бързали	бяха бързали

	Conditional Mood	**Imperative Mood**	
аз	бих бързал	**Positive**	**Negative**
ти	би бързал	бързай	не бързай
той	би бързал		
ние	бихме бързали		
вие	бихте бързали	бързайте	не бързайте
те	биха бързали		

Past Passive Participles

M	**F**	**N**	**Pl**
N/A	N/A	N/A	N/A

10) **бягам;** *run, jog*

	Present	Past Simple	Past Continuous
аз	бягам	бягах	бягах
ти	бягаш	бяга	бягаше
той	бяга	бяга	бягаше
ние	бягаме	бягахме	бягахме
вие	бягате	бягахте	бягахте
те	бягат	бягаха	бягаха

	Future	Future in the Past
	(For negative, replace **ще** with **няма да**)	(For negative, replace **щях/щеше/щяхме/щяхте/щяха** with **нямаше**)
аз	ще бягам	щях да бягам
ти	ще бягаш	щеше да бягаш
той	ще бяга	щеше да бяга
ние	ще бягаме	щяхме да бягаме
вие	ще бягате	щяхте да бягате
те	ще бягат	щяха да бягат

Past Active Participles

M	**F**	**N**	**Pl**
бягал	бягала	бягало	бягали

	Present Perfect	Past Perfect
аз	съм бягал	бях бягал
ти	си бягал	беше бягал
той	е бягал	беше бягал
ние	сме бягали	бяхме бягали
вие	сте бягали	бяхте бягали
те	са бягали	бяха бягали

	Conditional Mood	Imperative Mood	
аз	бих бягал	**Positive**	**Negative**
ти	би бягал	бягай	не бягай
той	би бягал		
ние	бихме бягали		
вие	бихте бягали	бягайте	не бягайте
те	биха бягали		

Past Passive Participles

M	**F**	**N**	**Pl**
N/A	N/A	N/A	N/A

11) **варя;** *boil*

	Present	**Past Simple**	**Past Continuous**
аз	варя	варих	варях
ти	вариш	вари	вареше
той	вари	вари	вареше
ние	варим	варихме	варяхме
вие	варите	варихте	варяхте
те	варят	вариха	варяха

	Future	**Future in the Past**
	(For negative, replace **ще** with **няма да**)	(For negative, replace **щях/щеше/щяхме/щяхте/щяха** with **нямаше**)
аз	ще варя	щях да варя
ти	ще вариш	щеше да вариш
той	ще вари	щеше да вари
ние	ще варим	щяхме да варим
вие	ще варите	щяхте да варите
те	ще варят	щяха да варят

Past Active Participles

M	**F**	**N**	**Pl**
варил	варила	варило	варили

	Present Perfect	**Past Perfect**
аз	съм варил	бях варил
ти	си варил	беше варил
той	е варил	беше варил
ние	сме варили	бяхме варили
вие	сте варили	бяхте варили
те	са варили	бяха варили

	Conditional Mood	**Imperative Mood**	
аз	бих варил	**Positive**	**Negative**
ти	би варил	вари	не вари
той	би варил		
ние	бихме варили		
вие	бихте варили	варете	не варете
те	биха варили		

Past Passive Participles

M	**F**	**N**	**Pl**
варен	варена	варено	варени

12) **вдигам/вдигна;** *lift, pick up, raise*

	Present	Past Simple	Past Continuous
аз	вдигам	вдигнах	вдигах
ти	вдигаш	вдигна	вдигаше
той	вдига	вдигна	вдигаше
ние	вдигаме	вдигнахме	вдигахме
вие	вдигате	вдигнахте	вдигахте
те	вдигат	вдигнаха	вдигаха

	Future	Future in the Past
	(For negative, replace **ще** with **няма да**)	(For negative, replace **щях/щеше/щяхме/щяхте/щяха** with **нямаше**)
аз	ще вдигам/вдигна	щях да вдигам/вдигна
ти	ще вдигаш/вдигнеш	щеше да вдигаш/вдигнеш
той	ще вдига/вдигне	щеше да вдига/вдигне
ние	ще вдигаме/вдигнем	щяхме да вдигаме/вдигнем
вие	ще вдигате/вдигнете	щяхте да вдигате/вдигнете
те	ще вдигат/вдигнат	щяха да вдигат/вдигнат

Past Active Participles

M	F	N	Pl
вдигал/вдигнал	вдигала/вдигнала	вдигало/вдигнало	вдигали/вдигнали

	Present Perfect	Past Perfect
аз	съм вдигал/вдигнал	бях вдигал/вдигнал
ти	си вдигал/вдигнал	беше вдигал/вдигнал
той	е вдигал/вдигнал	беше вдигал/вдигнал
ние	сме вдигали/вдигнали	бяхме вдигали/вдигнали
вие	сте вдигали/вдигнали	бяхте вдигали/вдигнали
те	са вдигали/вдигнали	бяха вдигали/вдигнали

	Conditional Mood	Imperative Mood	
аз	бих вдигал/вдигнал	**Positive**	**Negative**
ти	би вдигал/вдигнал	вдигай/вдигни	не вдигай
той	би вдигал/вдигнал		
ние	бихме вдигали/вдигнали		
вие	бихте вдигали/вдигнали	вдигайте/вдигнете	не вдигайте
те	биха вдигали/вдигнали		

Past Passive Participles

M	F	N	Pl
вдиган/вдигнат	вдигана/вдигната	вдигано/вдигнато	вдигани/вдигнати

13) **вдишвам/вдишам;** *breath in, inhale*

	Present	Past Simple	Past Continuous
аз	вдишвам	вдишах	вдишвах
ти	вдишваш	вдиша	вдишваше
той	вдишва	вдиша	вдишваше
ние	вдишваме	вдишахме	вдишвахме
вие	вдишвате	вдишахте	вдишвахте
те	вдишват	вдишаха	вдишваха

	Future	Future in the Past
	(For negative, replace **ще** With **няма да**)	(For negative, replace **щях/щеше/щяхме/щяхте/щяха** with **нямаше**)
аз	ще вдишвам/вдишам	щях да вдишвам/вдишам
ти	ще вдишваш/вдишаш	щеше да вдишваш/вдишаш
той	ще вдишва/вдиша	щеше да вдишва/вдиша
ние	ще вдишваме/вдишаме	щяхме да вдишваме/вдишаме
вие	ще вдишвате/вдишате	щяхте да вдишвате/вдишате
те	ще вдишват/вдишат	щяха да вдишват/вдишат

Past Active Participles

M	F	N	Pl
вдишвал/вдишал	вдишвала/вдишала	вдишвало/вдишало	вдишвали/вдишали

	Present Perfect	Past Perfect
аз	съм вдишвал/вдишал	бях вдишвал/вдишал
ти	си вдишвал/вдишал	беше вдишвал/вдишал
той	е вдишвал/вдишал	беше вдишвал/вдишал
ние	сме вдишвали/вдишали	бяхме вдишвали/вдишали
вие	сте вдишвали/вдишали	бяхте вдишвали/вдишали
те	са вдишвали/вдишали	бяха вдишвали/вдишали

	Conditional Mood	Imperative Mood	
аз	бих вдишвал/вдишал	**Positive**	**Negative**
ти	би вдишвал/вдишал	вдишвай/вдишай	не вдишвай
той	би вдишвал/вдишал		
ние	бихме вдишвали/вдишали		
вие	бихте вдишвали/вдишали	вдишвайте/вдишайте	не вдишвайте
те	биха вдишвали/вдишали		

Past Passive Participles

M	F	N	Pl
вдишван/вдишан	вдишвана/вдишана	вдишвано/вдишано	вдишвани/вдишани

14) **вечерям;** *dine, have dinner*

	Present	**Past Simple**	**Past Continuous**
аз	вечерям	вечерях	вечерях
ти	вечеряш	вечеря	вечеряше
той	вечеря	вечеря	вечеряше
ние	вечеряме	вечеряхме	вечеряхме
вие	вечеряте	вечеряхте	вечеряхте
те	вечерят	вечеряха	вечеряха

	Future	**Future in the Past**
	(For negative, replace **ще** with **няма да**)	(For negative, replace **щях/щеше/щяхме/щяхте/щяха** with **нямаше**)
аз	ще вечерям	щях да вечерям
ти	ще вечеряш	щеше да вечеряш
той	ще вечеря	щеше да вечеря
ние	ще вечеряме	щяхме да вечеряме
вие	ще вечеряте	щяхте да вечеряте
те	ще вечерят	щяха да вечерят

Past Active Participles

M	**F**	**N**	**Pl**
Вечерял	вечеряла	вечеряло	вечеряли

	Present Perfect	**Past Perfect**
аз	съм вечерял	бях вечерял
ти	си вечерял	беше вечерял
той	е вечерял	беше вечерял
ние	сме вечеряли	бяхме вечеряли
вие	сте вечеряли	бяхте вечеряли
те	са вечеряли	бяха вечеряли

	Conditional Mood	**Imperative Mood**	
аз	бих вечерял	**Positive**	**Negative**
ти	би вечерял	вечеряй	не вечеряй
той	би вечерял		
ние	бихме вечеряли		
вие	бихте вечеряли	вечеряйте	не вечеряйте
те	биха вечеряли		

Past Passive Participles

M	**F**	**N**	**Pl**
N/A	N/A	N/A	N/A

15) **вземам/взема;** *take, get, pick up*

	Present	Past Simple	Past Continuous
аз	вземам	взех	вземах
ти	вземаш	взе	вземаше
той	взема	взе	вземаше
ние	вземаме	взехме	вземахме
вие	вземате	взехте	вземахте
те	вземат	взеха	вземаха

	Future	Future in the Past
	(For negative, replace **ще** with **няма да**)	(For negative, replace **щях/щеше/щяхме/щяхте/щяха** with **нямаше**)
аз	ще вземам/взема	щях да вземам/взема
ти	ще вземаш/вземеш	щеше да вземаш/вземеш
той	ще взема/вземе	щеше да взема/вземе
ние	ще вземаме/вземем	щяхме да вземаме/вземем
вие	ще вземате/вземете	щяхте да вземате/вземете
те	ще вземат/вземат	щяха да вземат/вземат

Past Active Participles

M	F	N	Pl
вземал/взел	вземала/взела	вземало/взело	вземали/взели

	Present Perfect	Past Perfect
аз	съм вземал/взел	бях вземал/взел
ти	си вземал/взел	беше вземал/взел
той	е вземал/взел	беше вземал/взел
ние	сме вземали/взели	бяхме вземали/взели
вие	сте вземали/взели	бяхте вземали/взели
те	са вземали/взели	бяха вземали/взели

	Conditional Mood	Imperative Mood	
аз	бих вземал/взел	**Positive**	**Negative**
ти	би вземал/взел	вземай/вземи	не вземай
той	би вземал/взел		
ние	бихме вземали/взели		
вие	бихте вземали/взели	вземайте/вземете	не вземайте
те	биха вземали/взели		

Past Passive Participles

M	F	N	Pl
вземан/взет	вземана/взета	вземано/взето	вземани/взети

16) **виждам/видя;** *see, observe*

	Present	**Past Simple**	**Past Continuous**
аз	виждам	видях	виждах
ти	виждаш	видя	виждаше
той	вижда	видя	виждаше
ние	виждаме	видяхме	виждахме
вие	виждате	видяхте	виждахте
те	виждат	видяха	виждаха

	Future	**Future in the Past**
	(For negative, replace **ще** with **няма да**)	(For negative, replace **щях/щеше/щяхме/щяхте/щяха** with **нямаше**)
аз	ще виждам/видя	щях да виждам/видя
ти	ще виждаш/видиш	щеше да виждаш/видиш
той	ще вижда/види	щеше да вижда/види
ние	ще виждаме/видим	щяхме да виждаме/видим
вие	ще виждате/видите	щяхте да виждате/видите
те	ще виждат/видят	щяха да виждат/видят

Past Active Participles

M	**F**	**N**	**Pl**
виждал/видял	виждала/видяла	виждало/видяло	виждали/видели

	Present Perfect	**Past Perfect**
аз	съм виждал/видял	бях виждал/видял
ти	си виждал/видял	беше виждал/видял
той	е виждал/видял	беше виждал/видял
ние	сме виждали/видели	бяхме виждали/видели
вие	сте виждали/видели	бяхте виждали/видели
те	са виждали/видели	бяха виждали/видели

	Conditional Mood	**Imperative Mood**	
аз	бих виждал/видял	**Positive**	**Negative**
ти	би виждал/видял	виждай/виж	не виждай
той	би виждал/видял		
ние	бихме виждали/видели		
вие	бихте виждали/видели	виждайте/вижте	не виждайте
те	биха виждали/видели		

Past Passive Participles

M	**F**	**N**	**Pl**
виждан/видян	виждана/видяна	виждано/видяно	виждани/видени

17) **викам/викна;** *call; shout, yell, scream*

	Present	**Past Simple**	**Past Continuous**
аз	викам	викнах	виках
ти	викаш	викна	викаше
той	вика	викна	викаше
ние	викаме	викнахме	викахме
вие	викате	викнахте	викахте
те	викат	викнаха	викаха

	Future	**Future in the Past**
	(For negative, replace **ще** with **няма да**)	(For negative, replace **щях/щеше/щяхме/щяхте/щяха** with **нямаше**)
Аз	ще викам/викна	щях да викам/викна
ти	ще викаш/викнеш	щеше да викаш/викнеш
той	ще вика/викне	щеше да вика/викне
ние	ще викаме/викнем	щяхме да викаме/викнем
вие	ще викате/викнете	щяхте да викате/викнете
те	ще викат/викнат	щяха да викат/викнат

Past Active Participles

M	**F**	**N**	**Pl**
викал/викнал	викала/викнала	викало/викнало	викали/викнали

	Present Perfect	**Past Perfect**
аз	съм викал/викнал	бях викал/викнал
ти	си викал/викнал	беше викал/викнал
той	е викал/викнал	беше викал/викнал
ние	сме викали/викнали	бяхме викали/викнали
вие	сте викали/викнали	бяхте викали/викнали
те	са викали/викнали	бяха викали/викнали

	Conditional Mood	**Imperative Mood**	
аз	бих викал/викнал	**Positive**	**Negative**
ти	би викал/викнал	викай/викни	не викай
той	би викал/викнал		
ние	бихме викали/викнали		
вие	бихте викали/викнали	викайте/викнете	не викайте
те	биха викали/викнали		

Past Passive Participles

M	**F**	**N**	**Pl**
викан/викнат	викана/викната	викано/викнато	викани/викнати

18) **включвам/включа;** *include; turn on, plug in*

	Present	Past Simple	Past Continuous
аз	включвам	включих	включвах
ти	включваш	включи	включваше
той	включва	включи	включваше
ние	включваме	включихме	включвахме
вие	включвате	включихте	включвахте
те	включват	включиха	включваха

	Future	Future in the Past
	(For negative, replace **ще** with **няма да**)	(For negative, replace **щях/щеше/щяхме/щяхте/щяха** with **нямаше**)
аз	ще включвам/включа	щях да включвам/включа
ти	ще включваш/включиш	щеше да включваш/включиш
той	ще включва/включи	щеше да включва/включи
ние	ще включваме/включим	щяхме да включваме/включим
вие	ще включвате/включите	щяхте да включвате/включите
те	ще включват/включат	щяха да включват/включат

Past Active Participles

M	F	N	Pl
включвал/включил	включвала/включила	включвало/включило	включвали/ включили

	Present Perfect	Past Perfect
аз	съм включвал/включил	бях включвал/включил
ти	си включвал/включил	беше включвал/включил
той	е включвал/включил	беше включвал/включил
ние	сме включвали/включили	бяхме включвали/включили
вие	сте включвали/включили	бяхте включвали/включили
те	са включвали/включили	бяха включвали/включили

	Conditional Mood	Imperative Mood	
		Positive	**Negative**
аз	бих включвал/включил		
ти	би включвал/включил	включвай/включи	не включвай
той	би включвал/включил		
ние	бихме включвали/включили		
вие	бихте включвали/включили	включвайте/включете	не включвайте
те	биха включвали/включили		

Past Passive Participles

M	F	N	Pl
включван/ включен	включвана/включена	включвано/включено	включвани/включени

19) **влагам/вложа;** *put in, deposit, invest*

	Present	Past Simple	Past Continuous
аз	влагам	вложих	влагах
ти	влагаш	вложи	влагаше
той	влага	вложи	влагаше
ние	влагаме	вложихме	влагахме
вие	влагате	вложихте	влагахте
те	влагат	вложиха	влагаха

	Future	Future in the Past
	(For negative, replace **ще** with **няма да**)	(For negative, replace **щях/щеше/щяхме/щяхте/щяха** with **нямаше**)
аз	ще влагам/вложа	щях да влагам/вложа
ти	ще влагаш/вложиш	щеше да влагаш/вложиш
той	ще влага/вложи	щеше да влага/вложи
ние	ще влагаме/вложим	щяхме да влагаме/вложим
вие	ще влагате/вложите	щяхте да влагате/вложите
те	ще влагат/вложат	щяха да влагат/вложат

Past Active Participles

M	F	N	Pl
влагал/ вложил	влагала/вложила	влагало/вложило	влагали/вложили

	Present Perfect	Past Perfect
аз	сьм влагал/вложил	бях влагал/вложил
ти	си влагал/вложил	беше влагал/вложил
той	е влагал/вложил	беше влагал/ вложил
ние	сме влагали/вложили	бяхме влагали/вложили
вие	сте влагали/вложили	бяхте влагали/вложили
те	са влагали/вложили	бяха влагали/вложили

	Conditional Mood	Imperative Mood	
		Positive	**Negative**
аз	бих влагал/вложил		
ти	би влагал/вложил	влагай/вложи	не влагай
той	би влагал/вложил		
ние	бихме влагали/вложили		
вие	бихте влагали/вложили	влагайте/вложете	не влагайте
те	биха влагали/вложили		

Past Passive Participles

M	F	N	Pl
влаган/вложен	влагана/вложена	влагано/вложено	влагани/вложени

20) **влизам/вляза;** *enter, come in*

	Present	**Past Simple**	**Past Continuous**
аз	влизам	влизах	влизах
ти	влизаш	влиза	влизаше
той	влиза	влиза	влизаше
ние	влизаме	влизахме	влизахме
вие	влизате	влизахте	влизахте
те	влизат	влизаха	влизаха

	Future	**Future in the Past**
	(For negative, replace **ще** with **няма да**)	(For negative, replace **щях/щеше/щяхме/щяхте/щяха** with **нямаше**)
аз	ще влизам/вляза	щях да влизам/вляза
ти	ще влизаш/влезеш	щеше да влизаш/влезеш
той	ще влиза/влезе	щеше да влиза/влезе
ние	ще влизаме/влезем	щяхме да влизаме/влезем
вие	ще влизате/влезете	щяхте да влизате/влезете
те	ще влизат/влязат	щяха да влизат/влязат

Past Active Participles

M	**F**	**N**	**Pl**
влизал/влязъл	влизала/влязла	влизало/влязло	влизали/влезли

	Present Perfect	**Past Perfect**
аз	съм влизал/влязъл	бях влизал/влязъл
ти	си влизал/влязъл	беше влизал/влязъл
той	е влизал/влязъл	беше влизал/влязъл
ние	сме влизали/влезли	бяхме влизали/влезли
вие	сте влизали/влезли	бяхте влизали/влезли
те	са влизали/влезли	бяха влизали/влезли

	Conditional Mood	**Imperative Mood**	
Аз	бих влизал/влязъл	**Positive**	**Negative**
ти	би влизал/влязъл	влизай/влез	не влизай
той	би влизал/влязъл		
ние	бихме влизали/влезли		
вие	бихте влизали/влезли	влизайте/влезте	не влизайте
те	биха влизали/влезли		

Past Passive Participles

M	**F**	**N**	**Pl**
N/A	N/A	N/A	N/A

21) **влияя/повлияя;** *influence*

	Present	Past Simple	Past Continuous
аз	влияя	повлиях	влияех
ти	влияеш	повлия	влияеше
той	влияе	повлия	влияеше
ние	влияем	повлияхме	влияехме
вие	влияете	повлияхте	влияехте
те	влияят	повлияха	влияеха

	Future	Future in the Past
	(For negative, replace **ще** with **няма да**)	(For negative, replace **щях/щеше/щяхме/щяхте/щяха** with **нямаше**)
аз	ще влияя/повлияя	щях да влияя/повлияя
ти	ще влияеш/повлияеш	щеше да влияеш/повлияеш
той	ще влияе/повлияе	щеше да влияе/повлияе
ние	ще влияем/повлияем	щяхме да влияем/повлияем
вие	ще влияете/повлияете	щяхте да влияете/повлияете
те	ще влияят/повлияят	щяха да влияят/повлияят

Past Active Participles

M	F	N	Pl
влиял/повлиял	влияла/повлияла	влияло/повлияло	влияли/повлияли

	Present Perfect	Past Perfect
аз	съм влиял/повлиял	бях влиял/повлиял
ти	си влиял/повлиял	беше влиял/повлиял
той	е влиял/повлиял	беше влиял/повлиял
ние	сме влияли/повлияли	бяхме влияли/повлияли
вие	сте влияли/повлияли	бяхте влияли/повлияли
те	са влияли/повлияли	бяха влияли/повлияли

	Conditional Mood	Imperative Mood	
аз	бих влиял/повлиял	**Positive**	**Negative**
ти	би влиял/повлиял	влияй/повлияй	не влияй
той	би влиял/повлиял		
ние	бихме влияли/повлияли		
вие	бихте влияли/повлияли	влияйте/повлияйте	не влияйте
те	биха влияли/повлияли		

Past Passive Participles

M	F	N	Pl
повлиян	повлияна	повлияно	повлияни

22) **влюбвам се/влюбя се;** *fall in love*

	Present	**Past Simple**	**Past Continuous**
аз	се влюбвам	се влюбих	се влюбвах
ти	се влюбваш	се влюби	се влюбваше
той	се влюбва	се влюби	се влюбваше
ние	се влюбваме	се влюбихме	се влюбвахме
вие	се влюбвате	се влюбихте	се влюбвахте
те	се влюбват	се влюбиха	се влюбваха

	Future	**Future in the Past**
	(For negative, replace **ще** with **няма да**)	(For negative, replace **щях/щеше/щяхме/щяхте/щяха** with **нямаше**)
аз	ще се влюбвам/влюбя	щях да се влюбвам/влюбя
ти	ще се влюбваш/влюбиш	щеше да се влюбваш/влюбиш
той	ще се влюбва/влюби	щеше да се влюбва/влюби
ние	ще се влюбваме/влюбим	щяхме да се влюбваме/влюбим
вие	ще се влюбвате/влюбите	щяхте да се влюбвате/влюбите
те	ще се влюбват/влюбят	щяха да се влюбват/влюбят

Past Active Participles

M	**F**	**N**	**Pl**
влюбвал/влюбил	влюбвала/влюбила	влюбвало/влюбило	влюбвали/влюбили

	Present Perfect	**Past Perfect**
аз	съм се влюбвал/влюбил	бях се влюбвал/влюбил
ти	си се влюбвал/влюбил	беше се влюбвал/влюбил
той	се е влюбвал/влюбил	беше се влюбвал/влюбил
ние	сме се влюбвали/влюбили	бяхме се влюбвали/влюбили
вие	сте се влюбвали/влюбили	бяхте се влюбвали/влюбили
те	са се влюбвали/влюбили	бяха се влюбвали/влюбили

	Conditional Mood	**Imperative Mood**	
		Positive	**Negative**
аз	бих се влюбвал/влюбил		
ти	би се влюбвал/влюбил	влюбвай се/влюби се	не се влюбвай
той	би се влюбвал/влюбил		
ние	бихме се влюбвали/влюбили		
вие	бихте се влюбвали/влюбили	влюбвайте се/влюбете се	не се влюбвайте
те	биха се влюбвали/влюбили		

Past Passive Participles

M	**F**	**N**	**Pl**
влюбен	влюбена	влюбено	влюбени

23) **внасям/внеса;** *carry in; import; deposit*

	Present	Past Simple	Past Continuous
аз	внасям	внесох	внасях
ти	внасяш	внесе	внасяше
той	внася	внесе	внасяше
ние	внасяме	внесохме	внасяхме
вие	внасяте	внесохте	внасяхте
те	внасят	внесоха	внасяха

	Future	Future in the Past
	(For negative, replace **ще** with **няма да**)	(For negative, replace **щях/щеше/щяхме/щяхте/щяха** with **нямаше**)
аз	ще внасям/внеса	щях да внасям/внеса
ти	ще внасяш/внесеш	щеше да внасяш/внесеш
той	ще внася/внесе	щеше да внася/внесе
ние	ще внасяме/внесем	щяхме да внасяме/внесем
вие	ще внасяте/внесете	щяхте да внасяте/внесете
те	ще внасят/внесат	щяха да внасят/внесат

Past Active Participles

M	F	N	Pl
внасял/внесъл	внасяла/внесла	внасяло/внесло	внасяли/внесли

	Present Perfect	Past Perfect
аз	съм внасял/внесъл	бях внасял/внесъл
ти	си внасял/внесъл	беше внасял/внесъл
той	е внасял/внесъл	беше внасял/внесъл
ние	сме внасяли/внесли	бяхме внасяли/внесли
вие	сте внасяли/внесли	бяхте внасяли/внесли
те	са внасяли/внесли	бяха внасяли/внесли

	Conditional Mood	Imperative Mood: Positive	Imperative Mood: Negative
аз	бих внасял/внесъл		
ти	би внасял/внесъл	внасяй/внеси	не внасяй
той	би внасял/внесъл		
ние	бихме внасяли/внесли		
вие	бихте внасяли/внесли	внасяйте/внесете	не внасяйте
те	биха внасяли/внесли		

Past Passive Participles

M	F	N	Pl
внасян/внесен	внасяна/внесена	внасяно/внесено	внасяни/внесени

24) **воювам;** *be at war, fight*

	Present	**Past Simple**	**Past Continuous**
аз	воювам	воювах	воювах
ти	воюваш	воюва	воюваше
той	воюва	воюва	воюваше
ние	воюваме	воювахме	воювахме
вие	воювате	воювахте	воювахте
те	воюват	воюваха	воюваха

	Future	**Future in the Past**
	(For negative, replace **ще** with **няма да**)	(For negative, replace **щях/щеше/щяхме/щяхте/щяха** with **нямаше**)
аз	ще воювам	щях да воювам
ти	ще воюваш	щеше да воюваш
той	ще воюва	щеше да воюва
ние	ще воюваме	щяхме да воюваме
вие	ще воювате	щяхте да воювате
те	ще воюват	щяха да воюват

Past Active Participles

M	**F**	**N**	**Pl**
воювал	воювала	воювало	воювали

	Present Perfect	**Past Perfect**
аз	съм воювал	бях воювала
ти	си воювал	беше воювал
той	е воювал	беше воювал
ние	сме воювали	бяхме воювали
вие	сте воювали	бяхте воювали
те	са воювали	бяха воювали

	Conditional Mood	**Imperative Mood**	
		Positive	**Negative**
аз	бих воювал		
ти	би воювал	воювай	не воювай
той	би воювал		
ние	бихме воювали		
вие	бихте воювали	воювайте	не воювайте
те	биха воювали		

Past Passive Participles

M	**F**	**N**	**Pl**
N/A	N/A	N/A	N/A

25) **връщам/върна;** *return, give back* **връщам се/върна се;** *go back, go home*

	Present	Past Simple	Past Continuous
аз	връщам	върнах	връщах
ти	връщаш	върна	връщаше
той	връща	върна	връщаше
ние	връщаме	върнахме	връщахме
вие	връщате	върнахте	връщахте
те	връщат	върнаха	връщаха

	Future	Future in the Past
	(For negative, replace **ще** with **няма да**)	(For negative, replace **щях/щеше/щяхме/щяхте/щяха** with **нямаше**)
аз	ще връщам/върна	щях да връщам/върна
ти	ще връщаш/върнеш	щеше да връщаш/върнеш
той	ще връща/върне	щеше да връща/върне
ние	ще връщаме/върнем	щяхме да връщаме/върнем
вие	ще връщате/върнете	щяхте да връщате/върнете
те	ще връщат/върнат	щяха да връщат/върнат

Past Active Participles

M	F	N	Pl
връщал/върнал	връщала/върнала	връщало/върнало	връщали/върнали

	Present Perfect	Past Perfect
аз	съм връщал/върнал	бях връщал/върнал
ти	си връщал/върнал	беше връщал/върнал
той	е връщал/върнал	беше връщал/върнал
ние	сме връщали/върнали	бяхме връщали/върнали
вие	сте връщали/върнали	бяхте връщали/върнали
те	са връщали/върнали	бяха връщали/върнали

	Conditional Mood	Imperative Mood	
аз	бих връщал/върнал	**Positive**	**Negative**
ти	би връщал/върнал	връщай/върни	не връщай
той	би връщал/върнал		
ние	бихме връщали/върнали		
вие	бихте връщали/върнали	връщайте/върнете	не връщайте
те	биха връщали/върнали		

Past Passive Participles

M	F	N	Pl
връщан/върнат	връщана/върната	връщано/върнато	връщани/върнати

26) **въвеждам/въведа**; *bring into; introduce; initiate*

	Present	**Past Simple**	**Past Continuous**
аз	въвеждам	въведох	въвеждах
ти	въвеждаш	въведе	въвеждаше
той	въвежда	въведе	въвеждаше
ние	въвеждаме	въведохме	въвеждахме
вие	въвеждате	въведохте	въвеждахте
те	въвеждат	въведоха	въвеждаха

	Future	**Future in the Past**
	(For negative, replace **ще** with **няма да**)	(For negative, replace **щях/щеше/щяхме/щяхте/щяха** with **нямаше**)
аз	ще въвеждам/въведа	щях да въвеждам/въведа
ти	ще въвеждаш/въведеш	щеше да въвеждаш/въведеш
той	ще въвежда/въведе	щеше да въвежда/въведе
ние	ще въвеждаме/въведем	щяхме да въвеждаме/въведем
вие	ще въвеждате/въведете	щяхте да въвеждате/въведете
те	ще въвеждат/въведат	щяха да въвеждат/въведат

Past Active Participles

M	**F**	**N**	**Pl**
въвеждал/въвел	въвеждала/въвела	въвеждало/въвело	въвеждали/въвели

	Present Perfect	**Past Perfect**
аз	съм въвеждал/въвел	бях въвеждал/въвел
ти	си въвеждал/въвел	беше въвеждал/въвел
той	е въвеждал/въвел	беше въвеждал/въвел
ние	сме въвеждали/въвели	бяхме въвеждали/въвели
вие	сте въвеждали/въвели	бяхте въвеждали/въвели
те	са въвеждали/въвели	бяха въвеждали/въвели

	Conditional Mood	**Imperative Mood**	
		Positive	**Negative**
аз	бих въвеждал/въвел		
ти	би въвеждал/въвел	въвеждай/въведи	не въвеждай
той	би въвеждал/въвел		
ние	бихме въвеждали/въвели		
вие	бихте въвеждали/въвели	въвеждайте/въведете	не въвеждайте
те	биха въвеждали/въвели		

Past Passive Participles

M	**F**	**N**	**Pl**
въвеждан/въведен	въвеждана/въведена	въвеждано/въведено	въвеждани/въведени

27) **възразявам/възразя;** *retort, object*

	Present	Past Simple	Past Continuous
аз	възразявам	възразих	възразявах
ти	възразяваш	възрази	възразяваше
той	възразява	възрази	възразяваше
ние	възразяваме	възразихме	възразявахме
вие	възразявате	възразихте	възразявахте
те	възразяват	възразиха	възразяваха

	Future	Future in the Past
	(For negative, replace **ще** with **няма да**)	(For negative, replace **щях/щеше/щяхме/щяхте/щяха** with **нямаше**)
аз	ще възразявам/възразя	щях да възразявам/възразя
ти	ще възразяваш/възразиш	щеше да възразяваш/възразиш
той	ще възразява/възрази	щеше да възразява/възрази
ние	ще възразяваме/възразим	щяхме да възразяваме/възразим
вие	ще възразявате/възразите	щяхте да възразявате/възразите
те	ще възразяват/възразят	щяха да възразяват/възразят

Past Active Participles

M	F	N	Pl
възразявал/ възразил	възразявала/възразила	възразявало/възразило	възразявали/възразили

	Present Perfect	Past Perfect
аз	съм възразявал/възразил	бях възразявал/възразил
ти	си възразявал/възразил	беше възразявал/възразил
той	е възразявал/възразил	беше възразявал/възразил
ние	сме възразявали/възразили	бяхме възразявали/възразили
вие	сте възразявали/възразили	бяхте възразявали/възразили
те	са възразявали/възразили	бяха възразявали/възразили

	Conditional Mood	Imperative Mood	
		Positive	**Negative**
аз	бих възразявал/възразил		
ти	би възразявал/възразил	възразявай/възрази	не възразявай
той	би възразявал/възразил		
ние	бихме възразявали/възразили		
вие	бихте възразявали/възразили	възразявайте/възразете	не възразявайте
те	биха възразявали/възразили		

Past Passive Participles

M	F	N	Pl
N/A	N/A	N/A	N/A

28) **вървя;** *walk, march, hike*

	Present	Past Simple	Past Continuous
аз	вървя	вървях	вървях
ти	вървиш	вървя	вървеше
той	върви	вървя	вървеше
ние	вървим	вървяхме	вървяхме
вие	вървите	вървяхте	вървяхте
те	вървят	вървяха	вървяха

	Future	Future in the Past
	(For negative, replace **ще** with **няма да**)	(For negative, replace **щях/щеше/щяхме/щяхте/щяха** with **нямаше**)
аз	ще вървя	щях да вървя
ти	ще вървиш	щеше да вървиш
той	ще върви	щеше да върви
ние	ще вървим	щяхме да вървим
вие	ще вървите	щяхте да вървите
те	ще вървят	щяха да вървят

Past Active Participles

M	F	N	Pl
вървял	вървяла	вървяло	вървели

	Present Perfect	Past Perfect
аз	съм вървял	бях вървял
ти	си вървял	беше вървял
той	е вървял	беше вървял
ние	сме вървели	бяхме вървели
вие	сте вървели	бяхте вървели
те	са вървели	бяха вървели

	Conditional Mood	Imperative Mood	
		Positive	**Negative**
аз	бих вървял		
ти	би вървял	върви	не върви
той	би вървял		
ние	бихме вървели		
вие	бихте вървели	вървете	не вървете
те	биха вървели		

Past Passive Participles

M	F	N	Pl
N/A	N/A	N/A	N/A

29) **вярвам/повярвам;** *trust, believe*

	Present	Past Simple	Past Continuous
аз	вярвам	повярвах	вярвах
ти	вярваш	повярва	вярваше
той	вярва	повярва	вярваше
ние	вярваме	повярвахме	вярвахме
вие	вярвате	повярвахте	вярвахте
те	вярват	повярваха	вярваха

	Future	Future in the Past
	(For negative, replace **ще** with **няма да**)	(For negative, replace **щях/щеше/щяхме/щяхте/щяха** with **нямаше**)
аз	ще вярвам/повярвам	щях да вярвам/повярвам
ти	ще вярваш/повярваш	щеше да вярваш/повярваш
той	ще вярва/повярва	щеше да вярва/повярва
ние	ще вярваме/повярваме	щяхме да вярваме/повярваме
вие	ще вярвате/повярвате	щяхте да вярвате/повярвате
те	ще вярват/повярват	щяха да вярват/повярват

Past Active Participles

M	F	N	Pl
вярвал/повярвал	вярвала/повярвала	вярвало/повярвало	вярвали/повярвали

	Present Perfect	Past Perfect
аз	съм вярвал/повярвал	бях вярвал/повярвал
ти	си вярвал/повярвал	беше вярвал/повярвал
той	е вярвал/повярвал	беше вярвал/повярвал
ние	сме вярвали/повярвали	бяхме вярвали/повярвали
вие	сте вярвали/повярвали	бяхте вярвали/повярвали
те	са вярвали/повярвали	бяха вярвали/повярвали

	Conditional Mood	Imperative Mood	
аз	би вярвал/повярвал	**Positive**	**Negative**
ти	би вярвал/повярвал	вярвай/повярвай	не вярвай
той	бихме вярвали/повярвали		
ние	бихте вярвали/повярвали		
вие	биха вярвали/повярвали	вярвайте/повярвайте	не вярвайте
те	бих вярвал/повярвал		

Past Passive Participles

M	F	N	Pl
вярван/повярван	вярвана/повярвана	вярвано/повярвано	вярвани/повярвани

30) **гледам;** *watch, look at, observe*

	Present	Past Simple	Past Continuous
аз	гледам	гледах	гледах
ти	гледаш	гледа	гледаше
той	гледа	гледа	гледаше
ние	гледаме	гледахме	гледахме
вие	гледате	гледахте	гледахте
те	гледат	гледаха	гледаха

	Future	Future in the Past
	(For negative, replace **ще** with **няма да**)	(For negative, replace **щях/щеше/щяхме/щяхте/щяха** with **нямаше**)
аз	ще гледам	щях да гледам
ти	ще гледаш	щеше да гледаш
той	ще гледа	щеше да гледа
ние	ще гледаме	щяхме да гледаме
вие	ще гледате	щяхте да гледате
те	ще гледат	щяха да гледат

Past Active Participles

M	F	N	Pl
гледал	гледала	гледало	гледали

	Present Perfect	Past Perfect
аз	съм гледал	бях гледал
ти	си гледал	беше гледал
той	е гледал	беше гледал
ние	сме гледали	бяхме гледали
вие	сте гледали	бяхте гледали
те	са гледали	бяха гледали

	Conditional Mood	Imperative Mood	
аз	бих гледал	**Positive**	**Negative**
ти	би гледал	гледай	не гледай
той	би гледал		
ние	бихме гледали		
вие	бихте гледали	гледайте	не гледайте
те	биха гледали		

Past Passive Participles

M	F	N	Pl
гледан	гледана	гледано	гледани

31) **глезя;** *spoil, overindulge* **глезя се;** *behave badly*

	Present	Past Simple	Past Continuous
аз	глезя	глезих	глезех
ти	глезиш	глези	глезеше
той	глези	глези	глезеше
ние	глезим	глезихме	глезехме
вие	глезите	глезихте	глезехте
те	глезят	глезиха	глезеха

	Future	Future in the Past
	(For negative, replace **ще** with **няма да**)	(For negative, replace **щях/щеше/щяхме/щяхте/щяха** with **нямаше**)
аз	ще глезя	щях да глезя
ти	ще глезиш	щеше да глезиш
той	ще глези	щеше да глези
ние	ще глезим	щяхме да глезим
вие	ще глезите	щяхте да глезите
те	ще глезят	щяха да глезят

Past Active Participles

M	F	N	Pl
Глезил	глезила	глезило	глезили

	Present Perfect	Past Perfect
аз	съм глезил	бях глезил
ти	си глезил	беше глезил
той	е глезил	беше глезил
ние	сме глезили	бяхме глезили
вие	сте глезили	бяхте глезили
те	са глезили	бяха глезили

	Conditional Mood	Imperative Mood	
аз	бих глезил	**Positive**	**Negative**
ти	би глезил	глези	не глези
той	би глезил		
ние	бихме глезили		
вие	бихте глезили	глезете	не глезете
те	биха глезили		

Past Passive Participles

M	F	N	Pl
Глезен	глезена	глезено	глезени

32) **глобявам/глобя;** *fine, impose a fine*

	Present	**Past Simple**	**Past Continuous**
аз	глобявам	глобих	глобявах
ти	глобяваш	глоби	глобяваше
той	глобява	глоби	глобяваше
ние	глобяваме	глобихме	глобявахме
вие	глобявате	глобихте	глобявахте
те	глобяват	глобиха	глобяваха

	Future	**Future in the Past**
	(For negative, replace **ще** with **няма да**)	(For negative, replace **щях/щеше/щяхме/щяхте/щяха** with **нямаше**)
аз	ще глобявам/глобя	щях да глобявам/глобя
ти	ще глобяваш/глобиш	щеше да глобяваш/глобиш
той	ще глобява/глоби	щеше да глобява/глоби
ние	ще глобяваме/глобим	щяхме да глобяваме/глобим
вие	ще глобявате/глобите	щяхте да глобявате/глобите
те	ще глобяват/глобят	щяха да глобяват/глобят

Past Active Participles

M	**F**	**N**	**Pl**
глобявал/глобил	глобявала/глобила	глобявало/глобило	глобявали/глобили

	Present Perfect	**Past Perfect**
аз	съм глобявал/глобил	бях глобявал/глобил
ти	си глобявал/глобил	беше глобявал/глобил
той	е глобявал/глобил	беше глобявал/глобил
ние	сме глобявали/глобили	бяхме глобявали/глобили
вие	сте глобявали/глобили	бяхте глобявали/глобили
те	са глобявали/глобили	бяха глобявали/глобили

	Conditional Mood	**Imperative Mood**	
аз	бих глобявал/глобил	**Positive**	**Negative**
ти	би глобявал/глобил	глобявай/глоби	не глобявай
той	би глобявал/глобил		
ние	бихме глобявали/глобили		
вие	бихте глобявали/глобили	глобявайте/глобете	не глобявайте
те	биха глобявали/глобили		

Past Passive Participles

M	**F**	**N**	**Pl**
глобяван/глобен	глобявана/глобена	глобявано/глобено	глобявани/глобени

33) **говоря;** *talk, speak*

	Present	Past Simple	Past Continuous
аз	говоря	говорих	говорех
ти	говориш	говори	говореше
той	говори	говори	говореше
ние	говорим	говорихме	говорехме
вие	говорите	говорихте	говорехте
те	говорят	говориха	говореха

	Future	Future in the Past
	(For negative, replace **ще** with **няма да**)	(For negative, replace **щях/щеше/щяхме/щяхте/щяха** with **нямаше**)
аз	ще говоря	щях да говоря
ти	ще говориш	щеше да говориш
той	ще говори	щеше да говори
ние	ще говорим	щяхме да говорим
вие	ще говорите	щяхте да говорите
те	ще говорят	щяха да говорят

Past Active Participles

M	F	N	Pl
говорил	говорила	говорило	говорили

	Present Perfect	Past Perfect
аз	съм говорил	бях говорил
ти	си говорил	беше говорил
той	е говорил	беше говорил
ние	сме говорили	бяхме говорили
вие	сте говорили	бяхте говорили
те	са говорили	бяха говорили

	Conditional Mood	Imperative Mood	
аз	бих говорил	**Positive**	**Negative**
ти	би говорил	говори	не говори
той	би говорил		
ние	бихме говорили		
вие	бихте говорили	говорете	не говорете
те	биха говорили		

Past Passive Participles

M	F	N	Pl
говорен	говорена	говорено	говорени

34) **гордея се;** *be proud, take pride*

	Present	**Past Simple**	**Past Continuous**
аз	се гордея	се гордях	се гордеех
ти	се гордееш	се гордя	се гордееше
той	се гордее	се гордя	се гордееше
ние	се гордеем	се гордяхме	се гордеехме
вие	се гордеете	се гордяхте	се гордеехте
те	се гордеят	се гордяха	се гордееха

	Future	**Future in the Past**
	(For negative, replace **ще** with **няма да**)	(For negative, replace **щях/щеше/щяхме/щяхте/щяха** with **нямаше**)
аз	ще се гордея	щях да се гордея
ти	ще се гордееш	щеше да се гордееш
той	ще се гордее	щеше да се гордее
ние	ще се гордеем	щяхме да се гордеем
вие	ще се гордеете	щяхте да се гордеете
те	ще се гордеят	щяха да се гордеят

Past Active Participles

M	**F**	**N**	**Pl**
гордял	гордяла	гордяло	гордели

	Present Perfect	**Past Perfect**
аз	съм се гордял	бях се гордял
ти	си се гордял	беше се гордял
той	се е гордял	беше се гордял
ние	сме се гордели	бяхме се гордели
вие	сте се гордели	бяхте се гордели
те	са се гордели	бяха се гордели

	Conditional Mood	**Imperative Mood**	
аз	бих се гордял	**Positive**	**Negative**
ти	би се гордял	гордей се	не се гордей
той	би се гордял		
ние	бихме се гордели		
вие	бихте се гордели	гордейте се	не се гордейте
те	биха се гордели		

Past Passive Participles

M	**F**	**N**	**Pl**
N/A	N/A	N/A	N/A

35) **горя;** *burn, burn up, be on fire*

	Present	**Past Simple**	**Past Continuous**
аз	горя	горих	горях
ти	гориш	гори	гореше
той	гори	гори	гореше
ние	горим	горихме	горяхме
вие	горите	горихте	горяхте
те	горят	гориха	горяха

	Future	**Future in the Past**
	(For negative, replace **ще** with **няма да**)	(For negative, replace **щях/щеше/щяхме/щяхте/щяха** with **нямаше**)
аз	ще горя	щях да горя
ти	ще гориш	щеше да гориш
той	ще гори	щеше да гори
ние	ще горим	щяхме да горим
вие	ще горите	щяхте да горите
те	ще горят	щяха да горят

Past Active Participles

M	**F**	**N**	**Pl**
горил	горила	горило	горили

	Present Perfect	**Past Perfect**
аз	съм горил	бях горил
ти	си горил	беше горил
той	е горил	беше горил
ние	сме горили	бяхме горили
вие	сте горили	бяхте горили
те	са горили	бяха горили

	Conditional Mood	**Imperative Mood**	
		Positive	**Negative**
аз	бих горил		
ти	би горил	гори	не гори
той	би горил		
ние	бихме горили		
вие	бихте горили	горете	не горете
те	биха горили		

Past Passive Participles

M	**F**	**N**	**Pl**
горен	горена	горено	горени

36) **готвя;** *cook*

	Present	Past Simple	Past Continuous
аз	готвя	готвих	готвех
ти	готвиш	готви	готвеше
той	готви	готви	готвеше
ние	готвим	готвихме	готвехме
вие	готвите	готвихте	готвехте
те	готвят	готвиха	готвеха

	Future	Future in the Past
	(For negative, replace **ще** with **няма да**)	(For negative, replace **щях/щеше/щяхме/щяхте/щяха** with **нямаше**)
аз	ще готвя	щях да готвя
ти	ще готвиш	щеше да готвиш
той	ще готви	щеше да готви
ние	ще готвим	щяхме да готвим
вие	ще готвите	щяхте да готвите
те	ще готвят	щяха да готвят

Past Active Participles

M	F	N	Pl
готвил	готвила	готвило	готвили

	Present Perfect	Past Perfect
аз	съм готвил	бях готвил
ти	си готвил	беше готвил
той	е готвил	беше готвил
ние	сме готвили	бяхме готвили
вие	сте готвили	бяхте готвили
те	са готвили	бяха готвили

	Conditional Mood	Imperative Mood	
аз	бих готвил	**Positive**	**Negative**
ти	би готвил	готви	не готви
той	би готвил		
ние	бихме готвили		
вие	бихте готвили	гответе	не гответе
те	биха готвили		

Past Passive Participles

M	F	N	Pl
готвен	готвена	готвено	готвени

37) **греша/сгреша;** *make a mistake, be wrong*

	Present	**Past Simple**	**Past Continuous**
аз	греша	сгреших	грешах
ти	грешиш	сгреши	грешеше
той	греши	сгреши	грешеше
ние	грешим	сгрешихме	грешахме
вие	грешите	сгрешихте	грешахте
те	грешат	сгрешиха	грешаха

	Future	**Future in the Past**
	(For negative, replace **ще** with **няма да**)	(For negative, replace **щях/щеше/щяхме/щяхте/щяха** with **нямаше**)
аз	ще греша/сгреша	щях да греша/сгреша
ти	ще грешиш/сгрешиш	щеше да грешиш/сгрешиш
той	ще греши/сгреши	щеше да греши/сгреши
ние	ще грешим/сгрешим	щяхме да грешим/сгрешим
вие	ще грешите/сгрешите	щяхте да грешите/сгрешите
те	ще грешат/сгрешат	щяха да грешат/сгрешат

Past Active Participles

M	**F**	**N**	**Pl**
грешил/сгрешил	грешила/сгрешила	грешило/сгрешило	грешили/сгрешили

	Present Perfect	**Past Perfect**
аз	съм грешил/сгрешил	бях грешил/сгрешил
ти	си грешил/сгрешил	беше грешил/сгрешил
той	е грешил/сгрешил	беше грешил/сгрешил
ние	сме грешили/сгрешили	бяхме грешили/сгрешили
вие	сте грешили/сгрешили	бяхте грешили/сгрешили
те	са грешили/сгрешили	бяха грешили/сгрешили

	Conditional Mood	**Imperative Mood**	
аз	бих грешил/сгрешил	**Positive**	**Negative**
ти	би грешил/сгрешил	греши/сгреши	не греши
той	би грешил/сгрешил		
ние	бихме грешили/сгрешили		
вие	бихте грешили/сгрешили	грешете/сгрешете	не грешете
те	биха грешили/сгрешили		

Past Passive Participles

M	**F**	**N**	**Pl**
грешен/сгрешен	грешена/сгрешена	грешено/сгрешено	грешени/сгрешени

38) **губя/изгубя;** *lose, drop, be defeated*

	Present	**Past Simple**	**Past Continuous**
аз	губя	изгубих	губех
ти	губиш	изгуби	губеше
той	губи	изгуби	губеше
ние	губим	изгубихме	губехме
вие	губите	изгубихте	губехте
те	губят	изгубиха	губеха

	Future	**Future in the Past**
	(For negative, replace **ще** with **няма да**)	(For negative, replace **щях/щеше/щяхме/щяхте/щяха** with **нямаше**)
аз	ще губя/изгубя	щях да губя/изгубя
ти	ще губиш/изгубиш	щеше да губиш/изгубиш
той	ще губи/изгуби	щеше да губи/изгуби
ние	ще губим/изгубим	щяхме да губим/изгубим
вие	ще губите/изгубите	щяхте да губите/изгубите
те	ще губят/изгубят	щяха да губят/изгубят

Past Active Participles

M	**F**	**N**	**Pl**
губил/изгубил	губила/изгубила	губило/изгубило	губили/изгубили

	Present Perfect	**Past Perfect**
аз	съм губил/изгубил	бях губил/изгубил
ти	си губил/изгубил	беше губил/изгубил
той	е губил/изгубил	беше губил/изгубил
ние	сме губили/изгубили	бяхме губили/изгубили
вие	сте губили/изгубили	бяхте губили/изгубили
те	са губили/изгубили	бяха губили/изгубили

	Conditional Mood	**Imperative Mood**	
аз	би губил/изгубил	**Positive**	**Negative**
ти	би губил/изгубил	губи/изгуби	не губи
той	бихме губили/изгубили		
ние	бихте губили/изгубили		
вие	биха губили/изгубили	губете/изгубете	не губете
те	би губил/изгубил		

Past Passive Participles

M	**F**	**N**	**Pl**
губен/изгубен	губена/изгубена	губено/изгубено	губени/изгубени

39) **давам/дам;** *give, provide, offer*

	Present	Past Simple	Past Continuous
аз	давам	дадох	давах
ти	даваш	даде	даваше
той	дава	даде	даваше
ние	даваме	дадохме	давахме
вие	давате	дадохте	давахте
те	дават	дадоха	даваха

	Future	Future in the Past
	(For negative, replace **ще** with **няма да**)	(For negative, replace **щях/щеше/щяхме/щяхте/щяха** with **нямаше**)
аз	ще давам/дам	щях да давам/дам
ти	ще даваш/дадеш	щеше да даваш/дадеш
той	ще дава/даде	щеше да дава/даде
ние	ще даваме/дадем	щяхме да даваме/дадем
вие	ще давате/дадете	щяхте да давате/дадете
те	ще дават/дадат	щяха да дават/дадат

Past Active Participles

M	F	N	Pl
давал/дал	давала/дала	давало/дало	давали/дали

	Present Perfect	Past Perfect
аз	съм давал/дал	бях давал/дал
ти	си давал/дал	беше давал/дал
той	е давал/дал	беше давал/дал
ние	сме давали/дали	бяхме давали/дали
вие	сте давали/дали	бяхте давали/дали
те	са давали/дали	бяха давали/дали

	Conditional Mood	Imperative Mood	
аз	бих давал/дал	**Positive**	**Negative**
ти	би давал/дал	давай/дай	не давай
той	би давал/дал		
ние	бихме давали/дали		
вие	бихте давали/дали	давайте/дайте	не давайте
те	биха давали/дали		

Past Passive Participles

M	F	N	Pl
даван/даден	давана/дадена	давано/дадено	давани/дадени

40) **давя/удавя;** *drown, sink*

	Present	Past Simple	Past Continuous
аз	давя	удавих	давех
ти	давиш	удави	давеше
той	дави	удави	давеше
ние	давим	удавихме	давехме
вие	давите	удавихте	давехте
те	давят	удавиха	давеха

	Future	Future in the Past
	(For negative, replace **ще** with **няма да**)	(For negative, replace **щях/щеше/щяхме/щяхте/щяха** with **нямаше**)
аз	ще давя/удавя	щях да давя/удавя
ти	ще давиш/удавиш	щеше да давиш/удавиш
той	ще дави/удави	щеше да дави/удави
ние	ще давим/удавим	щяхме да давим/удавим
вие	ще давите/удавите	щяхте да давите/удавите
те	ще давят/удавят	щяха да давят/удавят

Past Active Participles

M	F	N	Pl
давил/удавил	давил/удавила	давило/удавило	давили/удавили

	Present Perfect	Past Perfect
аз	съм давил/удавил	бях давил/удавил
ти	си давил/удавил	беше давил/удавил
той	е давил/удавил	беше давил/удавил
ние	сме давили/удавили	бяхме давили/удавили
вие	сте давили/удавили	бяхте давили/удавили
те	са давили/удавили	бяха давили/удавили

	Conditional Mood	Imperative Mood: Positive	Imperative Mood: Negative
аз	бих давил/удавил		
ти	би давил/удавил	дави/удави	не дави
той	би давил/удавил		
ние	бихме давили/удавили		
вие	бихте давили/удавили	давете/удавете	не давете
те	биха давили/удавили		

Past Passive Participles

M	F	N	Pl
давен/удавен	давена/удавена	давено/удавено	давени/удавени

41) **движа;** *move, set in motion* **движа се;** *go, move*

	Present	Past Simple	Past Continuous
аз	движа	движих	движех
ти	движиш	движи	движеше
той	движи	движи	движеше
ние	движим	движихме	движехме
вие	движите	движихте	движехте
те	движат	движиха	движеха

	Future	Future in the Past
	(For negative, replace **ще** with **няма да**)	(For negative, replace **щях/щеше/щяхме/щяхте/щяха** with **нямаше**)
аз	ще движа	щях да движа
ти	ще движиш	щеше да движиш
той	ще движи	щеше да движи
ние	ще движим	щяхме да движим
вие	ще движите	щяхте да движите
те	ще движат	щяха да движат

Past Active Participles

M	F	N	Pl
движил	движила	движило	движили

	Present Perfect	Past Perfect
аз	съм движил	бях движил
ти	си движил	беше движил
той	е движил	беше движил
ние	сме движили	бяхме движили
вие	сте движили	бяхте движили
те	са движили	бяха движили

	Conditional Mood	Imperative Mood	
аз	бих движил	**Positive**	**Negative**
ти	би движил	движи	не движи
той	би движил		
ние	бихме движили		
вие	бихте движили	движете	не движете
те	биха движили		

Past Passive Participles

M	F	N	Pl
движен	движена	движено	движени

42) **добавям/добавя;** *add, append, insert*

	Present	Past Simple	Past Continuous
аз	добавям	добавих	добавях
ти	добавяш	добави	добавяше
той	добавя	добави	добавяше
ние	добавяме	добавихме	добавяхме
вие	добавяте	добавихте	добавяхте
те	добавят	добавиха	добавяха

	Future	Future in the Past
	(For negative, replace **ще** with **няма да**)	(For negative, replace **щях/щеше/щяхме/щяхте/щяха** with **нямаше**)
аз	ще добавям/добавя	щях да добавям/добавя
ти	ще добавяш/добавиш	щеше да добавяш/добавиш
той	ще добавя/добави	щеше да добавя/добави
ние	ще добавяме/добавим	щяхме да добавяме/добавим
вие	ще добавяте/добавите	щяхте да добавяте/добавите
те	ще добавят/добавят	щяха да добавят/добавят

Past Active Participles

M	F	N	Pl
добавял/добавил	добавяла/добавила	добавяло/добавило	добавяли/добавили

	Present Perfect	Past Perfect
аз	съм добавял/добавил	бях добавял/добавил
ти	си добавял/добавил	беше добавял/добавил
той	е добавял/добавил	беше добавял/добавил
ние	сме добавяли/добавили	бяхме добавяли/добавили
вие	сте добавяли/добавили	бяхте добавяли/добавили
те	са добавяли/добавили	бяха добавяли/добавили

	Conditional Mood	Imperative Mood	
аз	бих добавял/добавил	**Positive**	**Negative**
ти	би добавял/добавил	добавяй/добави	не добавяй
той	би добавял/добавил		
ние	бихме добавяли/добавили		
вие	бихте добавяли/добавили	добавяйте/добавете	не добавяйте
те	биха добавяли/добавили		

Past Passive Participles

M	F	N	Pl
добавян/добавен	добавяна/добавена	добавяно/добавено	добавяни/добавени

43) **довеждам/доведа;** *bring, take*

	Present	Past Simple	Past Continuous
аз	довеждам	доведох	довеждах
ти	довеждаш	доведе	довеждаше
той	довежда	доведе	довеждаше
ние	довеждаме	доведохме	довеждахме
вие	довеждате	доведохте	довеждахте
те	довеждат	доведоха	довеждаха

	Future	Future in the Past
	(For negative, replace **ще** with **няма да**)	(For negative, replace **щях/щеше/щяхме/щяхте/щяха** with **нямаше**)
аз	ще довеждам/доведа	щях да довеждам/доведа
ти	ще довеждаш/доведеш	щеше да довеждаш/доведеш
той	ще довежда/доведе	щеше да довежда/доведе
ние	ще довеждаме/доведем	щяхме да довеждаме/доведем
вие	ще довеждате/доведете	щяхте да довеждате/доведете
те	ще довеждат/доведат	щяха да довеждат/доведат

Past Active Participles

M	F	N	Pl
довеждал/довел	довеждала/довела	довеждало/довело	довеждали/довели

	Present Perfect	Past Perfect
аз	съм довеждал/довел	бях довеждал/довел
ти	си довеждал/довел	беше довеждал/довел
той	е довеждал/довел	беше довеждал/довел
ние	сме довеждали/довели	бяхме довеждали/довели
вие	сте довеждали/довели	бяхте довеждали/довели
те	са довеждали/довели	бяха довеждали/довели

	Conditional Mood	Imperative Mood	
аз	бих довеждал/довел	**Positive**	**Negative**
ти	би довеждал/довел	довеждай/доведи	не довеждай
той	би довеждал/довел		
ние	бихме довеждали/довели		
вие	бихте довеждали/довели	довеждайте/доведете	не довеждайте
те	биха довеждали/довели		

Past Passive Participles

M	F	N	Pl
довеждан/доведен	довеждана/доведена	довеждано/доведено	довеждани/доведени

44) **доверявам/доверя;** *confide, disclose* **доверявам/доверя се;** *trust, believe*

	Present	Past Simple	Past Continuous
аз	доверявам	довери х	доверявах
ти	доверяваш	довери	доверяваше
той	доверява	довери	доверяваше
ние	доверяваме	доверихме	доверявахме
вие	доверявате	доверихте	доверявахте
те	доверяват	довериха	доверяваха

	Future	Future in the Past
	(For negative, replace **ще** with **няма да**)	(For negative, replace **щях/щеше/щяхме/щяхте/щяха** with **нямаше**)
аз	ще доверявам/доверя	щях да доверявам/доверя
ти	ще доверяваш/довериш	щеше да доверяваш/довериш
той	ще доверява/довери	щеше да доверява/довери
ние	ще доверяваме/доверим	щяхме да доверяваме/доверим
вие	ще доверявате/доверите	щяхте да доверявате/доверите
те	ще доверяват/доверят	щяха да доверяват/доверят

Past Active Participles

M	F	N	Pl
доверявал/доверил	доверявала/доверила	доверявало/доверило	доверявали/доверили

	Present Perfect	Past Perfect
аз	съм доверявал/доверил	бях доверявал/доверил
ти	си доверявал/доверил	беше доверявал/доверил
той	е доверявал/доверил	беше доверявал/доверил
ние	сме доверявали/доверили	бяхме доверявали/доверили
вие	сте доверявали/доверили	бяхте доверявали/доверили
те	са доверявали/доверили	бяха доверявали/доверили

	Conditional Mood	Imperative Mood	
		Positive	**Negative**
аз	бих доверявал/доверил		
ти	би доверявал/доверил	доверявай/довери	не доверявай
той	би доверявал/доверил		
ние	бихме доверявали/доверили		
вие	бихте доверявали/доверили	доверявайте/доверете	не доверявайте
те	биха доверявали/доверили		

Past Passive Participles

M	F	N	Pl
доверяван/доверен	доверявана/доверена	доверявано/доверено	доверявани/доверени

45) **договарям/договоря;** *clear up, settle, resolve*

	Present	Past Simple	Past Continuous
аз	договарям	договорих	договарях
ти	договаряш	договори	договаряше
той	договаря	договори	договаряше
ние	договаряме	договорихме	договаряхме
вие	договаряте	договорихте	договаряхте
те	договарят	договориха	договаряха

	Future	Future in the Past
	(For negative, replace **ще** with **няма да**)	(For negative, replace **щях/щеше/щяхме/щяхте/щяха** with **нямаше**)
аз	ще договарям/договоря	щях да договарям/договоря
ти	ще договаряш/договориш	щеше да договаряш/договориш
той	ще договаря/договори	щеше да договаря/договори
ние	ще договаряме/договорим	щяхме да договаряме/договорим
вие	ще договаряте/договорите	щяхте да договаряте/договорите
те	ще договарят/договорят	щяха да договарят/договорят

Past Active Participles

M	F	N	Pl
договарял/ договорил	договаряла/договорила	договаряло/ договорило	договаряли/ договорили

	Present Perfect	Past Perfect
аз	съм договарял/договорил	бях договарял/договорил
ти	си договарял/договорил	беше договарял/договорил
той	е договарял/договорил	беше договарял/договорил
ние	сме договаряли/договорили	бяхме договаряли/договорили
вие	сте договаряли/договорили	бяхте договаряли/договорили
те	са договаряли/договорили	бяха договаряли/договорили

	Conditional Mood	Imperative Mood	
аз	бих договарял/договорил	**Positive**	**Negative**
ти	би договарял/договорил	договаряй/договори	не договаряй
той	би договарял/договорил		
ние	бихме договаряли/договорили		
вие	бихте договаряли/договорили	договаряйте/договорете	не договаряйте
те	биха договаряли/договорили		

Past Passive Participles

M	F	N	Pl
договарян/ договорен	договаряна/договорена	договаряно/ договорено	договаряни/ договорени

46) **донасям/донеса;** *bring, carry, take*

	Present	**Past Simple**	**Past Continuous**
аз	донасям	донесох	донасях
ти	донасяш	донесе	донасяше
той	донася	донесе	донасяше
ние	донасяме	донесохме	донасяхме
вие	донасяте	донесохте	донасяхте
те	донасят	донесоха	донасяха

	Future	**Future in the Past**
	(For negative, replace **ще** with **няма да**)	(For negative, replace **щях/щеше/щяхме/щяхте/щяха** with **нямаше**)
аз	ще донасям/донеса	щях да донасям/донеса
ти	ще донасяш/донесеш	щеше да донасяш/донесеш
той	ще донася/донесе	щеше да донася/донесе
ние	ще донасяме/донесем	щяхме да донасяме/донесем
вие	ще донасяте/донесете	щяхте да донасяте/донесете
те	ще донасят/донесат	щяха да донасят/донесат

Past Active Participles

M	**F**	**N**	**Pl**
донасял/донесъл	донасяла/донесла	донасяло/донесло	донасяли/донесли

	Present Perfect	**Past Perfect**
аз	съм донасял/донесъл	бях донасял/донесъл
ти	си донасял/донесъл	беше донасял/донесъл
той	е донасял/донесъл	беше донасял/донесъл
ние	сме донасяли/донесли	бяхме донасяли/донесли
вие	сте донасяли/донесли	бяхте донасяли/донесли
те	са донасяли/донесли	бяха донасяли/донесли

	Conditional Mood	**Imperative Mood**	
аз	бих донасял/донесъл	**Positive**	**Negative**
ти	би донасял/донесъл	донасяй/донеси	не донасяй
той	би донасял/донесъл		
ние	бихме донасяли/донесли		
вие	бихте донасяли/донесли	донасяйте/донесете	не донасяйте
те	биха донасяли/донесли		

Past Passive Participles

M	**F**	**N**	**Pl**
донасян/донесен	донасяна/донесена	донасяно/донесено	донасяни/донесени

47) **дръпвам/дръпна;** *pull, draw, drag*

	Present	Past Simple	Past Continuous
аз	дръпвам	дръпнах	дръпвах
ти	дръпваш	дръпна	дръпваше
той	дръпва	дръпна	дръпваше
ние	дръпваме	дръпнахме	дръпвахме
вие	дръпвате	дръпнахте	дръпвахте
те	дръпват	дръпнаха	дръпваха

	Future	Future in the Past
	(For negative replace **ще** with **няма да**)	(For negative replace **щях/щеше/щяхме/щяхте/щяха** with **нямаше**)
аз	ще дръпвам/дръпна	щях да дръпвам/дръпна
ти	ще дръпваш/дръпнеш	щеше да дръпваш/дръпнеш
той	ще дръпва/дръпне	щеше да дръпва/дръпне
ние	ще дръпваме/дръпнем	щяхме да дръпваме/дръпнем
вие	ще дръпвате/дръпнете	щяхте да дръпвате/дръпнете
те	ще дръпват/дръпнат	щяха да дръпват/дръпнат

Past Active Participles

M	F	N	Pl
дръпвал/дръпнал	дръпвала/дръпнала	дръпвало/дръпнало	дръпвали/дръпнали

	Present Perfect	Past Perfect
аз	съм дръпвал/дръпнал	бях дръпвал/дръпнал
ти	си дръпвал/дръпнал	беше дръпвал/дръпнал
той	е дръпвал/дръпнал	беше дръпвал/дръпнал
ние	сме дръпвали/дръпнали	бяхме дръпвали/дръпнали
вие	сте дръпвали/дръпнали	бяхте дръпвали/дръпнали
те	са дръпвали/дръпнали	бяха дръпвали/дръпнали

	Conditional Mood	Imperative Mood	
аз	бих дръпвал/дръпнал	**Positive**	**Negative**
ти	би дръпвал/дръпнал	дръпвай/дръпни	не дръпвай
той	би дръпвал/дръпнал		
ние	бихме дръпвали/дръпнали		
вие	бихте дръпвали/дръпнали	дръпвайте/дръпнете	не дръпвайте
те	биха дръпвали/дръпнали		

Past Passive Participles

M	F	N	Pl
дръпван/дръпнат	дръпвана/дръпната	дръпвано/дръпнато	дръпвани/дръпнати

48) **държа;** *hold, catch, keep; value; insist* **държа се;** *behave; be active/fit*

	Present	**Past Simple**	**Past Continuous**
аз	държа	държах	държах
ти	държиш	държа	държеше
той	държи	държа	държеше
ние	държим	държахме	държахме
вие	държите	държахте	държахте
те	държат	държаха	държаха

	Future	**Future in the Past**
	(For negative, replace **ще** with **няма да**)	(For negative, replace **щях/щеше/щяхме/щяхте/щяха** with **нямаше**)
аз	ще държа	щях да държа
ти	ще държиш	щеше да държиш
той	ще държи	щеше да държи
ние	ще държим	щяхме да държим
вие	ще държите	щяхте да държите
те	ще държат	щяха да държат

Past Active Participles

M	**F**	**N**	**Pl**
държал	държала	държало	държали

	Present Perfect	**Past Perfect**
аз	съм държал	бях държал
ти	си държал	беше държал
той	е държал	беше държал
ние	сме държали	бяхме държали
вие	сте държали	бяхте държали
те	са държали	бяха държали

	Conditional Mood	**Imperative Mood**	
		Positive	**Negative**
аз	бих държал		
ти	би държал	дръж	не дръж
той	би държал		
ние	бихме държали		
вие	бихте държали	дръжте	не дръжте
те	биха държали		

Past Passive Participles

M	**F**	**N**	**Pl**
държан	държана	държано	държани

49) **желая/пожелая;** *desire, wish*

	Present	Past Simple	Past Continuous
аз	желая	пожелах	желаех
ти	желаеш	пожела	желаеше
той	желае	пожела	желаеше
ние	желаем	пожелахме	желаехме
вие	желаете	пожелахте	желаехте
те	желаят	пожелаха	желаеха

	Future	Future in the Past
	(For negative, replace **ще** with **няма да**)	(For negative, replace **щях/щеше/щяхме/щяхте/щяха** with **нямаше**)
аз	ще желая/пожелая	щях да желая/пожелая
ти	ще желаеш/пожелаеш	щеше да желаеш/пожелаеш
той	ще желае/пожелае	щеше да желае/пожелае
ние	ще желаем/пожелаем	щяхме да желаем/пожелаем
вие	ще желаете/пожелаете	щяхте да желаете/пожелаете
те	ще желаят/пожелаят	щяха да желаят/пожелаят

Past Active Participles

M	F	N	Pl
желал/пожелал	желала/пожелала	желало/пожелало	желали/пожелали

	Present Perfect	Past Perfect
аз	съм желал/пожелал	бях желал/пожелал
ти	си желал/пожелал	беше желал/пожелал
той	е желал/пожелал	беше желал/пожелал
ние	сме желали/пожелали	бяхме желали/пожелали
вие	сте желали/пожелали	бяхте желали/пожелали
те	са желали/пожелали	бяха желали/пожелали

	Conditional Mood	Imperative Mood	
аз	бих желал/пожелал	**Positive**	**Negative**
ти	би желал/пожелал	желай/пожелай	не желай
той	би желал/пожелал		
ние	бихме желали/пожелали		
вие	бихте желали/пожелали	желайте/пожелайте	не желайте
те	биха желали/пожелали		

Past Passive Participles

M	F	N	Pl
желан/пожелан	желана/пожелана	желано/пожелано	желани/пожелани

50) **женя/оженя;** *marry, wed* **женя/оженя се;** *get married*

	Present	**Past Simple**	**Past Continuous**
аз	женя	ожених	женех
ти	жениш	ожени	женеше
той	жени	ожени	женеше
ние	женим	оженихме	женехме
вие	жените	оженихте	женехте
те	женят	ожениха	женеха

	Future	**Future in the Past**
	(For negative, replace **ще** with **няма да**)	(For negative, replace **щях/щеше/щяхме/щяхте/щяха** with **нямаше**)
аз	ще женя/оженя	щях да женя/оженя
ти	ще жениш/ожениш	щеше да жениш/ожениш
той	ще жени/ожени	щеше да жени/ожени
ние	ще женим/оженим	щяхме да женим/оженим
вие	ще жените/ожените	щяхте да жените/ожените
те	ще женят/оженят	щяха да женят/оженят

Past Active Participles

M	**F**	**N**	**Pl**
женил/оженил	женила/оженила	женило/оженило	женили/оженили

	Present Perfect	**Past Perfect**
аз	съм женил/оженил	бях женил/оженил
ти	си женил/оженил	беше женил/оженил
той	е женил/оженил	беше женил/оженил
ние	сме женили/оженили	бяхме женили/оженили
вие	сте женили/оженили	бяхте женили/оженили
те	са женили/оженили	бяха женили/оженили

	Conditional Mood	**Imperative Mood**	
аз	бих женил/оженил	**Positive**	**Negative**
ти	би женил/оженил	жени/ожени	не жени
той	би женил/оженил		
ние	бихме женили/оженили		
вие	бихте женили/оженили	женете/оженете	не женете
те	биха женили/оженили		

Past Passive Participles

M	**F**	**N**	**Pl**
женен/оженен	женена/оженена	женено/оженено	женени/оженени

51) **жертвам;** *sacrifice, give up, surrender*

	Present	**Past Simple**	**Past Continuous**
аз	жертвам	жертвах	жертвах
ти	жертваш	жертва	жертваше
той	жертва	жертва	жертваше
ние	жертваме	жертвахме	жертвахме
вие	жертвате	жертвахте	жертвахте
те	жертват	жертваха	жертваха

	Future	**Future in the Past**
	(For negative, replace **ще** with **няма да**)	(For negative, replace **щях/щеше/щяхме/щяхте/щяха** with **нямаше**)
аз	ще жертвам	щях да жертвам
ти	ще жертваш	щеше да жертваш
той	ще жертва	щеше да жертва
ние	ще жертваме	щяхме да жертваме
вие	ще жертвате	щяхте да жертвате
те	ще жертват	щяха да жертват

Past Active Participles

M	**F**	**N**	**Pl**
жертвал	жертвала	жертвало	жертвали

	Present Perfect	**Past Perfect**
аз	съм жертвал	бях жертвал
ти	си жертвал	беше жертвал
той	е жертвал	беше жертвал
ние	сме жертвали	бяхме жертвали
вие	сте жертвали	бяхте жертвали
те	са жертвали	бяха жертвали

	Conditional Mood	**Imperative Mood**	
аз	бих жертвал	**Positive**	**Negative**
ти	би жертвал	жертвай	не жертвай
той	би жертвал		
ние	бихме жертвали		
вие	бихте жертвали	жертвайте	не жертвайте
те	биха жертвали		

Past Passive Participles

M	**F**	**N**	**Pl**
жертван	жертвана	жертвано	жертвани

52) **живея;** *live, reside*

	Present	Past Simple	Past Continuous
аз	живея	живях	живеех
ти	живееш	живя	живееше
той	живее	живя	живееше
ние	живеем	живяхме	живеехме
вие	живеете	живяхте	живеехте
те	живеят	живяха	живееха

	Future	Future in the Past
	(For negative, replace **ще** with **няма да**)	(For negative, replace **щях/щеше/щяхме/щяхте/щяха** with **нямаше**)
аз	ще живея	щях да живея
ти	ще живееш	щеше да живееш
той	ще живее	щеше да живее
ние	ще живеем	щяхме да живеем
вие	ще живеете	щяхте да живеете
те	ще живеят	щяха да живеят

Past Active Participles

M	F	N	Pl
живял	живяла	живяло	живели

	Present Perfect	Past Perfect
аз	съм живял	бях живял
ти	си живял	беше живял
той	е живял	беше живял
ние	сме живели	бяхме живели
вие	сте живели	бяхте живели
те	са живели	бяха живели

	Conditional Mood	Imperative Mood	
аз	бих живял	**Positive**	**Negative**
ти	би живял	живей	не живей
той	би живял		
ние	бихме живели		
вие	бихте живели	живейте	не живейте
те	биха живели		

Past Passive Participles

M	F	N	Pl
N/A	N/A	N/A	N/A

53) **забавлявам;** *amuse, entertain* **забавлявам се;** *enjoy, have fun*

	Present	**Past Simple**	**Past Continuous**
аз	забавлявам	забавлявах	забавлявах
ти	забавляваш	забавлява	забавляваше
той	забавлява	забавлява	забавляваше
ние	забавляваме	забавлявахме	забавлявахме
вие	забавлявате	забавлявахте	забавлявахте
те	забавляват	забавляваха	забавляваха

	Future	**Future in the Past**
	(For negative, replace **ще** with **няма да**)	(For negative, replace **щях/щеше/щяхме/щяхте/щяха** with **нямаше**)
аз	ще забавлявам	щях да забавлявам
ти	ще забавляваш	щеше да забавляваш
той	ще забавлява	щеше да забавлява
ние	ще забавляваме	щяхме да забавляваме
вие	ще забавлявате	щяхте да забавлявате
те	ще забавляват	щяха да забавляват

Past Active Participles

M	**F**	**N**	**Pl**
забавлявал	забавлявала	забавлявало	забавлявали

	Present Perfect	**Past Perfect**
аз	съм забавлявал	бях забавлявал
ти	си забавлявал	беше забавлявал
той	е забавлявал	беше забавлявал
ние	сме забавлявали	бяхме забавлявали
вие	сте забавлявали	бяхте забавлявали
те	са забавлявали	бяха забавлявали

	Conditional Mood	**Imperative Mood**	
аз	бих забавлявал	**Positive**	**Negative**
ти	би забавлявал	забавлявай	не забавлявай
той	би забавлявал		
ние	бихме забавлявали		
вие	бихте забавлявали	забавлявайте	не забавлявайте
те	биха забавлявали		

Past Passive Participles

M	**F**	**N**	**Pl**
забавляван	забавлявана	забавлявано	забавлявани

54) **забавям/забавя;** *delay, be delayed*

	Present	Past Simple	Past Continuous
аз	забавям	забавих	забавях
ти	забавяш	забави	забавяше
той	забавя	забави	забавяше
ние	забавяме	забавихме	забавяхме
вие	забавяте	забавихте	забавяхте
те	забавят	забавиха	забавяха

	Future	Future in the Past
	(For negative, replace **ще** with **няма да**)	(For negative, replace **щях/щеше/щяхме/щяхте/щяха** with **нямаше**)
аз	ще забавям/забавя	щях да забавям/забавя
ти	ще забавяш/забавиш	щеше да забавяш/забавиш
той	ще забавя/забави	щеше да забавя/забави
ние	ще забавяме/забавим	щяхме да забавяме/забавим
вие	ще забавяте/забавите	щяхте да забавяте/забавите
те	ще забавят/забавят	щяха да забавят/забавят

Past Active Participles

M	F	N	Pl
забавял/забавил	забавяла/забавила	забавяло/забавило	забавяли/забавили

	Present Perfect	Past Perfect
аз	съм забавял/забавил	бях забавял/забавил
ти	си забавял/забавил	беше забавял/забавил
той	е забавял/забавил	беше забавял/забавил
ние	сме забавяли/забавили	бяхме забавяли/забавили
вие	сте забавяли/забавили	бяхте забавяли/забавили
те	са забавяли/забавили	бяха забавяли/забавили

	Conditional Mood	Imperative Mood	
аз	бих забавял/забавил	**Positive**	**Negative**
ти	би забавял/забавил	забавяй/забави	не забавяй
той	би забавял/забавил		
ние	бихме забавяли/забавили		
вие	бихте забавяли/забавили	забавяйте/забавете	не забавяйте
те	биха забавяли/забавили		

Past Passive Participles

M	F	N	Pl
забавян/забавен	забавяна/забавена	забавяно/забавено	забавяни/забавени

55) **забелязвам/забележа** ; *notice, detect, spot*

	Present	**Past Simple**	**Past Continuous**
аз	забелязвам	Забелязах	забелязвах
ти	забелязваш	забеляза	забелязваше
той	забелязва	забеляза	забелязваше
ние	забелязваме	забелязахме	забелязвахме
вие	забелязвате	забелязахте	забелязвахте
те	забелязват	забелязаха	забелязваха

	Future	**Future in the Past**
	(For negative, replace **ще** with **няма да**)	(For negative, replace **щях/щеше/щяхме/щяхте/щяха** with **нямаше**)
аз	ще забелязвам/забележа	щях да забелязвам/забележа
ти	ще забелязваш/забележиш	щеше да забелязваш/забележиш
той	ще забелязва/забележи	щеше да забелязва/забележи
ние	ще забелязваме/забележим	щяхме да забелязваме/забележим
вие	ще забелязвате/забележите	щяхте да забелязвате/забележите
те	ще забелязват/забележат	щяха да забелязват/забележат

Past Active Participles

M	F	N	Pl
забелязвал/ забелязал	забелязвала/забелязала	забелязвало/ забелязало	забелязвали/забелязали

	Present Perfect	**Past Perfect**
аз	съм забелязвал/забелязал	бях забелязвал/забелязал
ти	си забелязвал/забелязал	беше забелязвал/забелязал
той	е забелязвал/забелязал	беше забелязвал/забелязал
ние	сме забелязвали/забелязали	бяхме забелязвали/забелязали
вие	сте забелязвали/забелязали	бяхте забелязвали/забелязали
те	са забелязвали/забелязали	бяха забелязвали/забелязали

	Conditional Mood	**Imperative Mood**	
		Positive	**Negative**
аз	бих забелязвал/забелязал		
ти	би забелязвал/забелязал	забелязвай/забележи	не забелязвай
той	би забелязвал/забелязал		
ние	бихме забелязвали/забелязали		
вие	бихте забелязвали/забелязали	забелязвайте/забележете	не забелязвайте
те	биха забелязвали/забелязали		

Past Passive Participles

M	F	N	Pl
забелязван/ забелязан	забелязвана/забелязана	забелязвано/ забелязано	забелязвани/забелязани

56) **заблуждавам/заблудя;** *mislead, misinform; become disoriented*

	Present	**Past Simple**	**Past Continuous**
аз	заблуждавам	заблудих	заблуждавах
ти	заблуждаваш	заблуди	заблуждаваше
той	заблуждава	заблуди	заблуждаваше
ние	заблуждаваме	заблудихме	заблуждавахме
вие	заблуждавате	заблудихте	заблуждавахте
те	заблуждават	заблудиха	заблуждаваха

	Future	**Future in the Past**
	(For negative, replace **ще** with **няма да**)	(For negative, replace **щях/щеше/щяхме/щяхте/щяха** with **нямаше**)
аз	ще заблуждавам/заблудя	щях да заблуждавам/заблудя
ти	ще заблуждаваш/заблудиш	щеше да заблуждаваш/заблудиш
той	ще заблуждава/заблуди	щеше да заблуждава/заблуди
ние	ще заблуждаваме/заблудим	щяхме да заблуждаваме/заблудим
вие	ще заблуждавате/заблудите	щяхте да заблуждавате/заблудите
те	ще заблуждават/заблудят	щяха да заблуждават/заблудят

Past Active Participles

M	**F**	**N**	**Pl**
заблуждавал/заблудил	заблуждавала/заблудила	заблуждавало/заблудило	заблуждавали/заблудили

	Present Perfect	**Past Perfect**
аз	съм заблуждавал/заблудил	бях заблуждавал/заблудил
ти	си заблуждавал/заблудил	беше заблуждавал/заблудил
той	е заблуждавал/заблудил	беше заблуждавал/заблудил
ние	сме заблуждавали/заблудили	бяхме заблуждавали/заблудили
вие	сте заблуждавали/заблудили	бяхте заблуждавали/заблудили
те	са заблуждавали/заблудили	бяха заблуждавали/заблудили

	Conditional Mood	**Imperative Mood**	
		Positive	**Negative**
аз	бих заблуждавал/заблудил		
ти	би заблуждавал/заблудил	заблуждавай/заблуди	не заблуждавай
той	би заблуждавал/заблудил		
ние	бихме заблуждавали/заблудили		
вие	бихте заблуждавали/заблудили	заблуждавайте/заблудете	не заблуждавайте
те	биха заблуждавали/заблудили		

Past Passive Participles

M	**F**	**N**	**Pl**
заблуждаван/заблуден	заблуждавана/заблудена	заблуждавано/заблудено	заблуждавани/заблудени

57) **забогатявам/забогатея**; *grow rich, enrich, acquire wealth*

	Present	Past Simple	Past Continuous
аз	забогатявам	Забогатях	забогатявах
ти	забогатяваш	забогатя	забогатяваше
той	забогатява	забогатя	забогатяваше
ние	забогатяваме	забогатяхме	забогатявахме
вие	забогатявате	забогатяхте	забогатявахте
те	забогатяват	забогатяха	забогатяваха

	Future	Future in the Past
	(For negative, replace **ще** with **няма да**)	(For negative, replace **щях/щеше/щяхме/щяхте/щяха** with **нямаше**)
аз	ще забогатявам/забогатея	щях да забогатявам/забогатея
ти	ще забогатяваш/забогатееш	щеше да забогатяваш/забогатееш
той	ще забогатява/забогатее	щеше да забогатява/забогатее
ние	ще забогатяваме/забогатеем	щяхме да забогатяваме/забогатеем
вие	ще забогатявате/забогатеете	щяхте да забогатявате/забогатеете
те	ще забогатяват/забогатеят	щяха да забогатяват/забогатеят

Past Active Participles

M	F	N	Pl
забогатявал/забогатял	забогатявала/забогатяла	забогатявало/забогатяло	забогатявали/забогатели

	Present Perfect	Past Perfect
аз	съм забогатявал/забогатял	бях забогатявал/забогатял
ти	си забогатявал/забогатял	беше забогатявал/забогатял
той	е забогатявал/забогатял	беше забогатявал/забогатял
ние	сме забогатявали/забогатели	бяхме забогатявали/забогатели
вие	сте забогатявали/забогатели	бяхте забогатявали/забогатели
те	са забогатявали/забогатели	бяха забогатявали/забогатели

	Conditional Mood	Imperative Mood	
аз	бих забогатявал/забогатял	**Positive**	**Negative**
ти	би забогатявал/забогатял	забогатявай/забогатей	не забогатявай
той	би забогатявал/забогатял		
ние	бихме забогатявали/забогатели		
вие	бихте забогатявали/забогатели	забогатявайте/забогатейте	не забогатявайте
те	биха забогатявали/забогатели		

Past Passive Participles

M	F	N	Pl
N/A	N/A	N/A	N/A

58) **забравям/забравя**; *forget, disregard*

	Present	**Past Simple**	**Past Continuous**
аз	забравям	забравих	забравях
ти	забравяш	забрави	забравяше
той	забравя	забрави	забравяше
ние	забравяме	забравихме	забравяхме
вие	забравяте	забравихте	забравяхте
те	забравят	забравиха	забравяха

	Future	**Future in the Past**
	(For negative, replace **ще** with **няма да**)	(For negative, replace **щях/щеше/щяхме/щяхте/щяха** with **нямаше**)
аз	ще забравям/забравя	щях да забравям/забравя
ти	ще забравяш/забравиш	щеше да забравяш/забравиш
той	ще забравя/забрави	щеше да забравя/забрави
ние	ще забравяме/забравим	щяхме да забравяме/забравим
вие	ще забравяте/забравите	щяхте да забравяте/забравите
те	ще забравят/забравят	щяха да забравят/забравят

Past Active Participles

M	**F**	**N**	**Pl**
забравял/забравил	забравяла/забравила	забравяло/забравило	забравяли/забравили

	Present Perfect	**Past Perfect**
аз	съм забравял/забравил	бях забравял/забравил
ти	си забравял/забравил	беше забравял/забравил
той	е забравял/забравил	беше забравял/забравил
ние	сме забравяли/забравили	бяхме забравяли/забравили
вие	сте забравяли/забравили	бяхте забравяли/забравили
те	са забравяли/забравили	бяха забравяли/забравили

	Conditional Mood	**Imperative Mood**	**Negative**
аз	бих забравял/забравил	**Positive**	
ти	би забравял/забравил	забравяй/забрави	не забравяй
той	би забравял/забравил		
ние	бихме забравяли/забравили		
вие	бихте забравяли/забравили	забравяйте/забравете	не забравяйте
те	биха забравяли/забравили		

Past Passive Participles

M	**F**	**N**	**Pl**
забравян/забравен	забравяна/забравена	забравяно/забравено	забравяни/забравени

59) **забранявам /забраня;** *ban, forbid, prohibit*

	Present	Past Simple	Past Continuous
аз	забранявам	забраних	забранявах
ти	забраняваш	забрани	забраняваше
той	забранява	забрани	забраняваше
ние	забраняваме	забранихме	забранявахме
вие	забранявате	забранихте	забранявахте
те	забраняват	забраниха	забраняваха

	Future	Future in the Past
	(For negative, replace **ще** with **няма да**)	(For negative, replace **щях/щеше/щяхме/щяхте/щяха** with **нямаше**)
аз	ще забранявам/забраня	щях да забранявам/забраня
ти	ще забраняваш/забраниш	щеше да забраняваш/забраниш
той	ще забранява/забрани	щеше да забранява/забрани
ние	ще забраняваме/забраним	щяхме да забраняваме/забраним
вие	ще забранявате/забраните	щяхте да забранявате/забраните
те	ще забраняват/забранят	щяха да забраняват/забранят

Past Active Participles

M	F	N	Pl
забранявал/ забранил	забранявала/забранила	забранявало/забранило	забранявали/забранили

	Present Perfect	Past Perfect
аз	съм забранявал/забранил	бях забранявал/забранил
ти	си забранявал/забранил	беше забранявал/забранил
той	е забранявал/забранил	беше забранявал/забранил
ние	сме забранявали/забранили	бяхме забранявали/забранили
вие	сте забранявали/забранили	бяхте забранявали/забранили
те	са забранявали/забранили	бяха забранявали/забранили

	Conditional Mood	Imperative Mood	
		Positive	**Negative**
аз	бих забранявал/забранил		
ти	би забранявал/забранил	забранявай/забрани	не забранявай
той	би забранявал/забранил		
ние	бихме забранявали/забранили		
вие	бихте забранявали/забранили	забранявайте/забранете	не забранявайте
те	биха забранявали/забранили		

Past Passive Participles

M	F	N	Pl
забраняван/ забранен	забранявана/забранена	забранявано/забранено	забранявани/забранени

60) **завивам/завия;** *turn, take a turn, bend; cover*

	Present	Past Simple	Past Continuous
аз	завивам	завих	завивах
ти	завиваш	зави	завиваше
той	завива	зави	завиваше
ние	завиваме	завихме	завивахме
вие	завивате	завихте	завивахте
те	завиват	завиха	завиваха

	Future	Future in the Past
	(For negative, replace **ще** with **няма да**)	(For negative, replace **щях/щеше/щяхме/щяхте/щяха** with **нямаше**)
аз	ще завивам/завия	щях да завивам/завия
ти	ще завиваш/завиеш	щеше да завиваш/завиеш
той	ще завива/завие	щеше да завива/завие
ние	ще завиваме/завием	щяхме да завиваме/завием
вие	ще завивате/завиете	щяхте да завивате/завиете
те	ще завиват/завият	щяха да завиват/завият

Past Active Participles

M	F	N	Pl
завивал/завил	завивала/завила	завивало/завило	завивали/завили

	Present Perfect	Past Perfect
аз	съм завивал/завил	бях завивал/завил
ти	си завивал/завил	беше завивал/завил
той	е завивал/завил	беше завивал/завил
ние	сме завивали/завили	бяхме завивали/завили
вие	сте завивали/завили	бяхте завивали/завили
те	са завивали/завили	бяха завивали/завили

	Conditional Mood	Imperative Mood	
		Positive	**Negative**
аз	бих завивал/завил		
ти	би завивал/завил	завивай/завий	не завивай
той	би завивал/завил		
ние	бихме завивали/завили		
вие	бихте завивали/завили	завивайте/завийте	не завивайте
те	биха завивали/завили		

Past Passive Participles

M	F	N	Pl
завиван/завит	завивана/завита	завивано/завито	завивани/завити

61) **завися;** *depend*

	Present	**Past Simple**	**Past Continuous**
аз	завися	зависих	зависех
ти	зависиш	зависи	зависеше
той	зависи	зависи	зависеше
ние	зависим	зависихме	зависехме
вие	зависите	зависихте	зависехте
те	зависят	зависиха	зависеха

	Future	**Future in the Past**
	(For negative, replace **ще** with **няма да**)	(For negative, replace **щях/щеше/щяхме/щяхте/щяха** with **нямаше**)
аз	ще завися	щях да завися
ти	ще зависиш	щеше да зависиш
той	ще зависи	щеше да зависи
ние	ще зависим	щяхме да зависим
вие	ще зависите	щяхте да зависите
те	ще зависят	щяха да зависят

Past Active Participles

M	**F**	**N**	**Pl**
зависил	зависила	зависило	зависили

	Present Perfect	**Past Perfect**
аз	съм зависил	бях зависил
ти	си зависил	беше зависил
той	е зависил	беше зависил
ние	сме зависили	бяхме зависили
вие	сте зависили	бяхте зависили
те	са зависили	бяха зависили

	Conditional Mood	**Imperative Mood**	
аз	бих зависил	**Positive**	**Negative**
ти	би зависил	N/A	N/A
той	би зависил		
ние	бихме зависили		
вие	бихте зависили	N/A	N/A
те	биха зависили		

Past Passive Participles

M	**F**	**N**	**Pl**
N/A	N/A	N/A	N/A

62) **загивам/загина;** *perish, die*

	Present	**Past Simple**	**Past Continuous**
аз	загивам	загинах	загивах
ти	загиваш	загина	загиваше
той	загива	загина	загиваше
ние	загиваме	загинахме	загивахме
вие	загивате	загинахте	загивахте
те	загиват	загинаха	загиваха

	Future	**Future in the Past**
	(For negative, replace **ще** with **няма да**)	(For negative, replace **щях/щеше/щяхме/щяхте/щяха** with **нямаше**)
аз	ще загивам/загина	щях да загивам/загина
ти	ще загиваш/загинеш	щеше да загиваш/загинеш
той	ще загива/загине	щеше да загива/загине
ние	ще загиваме/загинем	щяхме да загиваме/загинем
вие	ще загивате/загинете	щяхте да загивате/загинете
те	ще загиват/загинат	щяха да загиват/загинат

Past Active Participles

M	**F**	**N**	**Pl**
загивал/загинал	загивала/загинала	загивало/загинало	загивали/загинали

	Present Perfect	**Past Perfect**
аз	съм загивал/загинал	бях загивал/загинал
ти	си загивал/загинал	беше загивал/загинал
той	е загивал/загинал	беше загивал/загинал
ние	сме загивали/загинали	бяхме загивали/загинали
вие	сте загивали/загинали	бяхте загивали/загинали
те	са загивали/загинали	бяха загивали/загинали

	Conditional Mood	**Imperative Mood**	
аз	бих загивал/загинал	**Positive**	**Negative**
ти	би загивал/загинал	загивай/загини	не загивай
той	би загивал/загинал		
ние	бихме загивали/загинали		
вие	бихте загивали/загинали	загивайте/загинете	не загивайте
те	биха загивали/загинали		

Past Passive Participles

M	**F**	**N**	**Pl**
N/A	N/A	N/A	N/A

63) **задушавам/задуша;** *stifle; stew* **задушавам/задуша се;** *suffocate*

	Present	Past Simple	Past Continuous
аз	задушавам	задуших	задушавах
ти	задушаваш	задуши	задушаваше
той	задушава	задуши	задушаваше
ние	задушаваме	задушихме	задушавахме
вие	задушавате	задушихте	задушавахте
те	задушават	задушиха	задушаваха

	Future	Future in the Past
	(For negative, replace **ще** with **няма да**)	(For negative, replace **щях/щеше/щяхме/щяхте/щяха** with **нямаше**)
аз	ще задушавам/задуша	щях да задушавам/задуша
ти	ще задушаваш/задушиш	щеше да задушаваш/задушиш
той	ще задушава/задуши	щеше да задушава/задуши
ние	ще задушаваме/задушим	щяхме да задушаваме/задушим
вие	ще задушавате/задушите	щяхте да задушавате/задушите
те	ще задушават/задушат	щяха да задушават/задушат

Past Active Participles

M	F	N	Pl
задушавал/ задушил	задушавала/задушила	задушавало/задушило	задушавали/задушили

	Present Perfect	Past Perfect
аз	съм задушавал/задушил	бях задушавал/задушил
ти	си задушавал/задушил	беше задушавал/задушил
той	е задушавал/задушил	беше задушавал/задушил
ние	сме задушавали/задушили	бяхме задушавали/задушили
вие	сте задушавали/задушили	бяхте задушавали/задушили
те	са задушавали/задушили	бяха задушавали/задушили

	Conditional Mood	Imperative Mood	
		Positive	**Negative**
аз	бих задушавал/задушил		
ти	би задушавал/задушил	задушавай/задуши	не задушавай
той	би задушавал/задушил		
ние	бихме задушавали/задушили		
вие	бихте задушавали/задушили	задушавайте/задушете	не задушавайте
те	биха задушавали/задушили		

Past Passive Participles

M	F	N	Pl
задушаван/ задушен	задушавана/задушена	задушавано/задушено	задушавани/задушени

64) **закусвам/закуся;** *have breakfast*

	Present	Past Simple	Past Continuous
аз	закусвам	закусих	закусвах
ти	закусваш	закуси	закусваше
той	закусва	закуси	закусваше
ние	закусваме	закусихме	закусвахме
вие	закусвате	закусихте	закусвахте
те	закусват	закусиха	закусваха

	Future	Future in the Past
	(For negative, replace **ще** with **няма да**)	(For negative, replace **щях/щеше/щяхме/щяхте/щяха** with **нямаше**)
аз	ще закусвам/закуся	щях да закусвам/закуся
ти	ще закусваш/закусиш	щеше да закусваш/закусиш
той	ще закусва/закуси	щеше да закусва/закуси
ние	ще закусваме/закусим	щяхме да закусваме/закусим
вие	ще закусвате/закусите	щяхте да закусвате/закусите
те	ще закусват/закусят	щяха да закусват/закусят

Past Active Participles

M	F	N	Pl
закусвал/закусил	закусвала/закусила	закусвало/закусило	закусвали/закусили

	Present Perfect	Past Perfect
аз	съм закусвал/закусил	бях закусвал/закусил
ти	си закусвал/закусил	беше закусвал/закусил
той	е закусвал/закусил	беше закусвал/закусил
ние	сме закусвали/закусили	бяхме закусвали/закусили
вие	сте закусвали/закусили	бяхте закусвали/закусили
те	са закусвали/закусили	бяха закусвали/закусили

	Conditional Mood	Imperative Mood	
		Positive	**Negative**
аз	бих закусвал/закусил		
ти	би закусвал/закусил	закусвай/закуси	не закусвай
той	би закусвал/закусил		
ние	бихме закусвали/закусили		
вие	бихте закусвали/закусили	закусвайте/закусете	не закусвайте
те	биха закусвали/закусили		

Past Passive Participles

M	F	N	Pl
N/A	N/A	N/A	N/A

65) **закъснявам/закъснея;** *be late, be delayed, be overdue*

	Present	**Past Simple**	**Past Continuous**
аз	закъснявам	закъснях	закъснявах
ти	закъсняваш	закъсня	закъсняваше
той	закъснява	закъсня	закъсняваше
ние	закъсняваме	закъсняхме	закъснявахме
вие	закъснявате	закъсняхте	закъснявахте
те	закъсняват	закъсняха	закъсняваха

	Future	**Future in the Past**
	(For negative, replace **ще** with **няма да**)	(For negative, replace **щях/щеше/щяхме/щяхте/щяха** with **нямаше**)
аз	ще закъснявам/закъснея	щях да закъснявам/закъснея
ти	ще закъсняваш/закъснееш	щеше да закъсняваш/закъснееш
той	ще закъснява/закъснее	щеше да закъснява/закъснее
ние	ще закъсняваме/закъснеем	щяхме да закъсняваме/закъснеем
вие	ще закъснявате/закъснеете	щяхте да закъснявате/закъснеете
те	ще закъсняват/закъснеят	щяха да закъсняват/закъснеят

Past Active Participles

M	**F**	**N**	**Pl**
закъснявал/ закъснял	закъснявала/закъсняла	закъснявало/закъсняло	закъснявали/закъснели

	Present Perfect	**Past Perfect**
аз	съм закъснявал/закъснял	бях закъснявал/закъснял
ти	си закъснявал/закъснял	беше закъснявал/закъснял
той	е закъснявал/закъснял	беше закъснявал/закъснял
ние	сме закъснявали/закъснели	бяхме закъснявали/закъснели
вие	сте закъснявали/закъснели	бяхте закъснявали/закъснели
те	са закъснявали/закъснели	бяха закъснявали/закъснели

	Conditional Mood	**Imperative Mood**	
аз	бих закъснявал/закъснял	**Positive**	**Negative**
ти	би закъснявал/закъснял	закъснявай/закъсней	не закъснявай
той	би закъснявал/закъснял		
ние	бихме закъснявали/закъснели		
вие	бихте закъснявали/закъснели	закъснявайте/закъснейте	не закъснявайте
те	биха закъснявали/закъснели		

Past Passive Participles

M	**F**	**N**	**Pl**
N/A	N/A	N/A	N/A

66) **заминавам/замина;** *depart, leave*

	Present	**Past Simple**	**Past Continuous**
аз	заминавам	заминах	заминавах
ти	заминаваш	замина	заминаваше
той	заминава	замина	заминаваше
ние	заминаваме	заминахме	заминавахме
вие	заминавате	заминахте	заминавахте
те	заминават	заминаха	заминаваха

	Future	**Future in the Past**
	(For negative, replace **ще** with **няма да**)	(For negative, replace **щях/щеше/щяхме/щяхте/щяха** with **нямаше**)
аз	ще заминавам/замина	щях да заминавам/замина
ти	ще заминаваш/заминеш	щеше да заминаваш/заминеш
той	ще заминава/замине	щеше да заминава/замине
ние	ще заминаваме/заминем	щяхме да заминаваме/заминем
вие	ще заминавате/заминете	щяхте да заминавате/заминете
те	ще заминават/заминат	щяха да заминават/заминат

Past Active Participles

M	**F**	**N**	**Pl**
заминавал/заминал	заминавала/заминала	заминавало/заминало	заминавали/заминали

	Present Perfect	**Past Perfect**
аз	съм заминавал/заминал	бях заминавал/заминал
ти	си заминавал/заминал	беше заминавал/заминал
той	е заминавал/заминал	беше заминавал/заминал
ние	сме заминавали/заминали	бяхме заминавали/заминали
вие	сте заминавали/заминали	бяхте заминавали/заминали
те	са заминавали/заминали	бяха заминавали/заминали

	Conditional Mood	**Imperative Mood**	
аз	бих заминавал/заминал	**Positive**	**Negative**
ти	би заминавал/заминал	заминавай/замини	не заминавай
той	би заминавал/заминал		
ние	бихме заминавали/заминали		
вие	бихте заминавали/заминали	заминавайте/заминете	не заминавайте
те	биха заминавали/заминали		

Past Passive Participles

M	**F**	**N**	**Pl**
N/A	N/A	N/A	N/A

67) **запалвам/запаля;** *light, fire up* **запалвам/запаля се;** *kindle, inspire*

	Present	**Past Simple**	**Past Continuous**
аз	запалвам	запалих	запалвах
ти	запалваш	запали	запалваше
той	запалва	запали	запалваше
ние	запалваме	запалихме	запалвахме
вие	запалвате	запалихте	запалвахте
те	запалват	запалиха	запалвах

	Future	**Future in the Past**
	(For negative, replace **ще** with **няма да**)	(For negative, replace **щях/щеше/щяхме/щяхте/щяха** with **нямаше**)
аз	ще запалвам/запаля	щях да запалвам/запаля
ти	ще запалваш/запалиш	щеше да запалваш/запалиш
той	ще запалва/запали	щеше да запалва/запали
ние	ще запалваме/запалим	щяхме да запалваме/запалим
вие	ще запалвате/запалите	щяхте да запалвате/запалите
те	ще запалват/запалят	щяха да запалват/запалят

Past Active Participles

M	**F**	**N**	**Pl**
запалвал/запалил	запалвала/запалила	запалвало/запалило	запалвали/запалили

	Present Perfect	**Past Perfect**
аз	съм запалвал/запалил	бях запалвал/запалил
ти	си запалвал/запалил	беше запалвал/запалил
той	е запалвал/запалил	беше запалвал/запалил
ние	сме запалвали/запалили	бяхме запалвали/запалили
вие	сте запалвали/запалили	бяхте запалвали/запалили
те	са запалвали/запалили	бяха запалвали/запалили

	Conditional Mood	**Imperative Mood**	
аз	бих запалвал/запалил	**Positive**	**Negative**
ти	би запалвал/запалил	запалвай/запали	не запалвай
той	би запалвал/запалил		
ние	бихме запалвали/запалили		
вие	бихте запалвали/запалили	запалвайте/запалете	не запалвайте
те	биха запалвали/запалили		

Past Passive Participles

M	**F**	**N**	**Pl**
N/A	N/A	N/A	N/A

68) **запознавам/запозная;** *introduce, meet*

	Present	**Past Simple**	**Past Continuous**
аз	запознавам	запознах	запознавах
ти	запознаваш	запозна	запознаваше
той	запознава	запозна	запознаваше
ние	запознаваме	запознахме	запознавахме
вие	запознавате	запознахте	запознавахте
те	запознават	запознаха	запознаваха

	Future	**Future in the Past**
	(For negative, replace **ще** with **няма да**)	(For negative, replace **щях/щеше/щяхме/щяхте/щяха** with **нямаше**)
аз	ще запознавам/запозная	щях да запознавам/запозная
ти	ще запознаваш/запознаеш	щеше да запознаваш/запознаеш
той	ще запознава/запознае	щеше да запознава/запознае
ние	ще запознаваме/запознаем	щяхме да запознаваме/запознаем
вие	ще запознавате/запознаете	щяхте да запознавате/запознаете
те	ще запознават/запознаят	щяха да запознават/запознаят

Past Active Participles

M	**F**	**N**	**Pl**
запознавал/ запознал	запознавала/запознала	запознавало/запознало	запознавали/запознали

	Present Perfect	**Past Perfect**
аз	съм запознавал/запознал	бях запознавал/запознал
ти	си запознавал/запознал	беше запознавал/запознал
той	е запознавал/запознал	беше запознавал/запознал
ние	сме запознавали/запознали	бяхме запознавали/запознали
вие	сте запознавали/запознали	бяхте запознавали/запознали
те	са запознавали/запознали	бяха запознавали/запознали

	Conditional Mood	**Imperative Mood**	
		Positive	**Negative**
аз	бих запознавал/запознал		
ти	би запознавал/запознал	запознавай/запознай	не запознавай
той	би запознавал/запознал		
ние	бихме запознавали/запознали		
вие	бихте запознавали/запознали	запознавайте/запознайте	не запознавайте
те	биха запознавали/запознали		

Past Passive Participles

M	**F**	**N**	**Pl**
запознаван/ запознат	запознавана/запозната	запознавано/запознато	запознавани/запознати

69) **запомням/запомня;** *remember, memorize, keep in mind*

	Present	Past Simple	Past Continuous
аз	запомням	запомних	запомнях
ти	запомняш	запомни	запомняше
той	запомня	запомни	запомняше
ние	запомняме	запомнихме	запомняхме
вие	запомняте	запомнихте	запомняхте
те	запомнят	запомниха	запомняха

	Future	Future in the Past
	(For negative, replace **ще** with **няма да**)	(For negative, replace **щях/щеше/щяхме/щяхте/щяха** with **нямаше**)
аз	ще запомням/запомня	щях да запомням/запомня
ти	ще запомняш/запомниш	щеше да запомняш/запомниш
той	ще запомня/запомни	щеше да запомня/запомни
ние	ще запомняме/запомним	щяхме да запомняме/запомним
вие	ще запомняте/запомните	щяхте да запомняте/запомните
те	ще запомнят/запомнят	щяха да запомнят/запомнят

Past Active Participles

M	F	N	Pl
запомнял/ запомнил	запомняла/запомнила	запомняло/запомнило	запомняли/запомнили

	Present Perfect	Past Perfect
аз	съм запомнял/запомнил	бях запомнял/запомнил
ти	си запомнял/запомнил	беше запомнял/запомнил
той	е запомнял/запомнил	беше запомнял/запомнил
ние	сме запомняли/запомнили	бяхме запомняли/запомнили
вие	сте запомняли/запомнили	бяхте запомняли/запомнили
те	са запомняли/запомнили	бяха запомняли/запомнили

	Conditional Mood	Imperative Mood	
		Positive	**Negative**
аз	бих запомнял/запомнил		
ти	би запомнял/запомнил	запомняй/запомни	не запомняй
той	би запомнял/запомнил		
ние	бихме запомняли/запомнили		
вие	бихте запомняли/запомнили	запомняйте/запомнете	не запомняйте
те	биха запомняли/запомнили		

Past Passive Participles

M	F	N	Pl
запомнян/ запомнен	запомняна/запомнена	запомняно/запомнено	запомняни/запомнени

70) **започвам/започна;** *begin, start, commence*

	Present	Past Simple	Past Continuous
аз	започвам	започнах	започвах
ти	започваш	започна	започваше
той	започва	започна	започваше
ние	започваме	започнахме	започвахме
вие	започвате	започнахте	започвахте
те	започват	започнаха	започваха

	Future	Future in the Past
	(For negative, replace **ще** with **няма да**)	(For negative, replace **щях/щеше/щяхме/щяхте/щяха** with **нямаше**)
аз	ще започвам/започна	щях да започвам/започна
ти	ще започваш/започнеш	щеше да започваш/започнеш
той	ще започва/започне	щеше да започва/започне
ние	ще започваме/започнем	щяхме да започваме/започнем
вие	ще започвате/започнете	щяхте да започвате/започнете
те	ще започват/започнат	щяха да започват/започнат

Past Active Participles

M	F	N	Pl
започвал/започнал	започвала/започнала	започвало/започнало	започвали/започнали

	Present Perfect	Past Perfect
аз	съм започвал/започнал	бях започвал/започнал
ти	си започвал/започнал	беше започвал/започнал
той	е започвал/започнал	беше започвал/започнал
ние	сме започвали/започнали	бяхме започвали/започнали
вие	сте започвали/започнали	бяхте започвали/започнали
те	са започвали/започнали	бяха започвали/започнали

	Conditional Mood	Imperative Mood	
		Positive	**Negative**
аз	бих започвал/започнал		
ти	би започвал/започнал	започвай/започни	не започвай
той	би започвал/започнал		
ние	бихме започвали/започнали		
вие	бихте започвали/започнали	започвайте/започнете	не започвайте
те	биха започвали/започнали		

Past Passive Participles

M	F	N	Pl
започван/започнат	започвана/започната	започвано/започнато	започвани/започнати

71) **заспивам/заспя;** *go to sleep, fall asleep*

	Present	Past Simple	Past Continuous
аз	заспивам	заспах	заспивах
ти	заспиваш	заспа	заспиваше
той	заспива	заспа	заспиваше
ние	заспиваме	заспахме	заспивахме
вие	заспивате	заспахте	заспивахте
те	заспиват	заспаха	заспиваха

	Future	Future in the Past
	(For negative, replace **ще** with **няма да**)	(For negative, replace **щях/щеше/щяхме/щяхте/щяха** with **нямаше**)
аз	ще заспивам/заспя	щях да заспивам/заспя
ти	ще заспиваш/заспиш	щеше да заспиваш/заспиш
той	ще заспива/заспи	щеше да заспива/заспи
ние	ще заспиваме/заспим	щяхме да заспиваме/заспим
вие	ще заспивате/заспите	щяхте да заспивате/заспите
те	ще заспиват/заспят	щяха да заспиват/заспят

Past Active Participles

M	F	N	Pl
заспивал/заспал	заспивала/заспала	заспивало/заспало	заспивали/заспали

	Present Perfect	Past Perfect
аз	съм заспивал/заспал	бях заспивал/заспал
ти	си заспивал/заспал	беше заспивал/заспал
той	е заспивал/заспал	беше заспивал/заспал
ние	сме заспивали/заспали	бяхме заспивали/заспали
вие	сте заспивали/заспали	бяхте заспивали/заспали
те	са заспивали/заспали	бяха заспивали/заспали

	Conditional Mood	Imperative Mood	
		Positive	**Negative**
аз	бих заспивал/заспал		
ти	би заспивал/заспал	заспивай/заспи	не заспивай
той	би заспивал/заспал		
ние	бихме заспивали/заспали		
вие	бихте заспивали/заспали	заспивайте/заспете	не заспивайте
те	биха заспивали/заспали		

Past Passive Participles

M	F	N	Pl
N/A	N/A	N/A	N/A

72) **зная;** *know*

	Present	**Past Simple = Past Continuous**
Аз	зная	знаех
ти	знаеш	знаеше
той	знае	знаеше
ние	знаем	знаехме
вие	знаете	знаехте
те	знаят	знаеха

	Future	**Future in the Past**
	(For negative, replace **ще** with **няма да**)	(For negative, replace **щях/щеше/щяхме/щяхте/щяха** with **нямаше**)
аз	ще зная	щях да зная
ти	ще знаеш	щеше да знаеш
той	ще знае	щеше да знае
ние	ще знаем	щяхме да знаем
вие	ще знаете	щяхте да знаете
те	ще знаят	щяха да знаят

Past Active Participles

M	**F**	**N**	**Pl**
знаел	знаела	знаело	знаели

	Present Perfect	**Past Perfect**
аз	съм знаел	бях знаел
ти	си знаел	беше знаел
той	е знаел	беше знаел
ние	сме знаели	бяхме знаели
вие	сте знаели	бяхте знаели
те	са знаели	бяха знаели

	Conditional Mood	**Imperative Mood**	
		Positive	**Negative**
аз	бих знаел		
ти	би знаел	знай	не знай
той	би знаел		
ние	бихме знаели		
вие	бихте знаели	знайте	не знайте
те	биха знаели		

Past Passive Participles

M	**F**	**P**	**Pl**
N/A	N/A	N/A	N/A

73) **играя;** *play, perform, participate*

	Present	**Past Simple**	**Past Continuous**
аз	играя	играх	играех
ти	играеш	игра	играеше
той	играе	игра	играеше
ние	играем	играхме	играехме
вие	играете	играхте	играехте
те	играят	играха	играеха

	Future	**Future in the Past**
	(For negative, replace **ще** with **няма да**)	(For negative, replace **щях/щеше/щяхме/щяхте/щяха** with **нямаше**)
аз	ще играя	щях да играя
ти	ще играеш	щеше да играеш
той	ще играе	щеше да играе
ние	ще играем	щяхме да играем
вие	ще играете	щяхте да играете
те	ще играят	щяха да играят

Past Active Participles

M	**F**	**N**	**Pl**
играл	играла	играло	играли

	Present Perfect	**Past Perfect**
аз	съм играл	бях играл
ти	си играл	беше играл
той	е играл	беше играл
ние	сме играли	бяхме играли
вие	сте играли	бяхте играли
те	са играли	бяха играли

	Conditional Mood	**Imperative Mood**	
аз	бих играл	**Positive**	**Negative**
ти	би играл	играй	не играй
той	би играл		
ние	бихме играли		
вие	бихте играли	играйте	не играйте
те	биха играли		

Past Passive Participles

M	**F**	**N**	**Pl**
игран	играна	играно	играни

74) **идвам/дойда;** *come, arrive*

	Present	**Past Simple**	**Past Continuous**
аз	идвам	дойдох	идвах
ти	идваш	дойде	идваше
той	идва	дойде	идваше
ние	идваме	дойдохме	идвахме
вие	идвате	дойдохте	идвахте
те	идват	дойдоха	идваха

	Future	**Future in the Past**
	(For negative, replace **ще** with **няма да**)	(For negative, replace **щях/щеше/щяхме/щяхте/щяха** with **нямаше**)
аз	ще идвам/дойда	щях да идвам/дойда
ти	ще идваш/дойдеш	щеше да идваш/дойдеш
той	ще идва/дойде	щеше да идва/дойде
ние	ще идваме/дойдем	щяхме да идваме/дойдем
вие	ще идвате/дойдете	щяхте да идвате/дойдете
те	ще идват/дойдат	щяха да идват/дойдат

Past Active Participles

M	**F**	**N**	**Pl**
идвал/дошъл	идвала/дошла	идвало/дошло	идвали/дошли

	Present Perfect	**Past Perfect**
аз	съм идвал/дошъл	бях идвал/дошъл
ти	си идвал/дошъл	беше идвал/дошъл
той	е идвал/дошъл	беше идвал/дошъл
ние	сме идвали/дошли	бяхме идвали/дошли
вие	сте идвали/дошли	бяхте идвали/дошли
те	са идвали/дошли	бяха идвали/дошли

	Conditional Mood	**Imperative Mood**	
аз	бих идвал/дошъл	**Positive**	**Negative**
ти	би идвал/дошъл	идвай/ела	не идвай
той	би идвал/дошъл		
ние	бихме идвали/дошли		
вие	бихте идвали/дошли	идвайте/елате	не идвайте
те	биха идвали/дошли		

Past Passive Participles

M	**F**	**N**	**Pl**
N/A	N/A	N/A	N/A

75) **избирам/избера;** *choose, select*

	Present	**Past Simple**	**Past Continuous**
аз	избирам	избрах	избирах
ти	избираш	избра	избираше
той	избира	избра	избираше
ние	избираме	избрахме	избирахме
вие	избирате	избрахте	избирахте
те	избират	избраха	избираха

	Future	**Future in the Past**
	(For negative, replace **ще** with **няма да**)	(For negative, replace **щях/щеше/щяхме/щяхте/щяха** with **нямаше**)
аз	ще избирам/избера	щях да избирам/избера
ти	ще избираш/избереш	щеше да избираш/избереш
той	ще избира/избере	щеше да избира/избере
ние	ще избираме/изберем	щяхме да избираме/изберем
вие	ще избирате/изберете	щяхте да избирате/изберете
те	ще избират/изберат	щяха да избират/изберат

Past Active Participles

M	**F**	**N**	**Pl**
избирал/избрал	избирала/избрала	избирало/избрало	избирали/избрали

	Present Perfect	**Past Perfect**
аз	съм избирал/избрал	бях избирал/избрал
ти	си избирал/избрал	беше избирал/избрал
той	е избирал/избрал	беше избирал/избрал
ние	сме избирали/избрали	бяхме избирали/избрали
вие	сте избирали/избрали	бяхте избирали/избрали
те	са избирали/избрали	бяха избирали/избрали

	Conditional Mood	**Imperative Mood**	
аз	бих избирал/избрал	**Positive**	**Negative**
ти	би избирал/избрал	избирай/избери	не избирай
той	би избирал/избрал		
ние	бихме избирали/избрали		
вие	бихте избирали/избрали	избирайте/изберете	не избирайте
те	биха избирали/избрали		

Past Passive Participles

M	**F**	**N**	**Pl**
избиран/избран	избирана/избрана	избирано/избрано	избирани/избрани

76) **извинявам се/извиня се;** *excuse, apologize*

	Present	**Past Simple**	**Past Continuous**
аз	се извинявам	се извиних	се извинявах
ти	се извиняваш	се извини	се извиняваше
той	се извинява	се извини	се извиняваше
ние	се извиняваме	се извинихме	се извинявахме
вие	се извинявате	се извинихте	се извинявахте
те	се извиняват	се извиниха	се извиняваха

	Future	**Future in the Past**
	(For negative, replace **ще** with **няма да**)	(For negative, replace **щях/щеше/щяхме/щяхте/щяха** with **нямаше**)
аз	ще се извинявам/извиня	щях да се извинявам/извиня
ти	ще се извиняваш/извиниш	щеше да се извиняваш/извиниш
той	ще се извинява/извини	щеше да се извинява/извини
ние	ще се извиняваме/извиним	щяхме да се извиняваме/извиним
вие	ще се извинявате/извините	щяхте да се извинявате/извините
те	ще се извиняват/извинят	щяха да се извиняват/извинят

Past Active Participles

M	**F**	**N**	**Pl**
извинявал/ извинил	извинявала/извинила	извинявало/извинило	извинявали/извинили

	Present Perfect	**Past Perfect**
аз	съм се извинявал/извинил	бях се извинявал/извинил
ти	си се извинявал/извинил	беше се извинявал/извинил
той	се е извинявал/извинил	беше се извинявал/извинил
ние	сме се извинявали/извинили	бяхме се извинявали/извинили
вие	сте се извинявали/извинили	бяхте се извинявали/извинили
те	са се извинявали/извинили	бяха се извинявали/извинили

	Conditional Mood	**Imperative Mood**	
		Positive	**Negative**
аз	бих се извинявал/извинил		
ти	би се извинявал/извинил	извинявай се/извини се	не се извинявай
той	би се извинявал/извинил		
ние	бихме се извинявали/извинили		
вие	бихте се извинявали/извинили	извинявайте се/извинете се	не се извинявайте
те	биха се извинявали/извинили		

Past Passive Participles

M	**F**	**N**	**Pl**
N/A	N/A	N/A	N/A

77) **изглеждам;** *look, appear, seem*

	Present	Past Simple = Past Continuous
аз	изглеждам	изглеждах
ти	изглеждаш	изглеждаше
той	изглежда	изглеждаше
ние	изглеждаме	изглеждахме
вие	изглеждате	изглеждахте
те	изглеждат	изглеждаха

	Future	Future in the Past
	(For negative, replace **ще** with **няма да**)	(For negative, replace **щях/щеше/щяхме/щяхте/щяха** with **нямаше**)
аз	ще изглеждам	щях да изглеждам
ти	ще изглеждаш	щеше да изглеждаш
той	ще изглежда	щеше да изглежда
ние	ще изглеждаме	щяхме да изглеждаме
вие	ще изглеждате	щяхте да изглеждате
те	ще изглеждат	щяха да изглеждат

Past Active Participles

M	F	N	Pl
изглеждал	изглеждала	изглеждало	изглеждали

	Present Perfect	Past Perfect
аз	съм изглеждал	бях изглеждал
ти	си изглеждал	беше изглеждал
той	е изглеждал	беше изглеждал
ние	сме изглеждали	бяхме изглеждали
вие	сте изглеждали	бяхте изглеждали
те	са изглеждали	бяха изглеждали

	Conditional Mood	Imperative Mood	
аз	бих изглеждал	**Positive**	**Negative**
ти	би изглеждал	изглеждай	не изглеждай
той	би изглеждал		
ние	бихме изглеждали		
вие	бихте изглеждали	изглеждайте	не изглеждайте
те	биха изглеждали		

Past Passive Participles

M	F	N	Pl
N/A	N/A	N/A	N/A

78) **излизам/изляза;** *go out, exit, leave*

	Present	**Past Simple**	**Past Continuous**
аз	излизам	излязох	излизах
ти	излизаш	излезе	излизаше
той	излиза	излезе	излизаше
ние	излизаме	излязохме	излизахме
вие	излизате	излязохте	излизахте
те	излизат	излязоха	излизаха

	Future	**Future in the Past**
	(For negative, replace **ще** with **няма да**)	(For negative, replace **щях/щеше/щяхме/щяхте/щяха** with **нямаше**)
аз	ще излизам/изляза	щях да излизам/изляза
ти	ще излизаш/излезеш	щеше да излизаш/излезеш
той	ще излиза/излезе	щеше да излиза/излезе
ние	ще излизаме/излезем	щяхме да излизаме/излезем
вие	ще излизате/излезете	щяхте да излизате/излезете
те	ще излизат/излязат	щяха да излизат/излязат

Past Active Participles

M	**F**	**N**	**Pl**
излизал/излязъл	излизала/излязла	излизало/излязло	излизали/излезли

	Present Perfect	**Past Perfect**
аз	съм излизал/излязъл	бях излизал/излязъл
ти	си излизал/излязъл	беше излизал/излязъл
той	е излизал/излязъл	беше излизал/излязъл
ние	сме излизали/излезли	бяхме излизали/излезли
вие	сте излизали/излезли	бяхте излизали/излезли
те	са излизали/излезли	бяха излизали/излезли

	Conditional Mood	**Imperative Mood**	
аз	бих излизал/излязъл	**Positive**	**Negative**
ти	би излизал/излязъл	излизай/излез	не излизай
той	би излизал/излязъл		
ние	бихме излизали/излезли		
вие	бихте излизали/излезли	излизайте/излезте	не излизайте
те	биха излизали/излезли		

Past Passive Participles

M	**F**	**N**	**Pl**
N/A	N/A	N/A	N/A

79) **изненадвам/изненадам;** *surprise, shock, astonish*

	Present	Past Simple	Past Continuous
аз	изненадвам	изненадах	изненадвах
ти	изненадваш	изненада	изненадваше
той	изненадва	изненада	изненадваше
ние	изненадваме	изненадахме	изненадвахме
вие	изненадвате	изненадахте	изненадвахте
те	изненадват	изненадаха	изненадваха

	Future	Future in the Past
	(For negative, replace **ще** with **няма да**)	(For negative, replace **щях/щеше/щяхме/щяхте/щяха** with **нямаше**)
аз	ще изненадвам/изненадам	щях да изненадвам/изненадам
ти	ще изненадваш/изненадаш	щеше да изненадваш/изненадаш
той	ще изненадва/изненада	щеше да изненадва/изненада
ние	ще изненадваме/изненадаме	щяхме да изненадваме/изненадаме
вие	ще изненадвате/изненадате	щяхте да изненадвате/изненадате
те	ще изненадват/изненадат	щяха да изненадват/изненадат

Past Active Participles

M	F	N	Pl
изненадвал/ изненадал	изненадвала/изненадала	изненадвало/изненадало	изненадвали/изненадали

	Present Perfect	Past Perfect
аз	съм изненадвал/изненадал	бях изненадвал/изненадал
ти	си изненадвал/изненадал	беше изненадвал/изненадал
той	е изненадвал/изненадал	беше изненадвал/изненадал
ние	сме изненадвали/изненадали	бяхме изненадвали/изненадали
вие	сте изненадвали/изненадали	бяхте изненадвали/изненадали
те	са изненадвали/изненадали	бяха изненадвали/изненадали

	Conditional Mood	Imperative Mood	
аз	бих изненадвал/изненадал	**Positive**	**Negative**
ти	би изненадвал/изненадал	изненадвай/изненадай	не изненадвай
той	би изненадвал/изненадал		
ние	бихме изненадвали/изненадали		
вие	бихте изненадвали/изненадали	изненадвайте/изненадайте	не изненадвайте
те	биха изненадвали/изненадали		

Past Passive Participles

M	F	N	Pl
изненадван/ изненадан	изненадвана/изненадана	изненадвано/изненадано	изненадвани/изненадани

80) **изобретявам/изобретя;** *invent, discover, create*

	Present	**Past Simple**	**Past Continuous**
аз	изобретявам	изобретих	изобретявах
ти	изобретяваш	изобрети	изобретяваше
той	изобретява	изобрети	изобретяваше
ние	изобретяваме	изобретихме	изобретявахме
вие	изобретявате	изобретихте	изобретявахте
те	изобретяват	изобретиха	изобретяваха

	Future	**Future in the Past**
	(For negative, replace **ще** with **няма да**)	(For negative, replace **щях/щеше/щяхме/щяхте/щяха** with **нямаше**)
аз	ще изобретявам/изобретя	щях да изобретявам/изобретя
ти	ще изобретяваш/изобретиш	щеше да изобретяваш/изобретиш
той	ще изобретява/изобрети	щеше да изобретява/изобрети
ние	ще изобретяваме/изобретим	щяхме да изобретяваме/изобретим
вие	ще изобретявате/изобретите	щяхте да изобретявате/изобретите
те	ще изобретяват/изобретят	щяха да изобретяват/изобретят

Past Active Participles

M	**F**	**N**	**Pl**
изобретявал/ изобретил	изобретявала/изобретила	изобретявало/изобретило	изобретявали/изобретили

	Present Perfect	**Past Perfect**
аз	съм изобретявал/изобретил	бях изобретявал/изобретил
ти	си изобретявал/изобретил	беше изобретявал/изобретил
той	е изобретявал/изобретил	беше изобретявал/изобретил
ние	сме изобретявали/изобретили	бяхме изобретявали/изобретили
вие	сте изобретявали/изобретили	бяхте изобретявали/изобретили
те	са изобретявали/изобретили	бяха изобретявали/изобретили

	Conditional Mood	**Imperative Mood**	
		Positive	**Negative**
аз	бих изобретявал/изобретил		
ти	би изобретявал/изобретил	изобретявай/изобрети	не изобретявай
той	би изобретявал/изобретил		
ние	бихме изобретявали/изобретили		
вие	бихте изобретявали/изобретили	изобретявайте/изобретете	не изобретявайте
те	биха изобретявали/изобретили		

Past Passive Participles

M	**F**	**N**	**Pl**
изобретяван/ изобретен	изобретявана/изобретена	изобретявано/изобретено	изобретявани/изобретени

81) **използвам;** *use, employ, utilize*

	Present	Past Simple	Past Continuous
аз	използвам	използвах	използвах
ти	използваш	използва	използваше
той	използва	използва	използваше
ние	използваме	използвахме	използвахме
вие	използвате	използвахте	използвахте
те	използват	използваха	използваха

	Future	Future in the Past
	(For negative, replace **ще** with **няма да**)	(For negative, replace **щях/щеше/щяхме/щяхте/щяха** with **нямаше**)
аз	ще използвам	щях да използвам
ти	ще използваш	щеше да използваш
той	ще използва	щеше да използва
ние	ще използваме	щяхме да използваме
вие	ще използвате	щяхте да използвате
те	ще използват	щяха да използват

Past Active Participles

M	F	N	Pl
използвал	използвала	използвало	използвали

	Present Perfect	Past Perfect
аз	съм използвал	бях използвал
ти	си използвал	беше използвал
той	е използвал	беше използвал
ние	сме използвали	бяхме използвали
вие	сте използвали	бяхте използвали
те	са използвали	бяха използвали

	Conditional Mood	Imperative Mood	
аз	бих използвал	**Positive**	**Negative**
ти	би използвал	използвай	не използвай
той	би използвал		
ние	бихме използвали		
вие	бихте използвали	използвайте	не използвайте
те	биха използвали		

Past Passive Participles

M	F	N	Pl
използван	използвана	използвано	използвани

82) **изпращам/изпратя;** *send, mail; accompany*

	Present	Past Simple	Past Continuous
аз	изпращам	изпратих	изпращах
ти	изпращаш	изпрати	изпращаше
той	изпраща	изпрати	изпращаше
ние	изпращаме	изпратихме	изпращахме
вие	изпращате	изпратихте	изпращахте
те	изпращат	изпратиха	изпращаха

	Future	Future in the Past
	(For negative, replace **ще** with **няма да**)	(For negative, replace **щях/щеше/щяхме/щяхте/щяха** with **нямаше**)
аз	ще изпращам/изпратя	щях да изпращам/изпратя
ти	ще изпращаш/изпратиш	щеше да изпращаш/изпратиш
той	ще изпраща/изпрати	щеше да изпраща/изпрати
ние	ще изпращаме/изпратим	щяхме да изпращаме/изпратим
вие	ще изпращате/изпратите	щяхте да изпращате/изпратите
те	ще изпращат/изпратят	щяха да изпращат/изпратят

Past Active Participles

M	F	N	Pl
изпращал/изпратил	изпращала/изпратила	изпращало/изпратило	изпращали/изпратили

	Present Perfect	Past Perfect
аз	съм изпращал/изпратил	бях изпращал/изпратил
ти	си изпращал/изпратил	беше изпращал/изпратил
той	е изпращал/изпратил	беше изпращал/изпратил
ние	сме изпращали/изпратили	бяхме изпращали/изпратили
вие	сте изпращали/изпратили	бяхте изпращали/изпратили
те	са изпращали/изпратили	бяха изпращали/изпратили

	Conditional Mood	Imperative Mood	
аз	бих изпращал/изпратил	**Positive**	**Negative**
ти	би изпращал/изпратил	изпращай/изпрати	не изпращай
той	би изпращал/изпратил		
ние	бихме изпращали/изпратили		
вие	бихте изпращали/изпратили	изпращайте/изпратете	не изпращайте
те	биха изпращали/изпратили		

Past Passive Participles

M	F	N	Pl
изпращан/ изпратен	изпращана/изпратена	изпращано/изпратено	изпращани/изпратени

83) **изпълнявам/изпълня;** *execute, carry out, perform*

	Present	**Past Simple**	**Past Continuous**
аз	изпълнявам	изпълних	изпълнявах
ти	изпълняваш	изпълни	изпълняваше
той	изпълнява	изпълни	изпълняваше
ние	изпълняваме	изпълнихме	изпълнявахме
вие	изпълнявате	изпълнихте	изпълнявахте
те	изпълняват	изпълниха	изпълняваха

	Future	**Future in the Past**
	(For negative, replace **ще** with **няма да**)	(For negative, replace **щях/щеше/щяхме/щяхте/щяха** with **нямаше**)
аз	ще изпълнявам/изпълня	щях да изпълнявам/изпълня
ти	ще изпълняваш/изпълниш	щеше да изпълняваш/изпълниш
той	ще изпълнява/изпълни	щеше да изпълнява/изпълни
ние	ще изпълняваме/изпълним	щяхме да изпълняваме/изпълним
вие	ще изпълнявате/изпълните	щяхте да изпълнявате/изпълните
те	ще изпълняват/изпълнят	щяха да изпълняват/изпълнят

Past Active Participles

M	**F**	**N**	**Pl**
изпълнявал/ изпълнил	изпълнявала/изпълнила	изпълнявало/изпълнило	изпълнявали/изпълнили

	Present Perfect	**Past Perfect**
аз	съм изпълнявал/изпълнил	бях изпълнявал/изпълнил
ти	си изпълнявал/изпълнил	беше изпълнявал/изпълнил
той	е изпълнявал/изпълнил	беше изпълнявал/изпълнил
ние	сме изпълнявали/изпълнили	бяхме изпълнявали/изпълнили
вие	сте изпълнявали/изпълнили	бяхте изпълнявали/изпълнили
те	са изпълнявали/изпълнили	бяха изпълнявали/изпълнили

	Conditional Mood	**Imperative Mood**	
аз	бих изпълнявал/изпълнил	**Positive**	**Negative**
ти	би изпълнявал/изпълнил	изпълнявай/изпълни	не изпълнявай
той	би изпълнявал/изпълнил		
ние	бихме изпълнявали/изпълнили		
вие	бихте изпълнявали/изпълнили	изпълнявайте/изпълнете	не изпълнявайте
те	биха изпълнявали/изпълнили		

Past Passive Participles

M	**F**	**N**	**Pl**
изпълняван/ изпълнен	изпълнявана/изпълнена	изпълнявано/изпълнено	изпълнявани/изпълнени

84) **изчезвам/изчезна;** *vanish, disappear*

	Present	**Past Simple**	**Past Continuous**
аз	изчезвам	изчезнах	изчезвах
ти	изчезваш	изчезна	изчезваше
той	изчезва	изчезна	изчезваше
ние	изчезваме	изчезнахме	изчезвахме
вие	изчезвате	изчезнахте	изчезвахте
те	изчезват	изчезнаха	изчезваха

	Future	**Future in the Past**
	(For negative, replace **ще** with **няма да**)	(For negative, replace **щях/щеше/щяхме/щяхте/щяха** with **нямаше**)
аз	ще изчезвам/изчезна	щях да изчезвам/изчезна
ти	ще изчезваш/изчезнеш	щеше да изчезваш/изчезнеш
той	ще изчезва/изчезне	щеше да изчезва/изчезне
ние	ще изчезваме/изчезнем	щяхме да изчезваме/изчезнем
вие	ще изчезвате/изчезнете	щяхте да изчезвате/изчезнете
те	ще изчезват/изчезнат	щяха да изчезват/изчезнат

Past Active Participles

M	**F**	**N**	**Pl**
изчезвал/изчезнал	изчезвала/изчезнала	изчезвало/изчезнало	изчезвали/изчезнали

	Present Perfect	**Past Perfect**
аз	съм изчезвал/изчезнал	бях изчезвал/изчезнал
ти	си изчезвал/изчезнал	беше изчезвал/изчезнал
той	е изчезвал/изчезнал	беше изчезвал/изчезнал
ние	сме изчезвали/изчезнали	бяхме изчезвали/изчезнали
вие	сте изчезвали/изчезнали	бяхте изчезвали/изчезнали
те	са изчезвали/изчезнали	бяха изчезвали/изчезнали

	Conditional Mood	**Imperative Mood**	
аз	бих изчезвал/изчезнал	**Positive**	**Negative**
ти	би изчезвал/изчезнал	изчезвай/изчезни	не изчезвай
той	би изчезвал/изчезнал		
ние	бихме изчезвали/изчезнали		
вие	бихте изчезвали/изчезнали	изчезвайте/изчезнете	не изчезвайте
те	биха изчезвали/изчезнали		

Past Passive Participles

M	**F**	**N**	**Pl**
N/A	N/A	N/A	N/A

85) **имам;** *have, possess, contain*

	Present	**Past Simple**	**Past Continuous**
аз	имам	имах	имах
ти	имаш	има	имаше
той	има	има	имаше
ние	имаме	имахме	имахме
вие	имате	имахте	имахте
те	имат	имаха	имаха

	Future	**Future in the Past**
	(For negative, replace **ще** with **няма да**)	(For negative, replace **щях/щеше/щяхме/щяхте/щяха** with **нямаше**)
аз	ще имам	щях да имам
ти	ще имаш	щеше да имаш
той	ще има	щеше да има
ние	ще имаме	щяхме да имаме
вие	ще имате	щяхте да имате
те	ще имат	щяха да имат

Past Active Participles

M	**F**	**N**	**Pl**
имал	имала	имало	имали

	Present Perfect	**Past Perfect**
аз	съм имал	бях имал
ти	си имал	беше имал
той	е имал	беше имал
ние	сме имали	бяхме имали
вие	сте имали	бяхте имали
те	са имали	бяха имали

	Conditional Mood	**Imperative Mood**	
аз	бих имал	**Positive**	**Negative**
ти	би имал	имай	нямай
той	би имал		
ние	бихме имали		
вие	бихте имали	имайте	нямайте
те	биха имали		

Past Passive Participles

M	**F**	**N**	**Pl**
N/A	N/A	N/A	N/A

86) **интересувам се;** *be interested*

	Present	Past Simple	Past Continuous
аз	се интересувам	се интересувах	се интересувах
ти	се интересуваш	се интересува	се интересуваше
той	се интересува	се интересува	се интересуваше
ние	се интересуваме	се интересувахме	се интересувахме
вие	се интересувате	се интересувахте	се интересувахте
те	се интересуват	се интересуваха	се интересуваха

	Future	Future in the Past
	(For negative, replace **ще** with **няма да**)	(For negative, replace **щях/щеше/щяхме/щяхте/щяха** with **нямаше**)
аз	ще се интересувам	щях да се интересувам
ти	ще се интересуваш	щеше да се интересуваш
той	ще се интересува	щеше да се интересува
ние	ще се интересуваме	щяхме да се интересуваме
вие	ще се интересувате	щяхте да се интересувате
те	ще се интересуват	щяха да се интересуват

Past Active Participles

M	F	N	Pl
интересувал	интересувала	интересувало	интересували

	Present Perfect	Past Perfect
аз	съм се интересувал	бях се интересувал
ти	си се интересувал	беше се интересувал
той	се е интересувал	беше се интересувал
ние	сме се интересували	бяхме се интересували
вие	сте се интересували	бяхте се интересували
те	са се интересували	бяха се интересували

	Conditional Mood	Imperative Mood	
аз	бих се интересувал	**Positive**	**Negative**
ти	би се интересувал	интересувай се	не се интересувай
той	би се интересувал		
ние	бихме се интересували		
вие	бихте се интересували	интересувайте се	не се интересувайте
те	биха се интересували		

Past Passive Participles

M	F	N	Pl
N/A	N/A	N/A	N/A

87) **искам;** *want, desire, like*

	Present	**Past Simple**	**Past Continuous**
аз	искам	исках	исках
ти	искаш	иска	искаше
той	иска	иска	искаше
ние	искаме	искахме	искахме
вие	искате	искахте	искахте
те	искат	искаха	искаха

	Future	**Future in the Past**
	(For negative, replace **ще** with **няма да**)	(For negative, replace **щях/щеше/щяхме/щяхте/щяха** with **нямаше**)
аз	ще искам	щях да искам
ти	ще искаш	щеше да искаш
той	ще иска	щеше да иска
ние	ще искаме	щяхме да искаме
вие	ще искате	щяхте да искате
те	ще искат	щяха да искат

Past Active Participles

M	**F**	**N**	**Pl**
искал	искала	искало	искали

	Present Perfect	**Past Perfect**
аз	съм искал	бях искал
ти	си искал	беше искал
той	е искал	беше искал
ние	сме искали	бяхме искали
вие	сте искали	бяхте искали
те	са искали	бяха искали

	Conditional Mood	**Imperative Mood**	
аз	бих искал	**Positive**	**Negative**
ти	би искал	искай	не искай
той	би искал		
ние	бихме искали		
вие	бихте искали	искайте	не искайте
те	биха искали		

Past Passive Participles

M	**F**	**N**	**Pl**
искан	искана	искано	искани

88) **казвам/кажа;** *say, state, declare, tell*

	Present	**Past Simple**	**Past Continuous**
аз	казвам	казах	казвах
ти	казваш	каза	казваше
той	казва	каза	казваше
ние	казваме	казахме	казвахме
вие	казвате	казахте	казвахте
те	казват	казаха	казваха

	Future	**Future in the Past**	
	(For negative, replace **ще** with **няма да**)	(For negative, replace **щях/щеше/щяхме/щяхте/щяха** with **нямаше**)	
аз	ще казвам/кажа	щях да казвам/кажа	
ти	ще казваш/кажеш	щеше да казваш/кажеш	
той	ще казва/каже	щеше да казва/каже	
ние	ще казваме/кажем	щяхме да казваме/кажем	
вие	ще казвате/кажете	щяхте да казвате/кажете	
те	ще казват/кажат	щяха да казват/кажат	

Past Active Participles

M	**F**	**N**	**Pl**
казвал/казал	казвала/казала	казвало/казало	казвали/казали

	Present Perfect	**Past Perfect**
аз	съм казвал/казал	бях казвал/казал
ти	си казвал/казал	беше казвал/казал
той	е казвал/казал	беше казвал/казал
ние	сме казвали/казали	бяхме казвали/казали
вие	сте казвали/казали	бяхте казвали/казали
те	са казвали/казали	бяха казвали/казали

	Conditional Mood	**Imperative Mood**	
аз	бих казвал/казал	**Positive**	**Negative**
ти	би казвал/казал	казвай/кажи	не казвай
той	би казвал/казал		
ние	бихме казвали/казали		
вие	бихте казвали/казали	казвайте/кажете	не казвайте
те	биха казвали/казали		

Past Passive Participles

M	**F**	**N**	**Pl**
казван/казан	казвана/казана	казвано/казано	казвани/казани

89) **каня/поканя;** *invite*

	Present	Past Simple	Past Continuous
аз	каня	поканих	канех
ти	каниш	покани	канеше
той	кани	покани	канеше
ние	каним	поканихме	канехме
вие	каните	поканихте	канехте
те	канят	поканиха	канеха

	Future	Future in the Past
	(For negative, replace **ще** with **няма да**)	(For negative, replace **щях/щеше/щяхме/щяхте/щяха** with **нямаше**)
аз	ще каня/поканя	щях да каня/поканя
ти	ще каниш/поканиш	щеше да каниш/поканиш
той	ще кани/покани	щеше да кани/покани
ние	ще каним/поканим	щяхме да каним/поканим
вие	ще каните/поканите	щяхте да каните/поканите
те	ще канят/поканят	щяха да канят/поканят

	Past Active Participles		
M	**F**	**N**	**Pl**
канил/поканил	канила/поканила	канило/поканило	канили/поканили

	Present Perfect	Past Perfect
аз	съм канил/поканил	бях канил/поканил
ти	си канил/поканил	беше канил/поканил
той	е канил/поканил	беше канил/поканил
ние	сме канили/поканили	бяхме канили/поканили
вие	сте канили/поканили	бяхте канили/поканили
те	са канили/поканили	бяха канили/поканили

	Conditional Mood	Imperative Mood	
аз	бих канил/поканил	**Positive**	**Negative**
ти	би канил/поканил	кани/покани	не кани
той	би канил/поканил		
ние	бихме канили/поканили		
вие	бихте канили/поканили	канете/поканете	не канете
те	биха канили/поканили		

	Past Passive Participles		
M	**F**	**N**	**Pl**
канен/поканен	канена/поканена	канено/поканено	канени/поканени

90) **карам;** *drive* **карам се;** *quarrel, argue*

	Present	**Past Simple**	**Past Continuous**
аз	карам	карах	карах
ти	караш	кара	караше
той	кара	кара	караше
ние	караме	карахме	карахме
вие	карате	карахте	карахте
те	карат	караха	караха

	Future	**Future in the Past**
	(For negative, replace **ще** with **няма да**)	(For negative, replace **щях/щеше/щяхме/щяхте/щяха** with **нямаше**)
аз	ще карам	щях да карам
ти	ще караш	щеше да караш
той	ще кара	щеше да кара
ние	ще караме	щяхме да караме
вие	ще карате	щяхте да карате
те	ще карат	щяха да карат

Past Active Participles

M	**F**	**N**	**Pl**
карал	карала	карало	карали

	Present Perfect	**Past Perfect**
аз	съм карал	бях карал
ти	си карал	беше карал
той	е карал	беше карал
ние	сме карали	бяхме карали
вие	сте карали	бяхте карали
те	са карали	бяха карали

	Conditional Mood	**Imperative Mood**	
аз	бих карал	**Positive**	**Negative**
ти	би карал	карай	не карай
той	би карал		
ние	бихме карали		
вие	бихте карали	карайте	не карайте
те	биха карали		

Past Passive Participles

M	**F**	**N**	**Pl**
каран	карана	карано	карани

91) **качвам/kaчa;** *carry up, take up* **качвам/качa ce;** *go up, climb; get on*

	Present	Past Simple	Past Continuous
аз	качвам	качих	качвах
ти	качваш	качи	качваше
той	качва	качи	качваше
ние	качваме	качихме	качвахме
вие	качвате	качихте	качвахте
те	качват	качиха	качваха

	Future	Future in the Past
	(For negative, replace **ще** with **няма да**)	(For negative, replace **щях/щеше/щяхме/щяхте/щяха** with **нямаше**)
аз	ще качвам/кача	щях да качвам/кача
ти	ще качваш/качиш	щеше да качваш/качиш
той	ще качва/качи	щеше да качва/качи
ние	ще качваме/качим	щяхме да качваме/качим
вие	ще качвате/качите	щяхте да качвате/качите
те	ще качват/качат	щяха да качват/качат

Past Active Participles

M	F	N	Pl
качвал/качил	качвала/качила	качвало/качило	качвали/качили

	Present Perfect	Past Perfect
аз	съм качвал/качил	бях качвал/качил
ти	си качвал/качил	беше качвал/качил
той	е качвал/качил	беше качвал/качил
ние	сме качвали/качили	бяхме качвали/качили
вие	сте качвали/качили	бяхте качвали/качили
те	са качвали/качили	бяха качвали/качили

	Conditional Mood	Imperative Mood	
аз	бих качвал/качил	**Positive**	**Negative**
ти	би качвал/качил	качвай/качи	не качвай
той	би качвал/качил		
ние	бихме качвали/качили		
вие	бихте качвали/качили	качвайте/качете	не качвайте
те	биха качвали/качили		

Past Passive Participles

M	F	N	Pl
качван/качен	качвана/качена	качвано/качено	качвани/качени

92) **кашлям**; *cough*

	Present	**Past Simple**	**Past Continuous**
аз	кашлям	кашлях	кашлях
ти	кашляш	кашля	кашляше
той	кашля	кашля	кашляше
ние	кашляме	кашляхме	кашляхме
вие	кашляте	кашляхте	кашляхте
те	кашлят	кашляха	кашляха

	Future	**Future in the Past**
	(For negative, replace **ще** with **няма да**)	(For negative, replace **щях/щеше/щяхме/щяхте/щяха** with **нямаше**)
аз	ще кашлям	щях да кашлям
ти	ще кашляш	щеше да кашляш
той	ще кашля	щеше да кашля
ние	ще кашляме	щяхме да кашляме
вие	ще кашляте	щяхте да кашляте
те	ще кашлят	щяха да кашлят

Past Active Participles

M	**F**	**N**	**Pl**
кашлял	кашляла	кашляло	кашляли

	Present Perfect	**Past Perfect**
аз	съм кашлял	бях кашлял
ти	си кашлял	беше кашлял
той	е кашлял	беше кашлял
ние	сме кашляли	бяхме кашляли
вие	сте кашляли	бяхте кашляли
те	са кашляли	бяха кашляли

	Conditional Mood	**Imperative Mood**	
аз	бих кашлял	**Positive**	**Negative**
ти	би кашлял	кашляй	не кашляй
той	би кашлял		
ние	бихме кашляли		
вие	бихте кашляли	кашляйте	не кашляйте
те	биха кашляли		

Past Passive Participles

M	**F**	**N**	**Pl**
N/A	N/A	N/A	N/A

93) **колебая се;** *hesitate*

	Present	Past Simple	Past Continuous
аз	се колебая	се колебах	се колебаех
ти	се колебаеш	се колеба	се колебаеше
той	се колебае	се колеба	се колебаеше
ние	се колебаем	се колебахме	се колебаехме
вие	се колебаете	се колебахте	се колебаехте
те	се колебаят	се колебаха	се колебаеха

	Future	Future in the Past
	(For negative, replace **ще** with **няма да**)	(For negative, replace **щях/щеше/щяхме/щяхте/щяха** with **нямаше**)
аз	ще се колебая	щях да се колебая
ти	ще се колебаеш	щеше да се колебаеш
той	ще се колебае	щеше да се колебае
ние	ще се колебаем	щяхме да се колебаем
вие	ще се колебаете	щяхте да се колебаете
те	ще се колебаят	щяха да се колебаят

Past Active Participles

M	F	N	Pl
колебал	колебала	колебало	колебали

	Present Perfect	Past Perfect
аз	съм се колебал	бях се колебал
ти	си се колебал	беше се колебал
той	се е колебал	беше се колебал
ние	сме се колебали	бяхме се колебали
вие	сте се колебали	бяхте се колебали
те	са се колебали	бяха се колебали

	Conditional Mood	Imperative Mood	
аз	бих се колебал	**Positive**	**Negative**
ти	би се колебал	колебай се	не се колебай
той	би се колебал		
ние	бихме се колебали		
вие	бихте се колебали	колебайте се	не се колебайте
те	биха се колебали		

Past Passive Participles

M	F	N	Pl
N/A	N/A	N/A	N/A

94) **крада;** *steal, pinch, rob*

	Present	**Past Simple**	**Past Continuous**
аз	крада	крадох	крадях
ти	крадеш	краде	крадеше
той	краде	краде	крадеше
ние	крадем	крадохме	крадяхме
вие	крадете	крадохте	крадяхте
те	крадат	крадоха	крадяха

	Future	**Future in the Past**
	(For negative replace **ще** with **няма да**)	(For negative replace **щях/щеше/щяхме/щяхте/щяха** with **нямаше**)
аз	ще крада	щях да крада
ти	ще крадеш	щеше да крадеш
той	ще краде	щеше да краде
ние	ще крадем	щяхме да крадем
вие	ще крадете	щяхте да крадете
те	ще крадат	щяха да крадат

Past Active Participles

M	**F**	**N**	**Pl**
крал	крала	крало	крали

	Present Perfect	**Past Perfect**
аз	съм крал	бях крал
ти	си крал	беше крал
той	е крал	беше крал
ние	сме крали	бяхме крали
вие	сте крали	бяхте крали
те	са крали	бяха крали

	Conditional Mood	**Imperative Mood**	
аз	бих крал	**Positive**	**Negative**
ти	би крал	кради	не кради
той	би крал		
ние	бихме крали		
вие	бихте крали	крадете	не крадете
те	биха крали		

Past Passive Participles

M	**F**	**N**	**Pl**
краден	крадена	крадено	крадени

95) **купувам/купя;** *buy, purchase*

	Present	**Past Simple**	**Past Continuous**
аз	купувам	купих	купувах
ти	купуваш	купи	купуваше
той	купува	купи	купуваше
ние	купуваме	купихме	купувахме
вие	купувате	купихте	купувахте
те	купуват	купиха	купуваха

	Future	**Future in the Past**
	(For negative, replace **ще** with **няма да**)	(For negative, replace **щях/щеше/щяхме/щяхте/щяха** with **нямаше**)
аз	ще купувам/купя	щях да купувам/купя
ти	ще купуваш/купиш	щеше да купуваш/купиш
той	ще купува/купи	щеше да купува/купи
ние	ще купуваме/купим	щяхме да купуваме/купим
вие	ще купувате/купите	щяхте да купувате/купите
те	ще купуват/купят	щяха да купуват/купят

Past Active Participles

M	**F**	**N**	**Pl**
купувал/купил	купувала/купила	купувало/купило	купували/купили

	Present Perfect	**Past Perfect**
аз	съм купувал/купил	бях купувал/купил
ти	си купувал/купил	беше купувал/купил
той	е купувал/купил	беше купувал/купил
ние	сме купували/купили	бяхме купували/купили
вие	сте купували/купили	бяхте купували/купили
те	са купували/купили	бяха купували/купили

	Conditional Mood	**Imperative Mood**	
аз	бих купувал/купил	**Positive**	**Negative**
ти	би купувал/купил	купувай/купи	не купувай
той	би купувал/купил		
ние	бихме купували/купили		
вие	бихте купували/купили	купувайте/купете	не купувайте
те	биха купували/купили		

Past Passive Participles

M	**F**	**N**	**Pl**
купуван/купен	купувана/купена	купувано/купено	купувани/купени

96) **къпя;** *bathe, give a bath* **къпя се;** *take a shower/bath*

	Present	Past Simple	Past Continuous
аз	къпя	къпах	къпех
ти	къпеш	къпа	къпеше
той	къпе	къпа	къпеше
ние	къпем	къпахме	къпехме
вие	къпете	къпахте	къпехте
те	къпят	къпаха	къпеха

	Future	Future in the Past
	(For negative, replace **ще** with **няма да**)	(For negative, replace **щях/щеше/щяхме/щяхте/щяха** with **нямаше**)
аз	ще къпя	щях да къпя
ти	ще къпеш	щеше да къпеш
той	ще къпе	щеше да къпе
ние	ще къпем	щяхме да къпем
вие	ще къпете	щяхте да къпете
те	ще къпят	щяха да къпят

Past Active Participles

M	F	N	Pl
къпал	къпала	къпало	къпали

	Present Perfect	Past Perfect
аз	съм къпал	бях къпал
ти	си къпал	беше къпал
той	е къпал	беше къпал
ние	сме къпали	бяхме къпали
вие	сте къпали	бяхте къпали
те	са къпали	бяха къпали

	Conditional Mood	Imperative Mood	
аз	бих къпал	**Positive**	**Negative**
ти	би къпал	къпи	не къпи
той	би къпал		
ние	бихме къпали		
вие	бихте къпали	къпете	не къпете
те	биха къпали		

Past Passive Participles

M	F	N	Pl
къпан	къпана	къпано	къпани

97) **лежа;** *lie, recline, lie down*

	Present	Past Simple	Past Continuous
аз	лежа	лежах	лежах
ти	лежиш	лежа	лежеше
той	лежи	лежа	лежеше
ние	лежим	лежахме	лежахме
вие	лежите	лежахте	лежахте
те	лежат	лежаха	лежаха

	Future	Future in the Past
	(For negative, replace **ще** with **няма да**)	(For negative, replace **щях/щеше/щяхме/щяхте/щяха** with **нямаше**)
аз	ще лежа	щях да лежа
ти	ще лежиш	щеше да лежиш
той	ще лежи	щеше да лежи
ние	ще лежим	щяхме да лежим
вие	ще лежите	щяхте да лежите
те	ще лежат	щяха да лежат

Past Active Participles

M	F	N	Pl
лежал	лежала	лежало	лежали

	Present Perfect	Past Perfect
аз	съм лежал	бях лежал
ти	си лежал	беше лежал
той	е лежал	беше лежал
ние	сме лежали	бяхме лежали
вие	сте лежали	бяхте лежали
те	са лежали	бяха лежали

	Conditional Mood	Imperative Mood	
аз	бих лежал	**Positive**	**Negative**
ти	би лежал	лежи	не лежи
той	би лежал		
ние	бихме лежали		
вие	бихте лежали	лежете	не лежете
те	биха лежали		

Past Passive Participles

M	F	N	Pl
N/A	N/A	N/A	N/A

98) **летя**; *fly*

	Present	Past Simple	Past Continuous
аз	летя	летях	летях
ти	летиш	летя	летеше
той	лети	летя	летеше
ние	летим	летяхме	летяхме
вие	летите	летяхте	летяхте
те	летят	летяха	летяха

	Future	Future in the Past
	(For negative, replace **ще** with **няма да**)	(For negative, replace **щях/щеше/щяхме/щяхте/щяха** with **нямаше**)
аз	ще летя	щях да летя
ти	ще летиш	щеше да летиш
той	ще лети	щеше да лети
ние	ще летим	щяхме да летим
вие	ще летите	щяхте да летите
те	ще летят	щяха да летят

Past Active Participles

M	F	N	Pl
летял	летяла	летяло	летели

	Present Perfect	Past Perfect
аз	съм летял	бях летял
ти	си летял	беше летял
той	е летял	беше летял
ние	сме летели	бяхме летели
вие	сте летели	бяхте летели
те	са летели	бяха летели

	Conditional Mood	Imperative Mood	
аз	бих летял	**Positive**	**Negative**
ти	би летял	лети	не лети
той	би летял		
ние	бихме летели		
вие	бихте летели	летете	не летете
те	биха летели		

Past Passive Participles

M	F	N	Pl
N/A	N/A	N/A	N/A

99) **ловя;** *catch, seize*

	Present	**Past Simple**	**Past Continuous**
аз	ловя	лових	ловях
ти	ловиш	лови	ловеше
той	лови	лови	ловеше
ние	ловим	ловихме	ловяхме
вие	ловите	ловихте	ловяхте
те	ловят	ловиха	ловяха

	Future	**Future in the Past**
	(For negative, replace **ще** with **няма да**)	(For negative, replace **щях/щеше/щяхме/щяхте/щяха** with **нямаше**)
аз	ще ловя	щях да ловя
ти	ще ловиш	щеше да ловиш
той	ще лови	щеше да лови
ние	ще ловим	щяхме да ловим
вие	ще ловите	щяхте да ловите
те	ще ловят	щяха да ловят

Past Active Participles

M	**F**	**N**	**Pl**
ловил	ловила	ловило	ловили

	Present Perfect	**Past Perfect**
аз	съм ловил	бях ловил
ти	си ловил	беше ловил
той	е ловил	беше ловил
ние	сме ловили	бяхме ловили
вие	сте ловили	бяхте ловили
те	са ловили	бяха ловили

	Conditional Mood	**Imperative Mood**	
аз	бих ловил	**Positive**	**Negative**
ти	би ловил	лови	не лови
той	би ловил		
ние	бихме ловили		
вие	бихте ловили	ловете	не ловете
те	биха ловили		

Past Passive Participles

M	**F**	**N**	**Pl**
ловен	ловена	ловено	ловени

100) **лъжа;** *lie, tell a lie*

	Present	**Past Simple**	**Past Continuous**
аз	лъжа	лъгах	лъжех
ти	лъжеш	лъга	лъжеше
той	лъже	лъга	лъжеше
ние	лъжем	лъгахме	лъжехме
вие	лъжете	лъгахте	лъжехте
те	лъжат	лъгаха	лъжеха

	Future	**Future in the Past**
	(For negative, replace **ще** with **няма да**)	(For negative, replace **щях/щеше/щяхме/щяхте/щяха** with **нямаше**)
аз	ще лъжа	щях да лъжа
ти	ще лъжеш	щеше да лъжеш
той	ще лъже	щеше да лъже
ние	ще лъжем	щяхме да лъжем
вие	ще лъжете	щяхте да лъжете
те	ще лъжат	щяха да лъжат

	Past Active Participles		
M	**F**	**N**	**Pl**
лъгал	лъгала	лъгало	лъгали

	Present Perfect	**Past Perfect**
аз	съм лъгал	бях лъгал
ти	си лъгал	беше лъгал
той	е лъгал	беше лъгал
ние	сме лъгали	бяхме лъгали
вие	сте лъгали	бяхте лъгали
те	са лъгали	бяха лъгали

	Conditional Mood	**Imperative Mood**	
аз	бих лъгал	**Positive**	**Negative**
ти	би лъгал	лъжи	не лъжи
той	би лъгал		
ние	бихме лъгали		
вие	бихте лъгали	лъжете	не лъжете
те	биха лъгали		

	Past Passive Participles		
M	**F**	**N**	**Pl**
лъган	лъгана	лъгано	лъгани

101) **лягам/легна;** *lie down* **лягам/легна си;** *go to bed*

	Present	Past Simple	Past Continuous
аз	лягам	легнах	лягах
ти	лягаш	легна	лягаше
той	ляга	легна	лягаше
ние	лягаме	легнахме	лягахме
вие	лягате	легнахте	лягахте
те	лягат	легнаха	лягаха

	Future	Future in the Past
	(For negative, replace **ще** with **няма да**)	(For negative, replace **щях/щеше/щяхме/щяхте/щяха** with **нямаше**)
аз	ще лягам/легна	щях да лягам/легна
ти	ще лягаш/легнеш	щеше да лягаш/легнеш
той	ще ляга/легне	щеше да ляга/легне
ние	ще лягаме/легнем	щяхме да лягаме/легнем
вие	ще лягате/легнете	щяхте да лягате/легнете
те	ще лягат/легнат	щяха да лягат/легнат

Past Active Participles

M	F	N	Pl
лягал/легнал	лягала/легнала	лягало/легнало	лягали/легнали

	Present Perfect	Past Perfect
аз	съм лягал/легнал	бях лягал/легнал
ти	си лягал/легнал	беше лягал/легнал
той	е лягал/легнал	беше лягал/легнал
ние	сме лягали/легнали	бяхме лягали/легнали
вие	сте лягали/легнали	бяхте лягали/легнали
те	са лягали/легнали	бяха лягали/легнали

	Conditional Mood	Imperative Mood	
аз	бих лягал/легнал	**Positive**	**Negative**
ти	би лягал/легнал	лягай/легни	не лягай
той	би лягал/легнал		
ние	бихме лягали/легнали		
вие	бихте лягали/легнали	лягайте/легнете	не лягайте
те	биха лягали/легнали		

Past Passive Participles

M	F	N	Pl
N/A	N/A	N/A	N/A

102) **меря;** *measure; try on*

	Present	Past Simple	Past Continuous
аз	меря	мерих	мерех
ти	мериш	мери	мереше
той	мери	мери	мереше
ние	мерим	мерихме	мерехме
вие	мерите	мерихте	мерехте
те	мерят	мериха	мереха

	Future	Future in the Past
	(For negative, replace **ще** with **няма да**)	(For negative, replace **щях/щеше/щяхме/щяхте/щяха** with **нямаше**)
аз	ще меря	щях да меря
ти	ще мериш	щеше да мериш
той	ще мери	щеше да мери
ние	ще мерим	щяхме да мерим
вие	ще мерите	щяхте да мерите
те	ще мерят	щяха да мерят

Past Active Participles

M	F	N	Pl
мерил	мерила	мерило	мерили

	Present Perfect	Past Perfect
аз	съм мерил	бях мерил
ти	си мерил	беше мерил
той	е мерил	беше мерил
ние	сме мерили	бяхме мерили
вие	сте мерили	бяхте мерили
те	са мерили	бяха мерили

	Conditional Mood	Imperative Mood	
аз	бих мерил	**Positive**	**Negative**
ти	би мерил	мери	не мери
той	би мерил		
ние	бихме мерили		
вие	бихте мерили	мерете	не мерете
те	биха мерили		

Past Passive Participles

M	F	N	Pl
мерен	мерена	мерено	мерени

103) **мечтая;** *dream, daydream*

	Present	**Past Simple**	**Past Continuous**
аз	мечтая	мечтах	мечтаех
ти	мечтаеш	мечта	мечтаеше
той	мечтае	мечта	мечтаеше
ние	мечтаем	мечтахме	мечтаехме
вие	мечтаете	мечтахте	мечтаехте
те	мечтаят	мечтаха	мечтаеха
аз	мечтая	мечтах	мечтаех

	Future	**Future in the Past**
	(For negative, replace **ще** with **няма да**)	(For negative, replace **щях/щеше/щяхме/щяхте/щяха** with **нямаше**)
аз	ще мечтая	щях да мечтая
ти	ще мечтаеш	щеше да мечтаеш
той	ще мечтае	щеше да мечтае
ние	ще мечтаем	щяхме да мечтаем
вие	ще мечтаете	щяхте да мечтаете
те	ще мечтаят	щяха да мечтаят

Past Active Participles

M	**F**	**N**	**Pl**
мечтал	мечтала	мечтало	мечтали

	Present Perfect	**Past Perfect**
аз	съм мечтал	бях мечтал
ти	си мечтал	беше мечтал
той	е мечтал	беше мечтал
ние	сме мечтали	бяхме мечтали
вие	сте мечтали	бяхте мечтали
те	са мечтали	бяха мечтали

	Conditional Mood	**Imperative Mood**	
аз	бих мечтал	**Positive**	**Negative**
ти	би мечтал	мечтай	не мечтай
той	би мечтал		
ние	бихме мечтали		
вие	бихте мечтали	мечтайте	не мечтайте
те	биха мечтали		

Past Passive Participles

M	**F**	**N**	**Pl**
N/A	N/A	N/A	N/A

104) **минавам/мина;** *pass, pass by, stop by*

	Present	Past Simple	Past Continuous
аз	минавам	минах	минавах
ти	минаваш	мина	минаваше
той	минава	мина	минаваше
ние	минаваме	минахме	минавахме
вие	минавате	минахте	минавахте
те	минават	минаха	минаваха

	Future	Future in the Past
	(For negative, replace **ще** with **няма да**)	(For negative, replace **щях/щеше/щяхме/щяхте/щяха** with **нямаше**)
аз	ще минавам/мина	щях да минавам/мина
ти	ще минаваш/минеш	щеше да минаваш/минеш
той	ще минава/мине	щеше да минава/мине
ние	ще минаваме/минем	щяхме да минаваме/минем
вие	ще минавате/минете	щяхте да минавате/минете
те	ще минават/минат	щяха да минават/минат

Past Active Participles

M	**F**	**N**	**Pl**
минавал/минал	минавала/минала	минавало/минало	минавали/минали

	Present Perfect	Past Perfect
аз	съм минавал/минал	бях минавал/минал
ти	си минавал/минал	беше минавал/минал
той	е минавал/минал	беше минавал/минал
ние	сме минавали/минали	бяхме минавали/минали
вие	сте минавали/минали	бяхте минавали/минали
те	са минавали/минали	бяха минавали/минали

	Conditional Mood	Imperative Mood	
аз	бих минавал/минал	**Positive**	**Negative**
ти	би минавал/минал	минавай/мини	не минавай
той	би минавал/минал		
ние	бихме минавали/минали		
вие	бихте минавали/минали	минавайте/минете	не минавайте
те	биха минавали/минали		

Past Passive Participles

M	**F**	**N**	**Pl**
минаван/минат	минавана/мината	минавано/минато	минавани/минати

105) **мириша;** *smell*

	Present	**Past Simple**	**Past Continuous**
аз	мириша	мирисах	миришех
ти	миришеш	мириса	миришеше
той	мирише	мириса	миришеше
ние	миришем	мирисахме	миришехме
вие	миришете	мирисахте	миришехте
те	миришат	мирисаха	миришеха

	Future	**Future in the Past**
	(For negative, replace **ще** with **няма да**)	(For negative, replace **щях/щеше/щяхме/щяхте/щяха** with **нямаше**)
аз	ще мириша	щях да мириша
ти	ще миришеш	щеше да миришеш
той	ще мирише	щеше да мирише
ние	ще миришем	щяхме да миришем
вие	ще миришете	щяхте да миришете
те	ще миришат	щяха да миришат

Past Active Participles

M	**F**	**N**	**Pl**
мирисал	мирисала	мирисало	мирисали

	Present Perfect	**Past Perfect**
аз	съм мирисал	бях мирисал
ти	си мирисал	беше мирисал
той	е мирисал	беше мирисал
ние	сме мирисали	бяхме мирисали
вие	сте мирисали	бяхте мирисали
те	са мирисали	бяха мирисали

	Conditional Mood	**Imperative Mood**	
аз	бих мирисал	**Positive**	**Negative**
ти	би мирисал	мириши	не мириши
той	би мирисал		
ние	бихме мирисали		
вие	бихте мирисали	миришете	не миришете
те	биха мирисали		

Past Passive Participles

M	**F**	**N**	**Pl**
мирисан	мирисана	мирисано	мирисани

106) **мисля;** *think, reflect, contemplate*

	Present	Past Simple	Past Continuous
аз	Мисля	мислих	мислех
ти	мислиш	мисли	мислеше
той	мисли	мисли	мислеше
ние	мислим	мислихме	мислехме
вие	мислите	мислихте	мислехте
те	мислят	мислиха	мислеха

	Future	Future in the Past
	(For negative, replace **ще** with **няма да**)	(For negative, replace **щях/щеше/щяхме/щяхте/щяха** with **нямаше**)
аз	ще мисля	щях да мисля
ти	ще мислиш	щеше да мислиш
той	ще мисли	щеше да мисли
ние	ще мислим	щяхме да мислим
вие	ще мислите	щяхте да мислите
те	ще мислят	щяха да мислят

Past Active Participles

M	F	N	Pl
мислил	мислила	мислило	мислили

	Present Perfect	Past Perfect
аз	съм мислил	бях мислил
ти	си мислил	беше мислил
той	е мислил	беше мислил
ние	сме мислили	бяхме мислили
вие	сте мислили	бяхте мислили
те	са мислили	бяха мислили

	Conditional Mood	Imperative Mood	
аз	бих мислил	**Positive**	**Negative**
ти	би мислил	мисли	не мисли
той	би мислил		
ние	бихме мислили		
вие	бихте мислили	мислете	не мислете
те	биха мислили		

Past Passive Participles

M	F	N	Pl
N/A	N/A	N/A	N/A

107) **мия;** *wash, mop*

	Present	**Past Simple**	**Past Continuous**
аз	мия	мих	миех
ти	миеш	ми	миеше
той	мие	ми	миеше
ние	мием	михме	миехме
вие	миете	михте	миехте
те	мият	миха	миеха

	Future	**Future in the Past**
	(For negative, replace **ще** with **няма да**)	(For negative, replace **щях/щеше/щяхме/щяхте/щяха** with **нямаше**)
аз	ще мия	щях да мия
ти	ще миеш	щеше да миеш
той	ще мие	щеше да мие
ние	ще мием	щяхме да мием
вие	ще миете	щяхте да миете
те	ще мият	щяха да мият

Past Active Participles

M	**F**	**N**	**Pl**
мил	мила	мило	мили

	Present Perfect	**Past Perfect**
аз	съм мил	бях мил
ти	си мил	беше мил
той	е мил	беше мил
ние	сме мили	бяхме мили
вие	сте мили	бяхте мили
те	са мили	бяха мили

	Conditional Mood	**Imperative Mood**	
аз	бих мил	**Positive**	**Negative**
ти	би мил	мий	не мий
той	би мил		
ние	бихме мили		
вие	бихте мили	мийте	не мийте
те	биха мили		

Past Passive Participles

M	**F**	**N**	**Pl**
мит	мита	мито	мити

108) **мога;** *can, may, be able to*

	Present	**Past Simple**	**Past Continuous**
аз	мога	можах	можех
ти	можеш	можа	можеше
той	може	можа	можеше
ние	можем	можахме	можехме
вие	можете	можахте	можехте
те	могат	можаха	можеха

	Future	**Future in the Past**
	(For negative, replace **ще** with **няма да**)	(For negative, replace **щях/щеше/щяхме/щяхте/щяха** with **нямаше**)
аз	ще мога	щях да мога
ти	ще можеш	щеше да можеш
той	ще може	щеше да може
ние	ще можем	щяхме да можем
вие	ще можете	щяхте да можете
те	ще могат	щяха да могат

Past Active Participles

M	**F**	**N**	**Pl**
могъл	могла	могло	могли

	Present Perfect	**Past Perfect**
аз	съм могъл	N/A
ти	си могъл	N/A
той	е могъл	N/A
ние	сме могли	N/A
вие	сте могли	N/A
те	са могли	N/A

	Conditional Mood	**Imperative Mood**	
аз	бих могъл	**Positive**	**Negative**
ти	би могъл	N/A	N/A
той	би могъл		
ние	бихме могли		
вие	бихте могли	N/A	N/A
те	биха могли		

Past Passive Participles

M	**F**	**N**	**Pl**
N/A	N/A	N/A	N/A

109) **моля/помоля;** *ask, beg, request*

	Present	**Past Simple**	**Past Continuous**
аз	Моля	помолих	молех
ти	молиш	помоли	молеше
той	моли	помоли	молеше
ние	молим	помолихме	молехме
вие	молите	помолихте	молехте
те	молят	помолиха	молеха

	Future	**Future in the Past**
	(For negative, replace **ще** with **няма да**)	(For negative, replace **щях/щеше/щяхме/щяхте/щяха** with **нямаше**)
аз	ще моля/помоля	щях да моля/помоля
ти	ще молиш/помолиш	щеше да молиш/помолиш
той	ще моли/помоли	щеше да моли/помоли
ние	ще молим/помолим	щяхме да молим/помолим
вие	ще молите/помолите	щяхте да молите/помолите
те	ще молят/помолят	щяха да молят/помолят

Past Active Participles

M	**F**	**N**	**Pl**
молил/помолил	молила/помолила	молило/помолило	молили/помолили

	Present Perfect	**Past Perfect**
аз	съм молил/помолил	бях молил/помолил
ти	си молил/помолил	беше молил/помолил
той	е молил/помолил	беше молил/помолил
ние	сме молили/помолили	бяхме молили/помолили
вие	сте молили/помолили	бяхте молили/помолили
те	са молили/помолили	бяха молили/помолили

	Conditional Mood	**Imperative Mood**	
аз	бих молил/помолил	**Positive**	**Negative**
ти	би молил/помолил	моли/помоли	не моли
той	би молил/помолил		
ние	бихме молили/помолили		
вие	бихте молили/помолили	молете/помолете	не молете
те	биха молили/помолили		

Past Passive Participles

M	**F**	**N**	**Pl**
молен/помолен	молена/помолена	молено/помолено	молени/помолени

110) **мълча;** *be silent, keep silence, remain silent*

	Present	**Past Simple**	**Past Continuous**
аз	мълча	мълчах	мълчах
ти	мълчиш	мълча	мълчеше
той	мълчи	мълча	мълчеше
ние	мълчим	мълчахме	мълчахме
вие	мълчите	мълчахте	мълчахте
те	мълчат	мълчаха	мълчаха

	Future	**Future in the Past**
	(For negative, replace **ще** with **няма да**)	(For negative, replace **щях/щеше/щяхме/щяхте/щяха** with **нямаше**)
аз	ще мълча	щях да мълча
ти	ще мълчиш	щеше да мълчиш
той	ще мълчи	щеше да мълчи
ние	ще мълчим	щяхме да мълчим
вие	ще мълчите	щяхте да мълчите
те	ще мълчат	щяха да мълчат

Past Active Participles

M	**F**	**N**	**Pl**
мълчал	мълчала	мълчало	мълчали

	Present Perfect	**Past Perfect**
аз	съм мълчал	бях мълчал
ти	си мълчал	беше мълчал
той	е мълчал	беше мълчал
ние	сме мълчали	бяхме мълчали
вие	сте мълчали	бяхте мълчали
те	са мълчали	бяха мълчали

	Conditional Mood	**Imperative Mood**	
аз	бих мълчал	**Positive**	**Negative**
ти	би мълчал	мълчи	не мълчи
той	би мълчал		
ние	бихме мълчали		
вие	бихте мълчали	мълчете	не мълчете
те	биха мълчали		

Past Passive Participles

M	**F**	**N**	**Pl**
N/A	N/A	N/A	N/A

111) **наближавам/наближа;** *approach, come close to*

	Present	Past Simple	Past Continuous
аз	наближавам	наближих	наближавах
ти	наближаваш	наближи	наближаваше
той	наближава	наближи	наближаваше
ние	наближаваме	наближихме	наближавахме
вие	наближавате	наближихте	наближавахте
те	наближават	наближиха	наближаваха

	Future	Future in the Past
	(For negative, replace **ще** with **няма да**)	(For negative, replace **щях/щеше/щяхме/щяхте/щяха** with **нямаше**)
аз	ще наближавам/наближа	щях да наближавам/наближа
ти	ще наближаваш/наближиш	щеше да наближаваш/наближиш
той	ще наближава/наближи	щеше да наближава/наближи
ние	ще наближаваме/наближим	щяхме да наближаваме/наближим
вие	ще наближавате/наближите	щяхте да наближавате/наближите
те	ще наближават/наближат	щяха да наближават/наближат

Past Active Participles

M	F	N	Pl
наближавал/ наближил	наближавала/наближила	наближавало/наближило	наближавали/наближили

	Present Perfect	Past Perfect
аз	съм наближавал/наближил	бях наближавал/наближил
ти	си наближавал/наближил	беше наближавал/наближил
той	е наближавал/наближил	беше наближавал/наближил
ние	сме наближавали/наближили	бяхме наближавали/наближили
вие	сте наближавали/наближили	бяхте наближавали/наближили
те	са наближавали/наближили	бяха наближавали/наближили

	Conditional Mood	Imperative Mood	
аз	бих наближавал/наближил	**Positive**	**Negative**
ти	би наближавал/наближил	наближавай/наближи	не наближавай
той	би наближавал/наближил		
ние	бихме наближавали/наближили		
вие	бихте наближавали/наближили	наближавайте/наближете	не наближавайте
те	биха наближавали/наближили		

Past Passive Participles

M	F	N	Pl
наближаван/ наближен	наближавана/наближена	наближавано/наближено	наближавани/наближени

112) **награждавам/наградя;** *reward, award*

	Present	Past Simple	Past Continuous
аз	награждавам	наградих	награждавах
ти	награждаваш	награди	награждаваше
той	награждава	награди	награждаваше
ние	награждаваме	наградихме	награждавахме
вие	награждавате	наградихте	награждавахте
те	награждават	наградиха	награждаваха

	Future	Future in the Past
	(For negative, replace **ще** with **няма да**)	(For negative, replace **щях/щеше/щяхме/щяхте/щяха** with **нямаше**)
аз	ще награждавам/наградя	щях да награждавам/наградя
ти	ще награждаваш/наградиш	щеше да награждаваш/наградиш
той	ще награждава/награди	щеше да награждава/награди
ние	ще награждаваме/наградим	щяхме да награждаваме/наградим
вие	ще награждавате/наградите	щяхте да награждавате/наградите
те	ще награждават/наградят	щяха да награждават/наградят

Past Active Participles

M	F	N	Pl
награждавал/ наградил	награждавала/наградила	награждавало/наградило	награждавали/наградили

	Present Perfect	Past Perfect
аз	съм награждавал/наградил	бях награждавал/наградил
ти	си награждавал/наградил	беше награждавал/наградил
той	е награждавал/наградил	беше награждавал/наградил
ние	сме награждавали/наградили	бяхме награждавали/наградили
вие	сте награждавали/наградили	бяхте награждавали/наградили
те	са награждавали/наградили	бяха награждавали/наградили

	Conditional Mood	Imperative Mood	
		Positive	**Negative**
аз	бих награждавал/наградил		
ти	би награждавал/наградил	награждавай/награди	не награждавай
той	би награждавал/наградил		
ние	бихме награждавали/наградили		
вие	бихте награждавали/наградили	награждавайте/наградете	не награждавайте
те	биха награждавали/наградили		

Past Passive Participles

M	F	N	Pl
награждаван/ награден	награждавана/наградена	награждавано/наградено	награждавани/ наградени

113) **надявам се;** *hope, expect, trust*

	Present	**Past Simple=Past Continuous**
аз	се надявам	се надявах
ти	се надяваш	се надяваше
той	се надява	се надяваше
ние	се надяваме	се надявахме
вие	се надявате	се надявахте
те	се надяват	се надяваха

	Future	**Future in the Past**
	(For negative, replace **ще** with **няма да**)	(For negative, replace **щях/щеше/щяхме/щяхте/щяха** with **нямаше**)
аз	ще се надявам	щях да се надявам
ти	ще се надяваш	щеше да се надяваш
той	ще се надява	щеше да се надява
ние	ще се надяваме	щяхме да се надяваме
вие	ще се надявате	щяхте да се надявате
те	ще се надяват	щяха да се надяват

Past Active Participles

M	**F**	**N**	**Pl**
надявал	надявала	надявало	надявали

	Present Perfect	**Past Perfect**
аз	съм се надявал	бях се надявал
ти	си се надявал	беше се надявал
той	се е надявал	беше се надявал
ние	сме се надявали	бяхме се надявали
вие	сте се надявали	бяхте се надявали
те	са се надявали	бяха се надявали

	Conditional Mood	**Imperative Mood**	
аз	бих се надявал	**Positive**	**Negative**
ти	би се надявал	надявайте се	не се надявайте
той	би се надявал		
ние	бихме се надявали		
вие	бихте се надявали	надявай се	не се надявай
те	биха се надявали		

Past Passive Participles

M	**F**	**N**	**Pl**
N/A	N/A	N/A	N/A

114) **намалявам/намаля;** *decrease, reduce*

	Present	**Past Simple**	**Past Continuous**
аз	намалявам	намалих	намалявах
ти	намаляваш	намали	намаляваше
той	намалява	намали	намаляваше
ние	намаляваме	намалихме	намалявахме
вие	намалявате	намалихте	намалявахте
те	намаляват	намалиха	намаляваха

	Future	**Future in the Past**
	(For negative, replace **ще** with **няма да**)	(For negative, replace **щях/щеше/щяхме/щяхте/щяха** with **нямаше**)
аз	ще намалявам/намаля	щях да намалявам/намаля
ти	ще намаляваш/намалиш	щеше да намаляваш/намалиш
той	ще намалява/намали	щеше да намалява/намали
ние	ще намаляваме/намалим	щяхме да намаляваме/намалим
вие	ще намалявате/намалите	щяхте да намалявате/намалите
те	ще намаляват/намалят	щяха да намаляват/намалят

Past Active Participles

M	**F**	**N**	**Pl**
намалявал/ намалил	намалявала/намалила	намалявало/намалило	намалявали/намалили

	Present Perfect	**Past Perfect**
аз	съм намалявал/намалил	бях намалявал/намалил
ти	си намалявал/намалил	беше намалявал/намалил
той	е намалявал/намалил	беше намалявал/намалил
ние	сме намалявали/намалили	бяхме намалявали/намалили
вие	сте намалявали/намалили	бяхте намалявали/намалили
те	са намалявали/намалили	бяха намалявали/намалили

	Conditional Mood	**Imperative Mood**	
аз	бих намалявал/намалил	**Positive**	**Negative**
ти	би намалявал/намалил	намалявай/намали	не намалявай
той	би намалявал/намалил		
ние	бихме намалявали/намалили		
вие	бихте намалявали/намалили	намалявайте/намалете	не намалявайте
те	биха намалявали/намалили		

Past Passive Participles

M	**F**	**N**	**Pl**
намаляван/ намален	намалявана/намалена	намалявано/намалено	намалявани/намалени

115) **намирам/намеря;** *find, discover, locate; think, consider*

	Present	Past Simple	Past Continuous
аз	намирам	намерих	намирах
ти	намираш	намери	намираше
той	намира	намери	намираше
ние	намираме	намерихме	намирахме
вие	намирате	намерихте	намирахте
те	намират	намериха	намираха

	Future	Future in the Past
	(For negative, replace **ще** with **няма да**)	(For negative, replace **щях/щеше/щяхме/щяхте/щяха** with **нямаше**)
аз	ще намирам/намеря	щях да намирам/намеря
ти	ще намираш/намериш	щеше да намираш/намериш
той	ще намира/намери	щеше да намира/намери
ние	ще намираме/намерим	щяхме да намираме/намерим
вие	ще намирате/намерите	щяхте да намирате/намерите
те	ще намират/намерят	щяха да намират/намерят

Past Active Participles

M	F	N	Pl
намирал/намерил	намирала/намерила	намирало/намерило	намирали/намерили

	Present Perfect	Past Perfect
аз	съм намирал/намерил	бях намирал/намерил
ти	си намирал/намерил	беше намирал/намерил
той	е намирал/намерил	беше намирал/намерил
ние	сме намирали/намерили	бяхме намирали/намерили
вие	сте намирали/намерили	бяхте намирали/намерили
те	са намирали/намерили	бяха намирали/намерили

	Conditional Mood	Imperative Mood	
аз	бих намирал/намерил	Positive	Negative
ти	би намирал/намерил	намирай/намери	не намирай
той	би намирал/намерил		
ние	бихме намирали/намерили		
вие	бихте намирали/намерили	намирайте/намерете	не намирайте
те	биха намирали/намерили		

Past Passive Participles

M	F	N	Pl
намиран/намерен	намирана/намерена	намирано/намерено	намирани/намерени

116) **напомням/напомня**; *remind; resemble*

	Present	**Past Simple**	**Past Continuous**
аз	напомням	напомних	напомнях
ти	напомняш	напомни	напомняше
той	напомня	напомни	напомняше
ние	напомняме	напомнихме	напомняхме
вие	напомняте	напомнихте	напомняхте
те	напомнят	напомниха	напомняха

	Future	**Future in the Past**
	(For negative, replace **ще** with **няма да**)	(For negative, replace **щях/щеше/щяхме/щяхте/щяха** with **нямаше**)
аз	ще напомням/напомня	щях да напомням/напомня
ти	ще напомняш/напомниш	щеше да напомняш/напомниш
той	ще напомня/напомни	щеше да напомня/напомни
ние	ще напомняме/напомним	щяхме да напомняме/напомним
вие	ще напомняте/напомните	щяхте да напомняте/напомните
те	ще напомнят/напомнят	щяха да напомнят/напомнят

Past Active Participles

M	**F**	**N**	**Pl**
напомнял/ напомнил	напомняла/напомнила	напомняло/напомнило	напомняли/напомнили

	Present Perfect	**Past Perfect**
аз	съм напомнял/напомнил	бях напомнял/напомнил
ти	си напомнял/напомнил	беше напомнял/напомнил
той	е напомнял/напомнил	беше напомнял/напомнил
ние	сме напомняли/напомнили	бяхме напомняли/напомнили
вие	сте напомняли/напомнили	бяхте напомняли/напомнили
те	са напомняли/напомнили	бяха напомняли/напомнили

	Conditional Mood	**Imperative Mood**	
аз	бих напомнял/напомнил	**Positive**	**Negative**
ти	би напомнял/напомнил	напомняй/напомни	не напомняй
той	би напомнял/напомнил		
ние	бихме напомняли/напомнили		
вие	бихте напомняли/напомнили	напомняйте/напомнете	не напомняйте
те	биха напомняли/напомнили		

Past Passive Participles

M	**F**	**N**	**Pl**
напомнян/ напомнен	напомняна/напомнена	напомняно/напомнено	напомняни/напомнени

117) **нарушавам/наруша;** *break, violate; disturb*

	Present	Past Simple	Past Continuous
аз	нарушавам	наруших	нарушавах
ти	нарушаваш	наруши	нарушаваше
той	нарушава	наруши	нарушаваше
ние	нарушаваме	нарушихме	нарушавахме
вие	нарушавате	нарушихте	нарушавахте
те	нарушават	нарушиха	нарушаваха

	Future	Future in the Past
	(For negative, replace **ще** with **няма да**)	(For negative, replace **щях/щеше/щяхме/щяхте/щяха** with **нямаше**)
аз	ще нарушавам/наруша	щях да нарушавам/наруша
ти	ще нарушаваш/нарушиш	щеше да нарушаваш/нарушиш
той	ще нарушава/наруши	щеше да нарушава/наруши
ние	ще нарушаваме/нарушим	щяхме да нарушаваме/нарушим
вие	ще нарушавате/нарушите	щяхте да нарушавате/нарушите
те	ще нарушават/нарушат	щяха да нарушават/нарушат

Past Active Participles

M	F	N	Pl
нарушавал/ нарушил	нарушавала/нарушила	нарушавало/нарушило	нарушавали/нарушили

	Present Perfect	Past Perfect
аз	съм нарушавал/нарушил	бях нарушавал/нарушил
ти	си нарушавал/нарушил	беше нарушавал/нарушил
той	е нарушавал/нарушил	беше нарушавал/нарушил
ние	сме нарушавали/нарушили	бяхме нарушавали/нарушили
вие	сте нарушавали/нарушили	бяхте нарушавали/нарушили
те	са нарушавали/нарушили	бяха нарушавали/нарушили

	Conditional Mood	Imperative Mood	
аз	бих нарушавал/нарушил	**Positive**	**Negative**
ти	би нарушавал/нарушил	нарушавай/наруши	не нарушавай
той	би нарушавал/нарушил		
ние	бихме нарушавали/нарушили		
вие	бихте нарушавали/нарушили	нарушавайте/нарушете	не нарушавайте
те	биха нарушавали/нарушили		

Past Passive Participles

M	F	N	Pl
нарушаван/ нарушен	нарушавана/нарушена	нарушавано/нарушено	нарушавани/нарушени

118) **настоявам/настоя;** *insist, persist, persevere*

	Present	Past Simple	Past Continuous
аз	настоявам	настоях	настоявах
ти	настояваш	настоя	настояваше
той	настоява	настоя	настояваше
ние	настояваме	настояхме	настоявахме
вие	настоявате	настояхте	настоявахте
те	настояват	настояха	настояваха

	Future	Future in the Past
	(For negative, replace **ще** with **няма да**)	(For negative, replace **щях/щеше/щяхме/щяхте/щяха** with **нямаше**)
аз	ще настоявам/настоя	щях да настоявам/настоя
ти	ще настояваш/настоиш	щеше да настояваш/настоиш
той	ще настоява/настои	щеше да настоява/настои
ние	ще настояваме/настоим	щяхме да настояваме/настоим
вие	ще настоявате/настоите	щяхте да настоявате/настоите
те	ще настояват/настоят	щяха да настояват/настоят

Past Active Participles

M	F	N	Pl
настоявал/ настоял	настоявала/настояла	настоявало/настояло	настоявали/настояли

	Present Perfect	Past Perfect
аз	съм настоявал/настоял	бях настоявал/настоял
ти	си настоявал/настоял	беше настоявал/настоял
той	е настоявал/настоял	беше настоявал/настоял
ние	сме настоявали/настояли	бяхме настоявали/настояли
вие	сте настоявали/настояли	бяхте настоявали/настояли
те	са настоявали/настояли	бяха настоявали/настояли

	Conditional Mood	Imperative Mood	
аз	бих настоявал/настоял	**Positive**	**Negative**
ти	би настоявал/настоял	настоявай	не настоявай
той	би настоявал/настоял		
ние	бихме настоявали/настояли		
вие	бихте настоявали/настояли	настоявайте	не настоявайте
те	биха настоявали/настояли		

Past Passive Participles

M	F	N	Pl
N/A	N/A	N/A	N/A

119) **научавам/науча;** *learn, find out, discover*

	Present	Past Simple	Past Continuous
аз	научавам	научих	научавах
ти	научаваш	научи	научаваше
той	научава	научи	научаваше
ние	научаваме	научихме	научавахме
вие	научавате	научихте	научавахте
те	научават	научиха	научаваха

	Future	Future in the Past
	(For negative, replace **ще** with **няма да**)	(For negative, replace **щях/щеше/щяхме/щяхте/щяха** with **нямаше**)
аз	ще научавам/науча	щях да научавам/науча
ти	ще научаваш/научиш	щеше да научаваш/научиш
той	ще научава/научи	щеше да научава/научи
ние	ще научаваме/научим	щяхме да научаваме/научим
вие	ще научавате/научите	щяхте да научавате/научите
те	ще научават/научат	щяха да научават/научат

Past Active Participles

M	F	N	Pl
научавал/научил	научавала/научила	научавало/научило	научавали/научили

	Present Perfect	Past Perfect
аз	съм научавал/научил	бях научавал/научил
ти	си научавал/научил	беше научавал/научил
той	е научавал/научил	беше научавал/научил
ние	сме научавали/научили	бяхме научавали/научили
вие	сте научавали/научили	бяхте научавали/научили
те	са научавали/научили	бяха научавали/научили

	Conditional Mood	Imperative Mood	
аз	бих научавал/научил	**Positive**	**Negative**
ти	би научавал/научил	научавай/научи	не научавай
той	би научавал/научил		
ние	бихме научавали/научили		
вие	бихте научавали/научили	научавайте/научете	не научавайте
те	биха научавали/научили		

Past Passive Participles

M	F	N	Pl
научаван/научен	научавана/научена	научавано/научено	научавани/научени

120) **нося;** *carry; wear*

	Present	**Past Simple**	**Past Continuous**
аз	нося	носих	носех
ти	носиш	носи	носеше
той	носи	носи	носеше
ние	носим	носихме	носехме
вие	носите	носихте	носехте
те	носят	носиха	носеха

	Future	**Future in the Past**
	(For negative, replace **ще** with **няма да**)	(For negative, replace **щях/щеше/щяхме/щяхте/щяха** with **нямаше**)
аз	ще нося	щях да нося
ти	ще носиш	щеше да носиш
той	ще носи	щеше да носи
ние	ще носим	щяхме да носим
вие	ще носите	щяхте да носите
те	ще носят	щяха да носят

Past Active Participles

M	**F**	**N**	**Pl**
носил	носила	носило	носили

	Present Perfect	**Past Perfect**
аз	съм носил	бях носил
ти	си носил	беше носил
той	е носил	беше носил
ние	сме носили	бяхме носили
вие	сте носили	бяхте носили
те	са носили	бяха носили

	Conditional Mood	**Imperative Mood**	
аз	бих носил	**Positive**	**Negative**
ти	би носил	носи	не носи
той	би носил		
ние	бихме носили		
вие	бихте носили	носете	не носете
те	биха носили		

Past Passive Participles

M	**F**	**N**	**Pl**
носен	носена	носено	носени

121) **нуждая се**; *need, require*

	Present	**Past Simple = Past Continuous**
аз	се нуждая	се нуждаех
ти	се нуждаеш	се нуждаеше
той	се нуждае	се нуждаеше
ние	се нуждаем	се нуждаехме
вие	се нуждаете	се нуждаехте
те	се нуждаят	се нуждаеха

	Future	**Future in the Past**
	(For negative, replace **ще** with **няма да**)	(For negative, replace **щях/щеше/щяхме/щяхте/щяха** with **нямаше**)
аз	ще се нуждая	щях да се нуждая
ти	ще се нуждаеш	щеше да се нуждаеш
той	ще се нуждае	щеше да се нуждае
ние	ще се нуждаем	щяхме да се нуждаем
вие	ще се нуждаете	щяхте да се нуждаете
те	ще се нуждаят	щяха да се нуждаят

Past Active Participles

M	**F**	**N**	**Pl**
Нуждаел	нуждаела	нуждаело	нуждаели

	Present Perfect	**Past Perfect**
аз	съм се нуждаел	бях се нуждаел
ти	си се нуждаел	беше се нуждаел
той	се е нуждаел	беше се нуждаел
ние	сме се нуждаели	бяхме се нуждаели
вие	сте се нуждаели	бяхте се нуждаели
те	са се нуждаели	бяха се нуждаели

	Conditional Mood	**Imperative Mood**	
аз	бих се нуждаел	**Positive**	**Negative**
ти	би се нуждаел	нуждай се	не се нуждай
той	би се нуждаел		
ние	бихме се нуждаели		
вие	бихте се нуждаели	нуждайте се	не се нуждайте
те	биха се нуждаели		

Past Passive Participles

M	**F**	**P**	**Pl**
N/A	N/A	N/A	N/A

122) **нямам;** *have not*

	Present	**Past Simple = Past Continuous**
аз	Нямам	нямах
ти	нямаш	нямаше
той	няма	нямаше
ние	нямаме	нямахме
вие	нямате	нямахте
те	нямат	нямаха

	Future	**Future in the Past**
	(For negative, replace **ще** with **няма да**)	(For negative, replace **щях/щеше/щяхме/щяхте/щяха** with **нямаше**)
аз	N/A	N/A
ти	N/A	N/A
той	N/A	N/A
ние	N/A	N/A
вие	N/A	N/A
те	N/A	N/A

Past Active Participles

M	**F**	**N**	**Pl**
Нямал	нямала	нямало	нямали

	Present Perfect	**Past Perfect**
аз	съм нямал	бях нямал
ти	си нямал	беше нямал
той	е нямал	беше нямал
ние	сме нямали	бяхме нямали
вие	сте нямали	бяхте нямали
те	са нямали	бяха нямали

	Conditional Mood	**Imperative Mood**	
аз	бих нямал	**Positive**	**Negative**
ти	би нямал	N/A	нямай
той	би нямал		
ние	бихме нямали		
вие	бихте нямали	N/A	нямайте
те	биха нямали		

Past Passive Participles

M	**F**	**N**	**Pl**
N/A	N/A	N/A	N/A

123) **обаждам се/обадя се;** *call, answer (a phone)*

	Present	**Past Simple**	**Past Continuous**
аз	се обаждам	се обадих	се обаждах
ти	се обаждаш	се обади	се обаждаше
той	се обажда	се обади	се обаждаше
ние	се обаждаме	се обадихме	се обаждахме
вие	се обаждате	се обадихте	се обаждахте
те	се обаждат	се обадиха	се обаждаха

	Future	**Future in the Past**
	(For negative, replace **ще** with **няма да**)	(For negative, replace **щях/щеше/щяхме/щяхте/щяха** with **нямаше**)
аз	ще се обаждам/обадя	щях да се обаждам/обадя
ти	ще се обаждаш/обадиш	щеше да се обаждаш/обадиш
той	ще се обажда/обади	щеше да се обажда/обади
ние	ще се обаждаме/обадим	щяхме да се обаждаме/обадим
вие	ще се обаждате/обадите	щяхте да се обаждате/обадите
те	ще се обаждат/обадят	щяха да се обаждат/обадят

Past Active Participles

M	**F**	**N**	**Pl**
обаждал/обадил	обаждала/обадила	обаждало/обадило	обаждали/обадили

	Present Perfect	**Past Perfect**
аз	съм се обаждал/обадил	бях се обаждал/обадил
ти	си се обаждал/обадил	беше се обаждал/обадил
той	се е обаждал/обадил	беше се обаждал/обадил
ние	сме се обаждали/обадили	бяхме се обаждали/обадили
вие	сте се обаждали/обадили	бяхте се обаждали/обадили
те	са се обаждали/обадили	бяха се обаждали/обадили

	Conditional Mood	**Imperative Mood**	
аз	бих се обаждал/обадил	**Positive**	**Negative**
ти	би се обаждал/обадил	обаждай /обади се	не се обаждай
той	би се обаждал/обадил		
ние	бихме се обаждали/обадили		
вие	бихте се обаждали/обадили	обаждайте/обадете се	не се обаждайте
те	биха се обаждали/обадили		

Past Passive Participles

M	**F**	**N**	**Pl**
N/A	N/A	N/A	N/A

124) **обещавам/обещая;** *promise*

	Present	Past Simple	Past Continuous
аз	обещавам	обещах	обещавах
ти	обещаваш	обеща	обещаваше
той	обещава	обеща	обещаваше
ние	обещаваме	обещахме	обещавахме
вие	обещавате	обещахте	обещавахте
те	обещават	обещаха	обещаваха

	Future	Future in the Past
	(For negative, replace **ще** with **няма да**)	(For negative, replace **щях/щеше/щяхме/щяхте/щяха** with **нямаше**)
аз	ще обещавам/обещая	щях да обещавам/обещая
ти	ще обещаваш/обещаеш	щеше да обещаваш/обещаеш
той	ще обещава/обещае	щеше да обещава/обещае
ние	ще обещаваме/обещаем	щяхме да обещаваме/обещаем
вие	ще обещавате/обещаете	щяхте да обещавате/обещаете
те	ще обещават/обещаят	щяха да обещават/обещаят

Past Active Participles

M	F	N	Pl
обещавал/обещал	обещавала/обещала	обещавало/обещало	обещавали/обещали

	Present Perfect	Past Perfect
аз	съм обещавал/обещал	бях обещавал/обещал
ти	си обещавал/обещал	беше обещавал/обещал
той	е обещавал/обещал	беше обещавал/обещал
ние	сме обещавали/обещали	бяхме обещавали/обещали
вие	сте обещавали/обещали	бяхте обещавали/обещали
те	са обещавали/обещали	бяха обещавали/обещали

	Conditional Mood	Imperative Mood	
аз	бих обещавал/обещал	**Positive**	**Negative**
ти	би обещавал/обещал	обещавай/обещай	не обещавай
той	би обещавал/обещал		
ние	бихме обещавали/обещали		
вие	бихте обещавали/обещали	обещавайте/обещайте	не обещавайте
те	биха обещавали/обещали		

Past Passive Participles

M	F	N	Pl
обещаван/обещан	обещавана/обещана	обещавано/обещано	обещавани/обещани

125) **обичам;** *love, like*

	Present	**Past Simple = Past Continuous**
аз	обичам	обичах
ти	обичаш	обичаше
той	обича	обичаше
ние	обичаме	обичахме
вие	обичате	обичахте
те	обичат	обичаха

	Future	**Future in the Past**
	(For negative, replace **ще** with **няма да**)	(For negative, replace **щях/щеше/щяхме/щяхте/щяха** with **нямаше**)
аз	ще обичам	щях да обичам
ти	ще обичаш	щеше да обичаш
той	ще обича	щеше да обича
ние	ще обичаме	щяхме да обичаме
вие	ще обичате	щяхте да обичате
те	ще обичат	щяха да обичат

Past Active Participles

M	**F**	**N**	**Pl**
обичал	обичала	обичало	обичали

	Present Perfect	**Past Perfect**
аз	съм обичал	бях обичал
ти	си обичал	беше обичал
той	е обичал	беше обичал
ние	сме обичали	бяхме обичали
вие	сте обичали	бяхте обичали
те	са обичали	бяха обичали

	Conditional Mood	**Imperative Mood**	
аз	бих обичал	**Positive**	**Negative**
ти	би обичал	обичай	не обичай
той	би обичал		
ние	бихме обичали		
вие	бихте обичали	обичайте	не обичайте
те	биха обичали		

Past Passive Participles

M	**F**	**N**	**Pl**
обичан	обичана	обичано	обичани

126) **облекчавам/облекча;** *relieve*

	Present	**Past Simple**	**Past Continuous**
аз	облекчавам	облекчих	облекчавах
ти	облекчаваш	облекчи	облекчаваше
той	облекчава	облекчи	облекчаваше
ние	облекчаваме	облекчихме	облекчавахме
вие	облекчавате	облекчихте	облекчавахте
те	облекчават	облекчиха	облекчаваха

	Future	**Future in the Past**
	(For negative, replace **ще** with **няма да**)	(For negative, replace **щях/щеше/щяхме/щяхте/щяха** with **нямаше**)
аз	ще облекчавам/облекча	щях да облекчавам/облекча
ти	ще облекчаваш/облекчиш	щеше да облекчаваш/облекчиш
той	ще облекчава/облекчи	щеше да облекчава/облекчи
ние	ще облекчаваме/облекчим	щяхме да облекчаваме/облекчим
вие	ще облекчавате/облекчите	щяхте да облекчавате/облекчите
те	ще облекчават/облекчат	щяха да облекчават/облекчат

Past Active Participles

M	**F**	**N**	**Pl**
облекчавал/ облекчил	облекчавала/облекчила	облекчавало/облекчило	облекчавали/облекчили

	Present Perfect	**Past Perfect**
аз	съм облекчавал/облекчил	бях облекчавал/облекчил
ти	си облекчавал/облекчил	беше облекчавал/облекчил
той	е облекчавал/облекчил	беше облекчавал/облекчил
ние	сме облекчавали/облекчили	бяхме облекчавали/облекчили
вие	сте облекчавали/облекчили	бяхте облекчавали/облекчили
те	са облекчавали/облекчили	бяха облекчавали/облекчили

	Conditional Mood	**Imperative Mood**	
аз	бих облекчавал/облекчил	**Positive**	**Negative**
ти	би облекчавал/облекчил	облекчавай/облекчи	не облекчавай
той	би облекчавал/облекчил		
ние	бихме облекчавали/облекчили		
вие	бихте облекчавали/облекчили	облекчавайте/облекчете	не облекчавайте
те	биха облекчавали/облекчили		

Past Passive Participles

M	**F**	**N**	**Pl**
облекчаван/ облекчен	облекчавана/облекчена	облекчавано/облекчено	облекчавани/облекчени

127) **обличам/облека;** *dress, put on*

	Present	**Past Simple**	**Past Continuous**
аз	обличам	облякох	обличах
ти	обличаш	облече	обличаше
той	облича	облече	обличаше
ние	обличаме	облякохме	обличахме
вие	обличате	облякохте	обличахте
те	обличат	облякоха	обличаха

	Future	**Future in the Past**
	(For negative, replace **ще** with **няма да**)	(For negative, replace **щях/щеше/щяхме/щяхте/щяха** with **нямаше**)
аз	ще обличам/облека	щях да обличам/облека
ти	ще обличаш/облечеш	щеше да обличаш/облечеш
той	ще облича/облече	щеше да облича/облече
ние	ще обличаме/облечем	щяхме да обличаме/облечем
вие	ще обличате/облечете	щяхте да обличате/облечете
те	ще обличат/облекат	щяха да обличат/облекат

Past Active Participles

M	**F**	**N**	**Pl**
обличал/облякъл	обличала/облякла	обличало/облякло	обличали/облекли

	Present Perfect	**Past Perfect**
аз	съм обличал/облякъл	бях обличал/облякъл
ти	си обличал/облякъл	беше обличал/облякъл
той	е обличал/облякъл	беше обличал/облякъл
ние	сме обличали/облекли	бяхме обличали/облекли
вие	сте обличали/облекли	бяхте обличали/облекли
те	са обличали/облекли	бяха обличали/облекли

	Conditional Mood	**Imperative Mood**	
аз	бих обличал/облякъл	**Positive**	**Negative**
ти	би обличал/облякъл	обличай/облечи	не обличай
той	би обличал/облякъл		
ние	бихме обличали/облекли		
вие	бихте обличали/облекли	обличайте/облечете	не обличайте
те	биха обличали/облекли		

Past Passive Participles

M	**F**	**N**	**Pl**
обличан/облечен	обличана/облечена	обличано/облечено	обличани/облечени

128) **обувам/обуя;** *put on (shoes, socks)*

	Present	**Past Simple**	**Past Continuous**
аз	обувам	обух	обувах
ти	обуваш	обу	обуваше
той	обува	обу	обуваше
ние	обуваме	обухме	обувахме
вие	обувате	обухте	обувахте
те	обуват	обуха	обуваха

	Future	**Future in the Past**
	(For negative, replace **ще** with **няма да**)	(For negative, replace **щях/щеше/щяхме/щяхте/щяха** with **нямаше**)
аз	ще обувам/обуя	щях да обувам/обуя
ти	ще обуваш/обуеш	щеше да обуваш/обуеш
той	ще обува/обуе	щеше да обува/обуе
ние	ще обуваме/обуем	щяхме да обуваме/обуем
вие	ще обувате/обуете	щяхте да обувате/обуете
те	ще обуват/обуят	щяха да обуват/обуят

Past Active Participles

M	**F**	**N**	**Pl**
обувал/обул	обувала/обула	обувало/обуло	обували/обули

	Present Perfect	**Past Perfect**
аз	съм обувал/обул	бях обувал/обул
ти	си обувал/обул	беше обувал/обул
той	е обувал/обул	беше обувал/обул
ние	сме обували/обули	бяхме обували/обули
вие	сте обували/обули	бяхте обували/обули
те	са обували/обули	бяха обували/обули

	Conditional Mood	**Imperative Mood**	
аз	бих обувал/обул	**Positive**	**Negative**
ти	би обувал/обул	обувай/обуй	не обувай
той	би обувал/обул		
ние	бихме обували/обули		
вие	бихте обували/обули	обувайте/обуйте	не обувайте
те	биха обували/обули		

Past Passive Participles

M	**F**	**N**	**Pl**
обуван/обут	обувана/обута	обувано/обуто	обувани/обути

129) **обядвам;** *have lunch*

	Present	**Past Simple**	**Past Continuous**
аз	обядвам	обядвах	обядвах
ти	обядваш	обядва	обядваше
той	обядва	обядва	обядваше
ние	обядваме	обядвахме	обядвахме
вие	обядвате	обядвахте	обядвахте
те	обядват	обядваха	обядваха

	Future	**Future in the Past**
	(For negative, replace **ще** with **няма да**)	(For negative, replace **щях/щеше/щяхме/щяхте/щяха** with **нямаше**)
аз	ще обядвам	щях да обядвам
ти	ще обядваш	щеше да обядваш
той	ще обядва	щеше да обядва
ние	ще обядваме	щяхме да обядваме
вие	ще обядвате	щяхте да обядвате
те	ще обядват	щяха да обядват

Past Active Participles

M	**F**	**N**	**Pl**
обядвал	обядвала	обядвало	обядвали

	Present Perfect	**Past Perfect**
аз	съм обядвал	бях обядвал
ти	си обядвал	беше обядвал
той	е обядвал	беше обядвал
ние	сме обядвали	бяхме обядвали
вие	сте обядвали	бяхте обядвали
те	са обядвали	бяха обядвали

	Conditional Mood	**Imperative Mood**	
аз	бих обядвал	**Positive**	**Negative**
ти	би обядвал	обядвай	не обядвай
той	би обядвал		
ние	бихме обядвали		
вие	бихте обядвали	обядвайте	не обядвайте
те	биха обядвали		

Past Passive Participles

M	**F**	**N**	**Pl**
N/A	N/A	N/A	N/A

130) **обяснявам/обясня;** *explain, describe*

	Present	**Past Simple**	**Past Continuous**
аз	обяснявам	обясних	обяснявах
ти	обясняваш	обясни	обясняваше
той	обяснява	обясни	обясняваше
ние	обясняваме	обяснихме	обяснявахме
вие	обяснявате	обяснихте	обяснявахте
те	обясняват	обясниха	обясняваха

	Future	**Future in the Past**
	(For negative, replace **ще** with **няма да**)	(For negative, replace **щях/щеше/щяхме/щяхте/щяха** with **нямаше**)
аз	ще обяснявам/обясня	щях да обяснявам/обясня
ти	ще обясняваш/обясниш	щеше да обясняваш/обясниш
той	ще обяснява/обясни	щеше да обяснява/обясни
ние	ще обясняваме/обясним	щяхме да обясняваме/обясним
вие	ще обяснявате/обясните	щяхте да обяснявате/обясните
те	ще обясняват/обяснят	щяха да обясняват/обяснят

Past Active Participles

M	**F**	**N**	**Pl**
обяснявал/обяснил	обяснявала/обяснила	обяснявало/обяснило	обяснявали/обяснили

	Present Perfect	**Past Perfect**
аз	съм обяснявал/обяснил	бях обяснявал/обяснил
ти	си обяснявал/обяснил	беше обяснявал/обяснил
той	е обяснявал/обяснил	беше обяснявал/обяснил
ние	сме обяснявали/обяснили	бяхме обяснявали/обяснили
вие	сте обяснявали/обяснили	бяхте обяснявали/обяснили
те	са обяснявали/обяснили	бяха обяснявали/обяснили

	Conditional Mood	**Imperative Mood**	
аз	бих обяснявал/обяснил	**Positive**	**Negative**
ти	би обяснявал/обяснил	обяснявай/обясни	не обяснявай
той	би обяснявал/обяснил		
ние	бихме обяснявали/обяснили		
вие	бихте обяснявали/обяснили	обяснявайте/обяснете	не обяснявайте
те	биха обяснявали/обяснили		

Past Passive Participles

M	**F**	**N**	**Pl**
обясняван/обяснен	обяснявана/обяснена	обяснявано/обяснено	обяснявани/обяснени

131) **опитвам/опитам;** *try; taste*

	Present	**Past Simple**	**Past Continuous**
аз	опитвам	опитах	опитвах
ти	опитваш	опита	опитваше
той	опитва	опита	опитваше
ние	опитваме	опитахме	опитвахме
вие	опитвате	опитахте	опитвахте
те	опитват	опитаха	опитваха

	Future	**Future in the Past**
	(For negative, replace **ще** with **няма да**)	(For negative, replace **щях/щеше/щяхме/щяхте/щяха** with **нямаше**)
аз	ще опитвам/опитам	щях да опитвам/опитам
ти	ще опитваш/опиташ	щеше да опитваш/опиташ
той	ще опитва/опита	щеше да опитва/опита
ние	ще опитваме/опитаме	щяхме да опитваме/опитаме
вие	ще опитвате/опитате	щяхте да опитвате/опитате
те	ще опитват/опитат	щяха да опитват/опитат

Past Active Participles

M	**F**	**N**	**Pl**
опитвал/опитал	опитвала/опитала	опитвало/опитало	опитвали/опитали

	Present Perfect	**Past Perfect**
аз	съм опитвал/опитал	бях опитвал/опитал
ти	си опитвал/опитал	беше опитвал/опитал
той	е опитвал/опитал	беше опитвал/опитал
ние	сме опитвали/опитали	бяхме опитвали/опитали
вие	сте опитвали/опитали	бяхте опитвали/опитали
те	са опитвали/опитали	бяха опитвали/опитали

	Conditional Mood	**Imperative Mood**	
аз	бих опитвал/опитал	**Positive**	**Negative**
ти	би опитвал/опитал	опитвай/опитай	не опитвай
той	би опитвал/опитал		
ние	бихме опитвали/опитали		
вие	бихте опитвали/опитали	опитвайте/опитайте	не опитвайте
те	биха опитвали/опитали		

Past Passive Participles

M	**F**	**N**	**Pl**
опитван/опитан	опитвана/опитана	опитвано/опитано	опитвани/опитани

132) **оплаквам се/оплача се;** *complain, grumble*

	Present	**Past Simple**	**Past Continuous**
аз	се оплаквам	се оплаках	се оплаквах
ти	се оплакваш	се оплака	се оплакваше
той	се оплаква	се оплака	се оплакваше
ние	се оплакваме	се оплакахме	се оплаквахме
вие	се оплаквате	се оплакахте	се оплаквахте
те	се оплакват	се оплакаха	се оплакваха

	Future	**Future in the Past**
	(For negative, replace **ще** with **няма да**)	(For negative, replace **щях/щеше/щяхме/щяхте/щяха** with **нямаше**)
аз	ще се оплаквам/оплача	щях да се оплаквам/оплача
ти	ще се оплакваш/оплачеш	щеше да се оплакваш/оплачеш
той	ще се оплаква/оплаче	щеше да се оплаква/оплаче
ние	ще се оплакваме/оплачем	щяхме да се оплакваме/оплачем
вие	ще се оплаквате/оплачете	щяхте да се оплаквате/оплачете
те	ще се оплакват/оплачат	щяха да се оплакват/оплачат

Past Active Participles

M	**F**	**N**	**Pl**
оплаквал/оплакал	оплаквала/оплакала	оплаквало/оплакало	оплаквали/оплакали

	Present Perfect	**Past Perfect**
аз	съм се оплаквал/оплакал	бях се оплаквал/оплакал
ти	си се оплаквал/оплакал	беше се оплаквал/оплакал
той	се е оплаквал/оплакал	беше се оплаквал/оплакал
ние	сме се оплаквали/оплакали	бяхме се оплаквали/оплакали
вие	сте се оплаквали/оплакали	бяхте се оплаквали/оплакали
те	са се оплаквали/оплакали	бяха се оплаквали/оплакали

	Conditional Mood	**Imperative Mood**	
аз	бих се оплаквал/оплакал	**Positive**	**Negative**
ти	би се оплаквал/оплакал	оплаквай се/оплачи се	не се оплаквай
той	би се оплаквал/оплакал		
ние	бихме се оплаквали/оплакали		
вие	бихте се оплаквали/оплакали	оплаквайте се/оплачете се	не се оплаквайте
те	биха се оплаквали/оплакали		

Past Passive Participles

M	**F**	**N**	**Pl**
N/A	N/A	N/A	N/A

133) **оставам/остана;** *remain, stay*

	Present	**Past Simple**	**Past Continuous**
аз	оставам	останах	оставах
ти	оставаш	остана	оставаше
той	остава	остана	оставаше
ние	оставаме	останахме	оставахме
вие	оставате	останахте	оставахте
те	остават	останаха	оставаха

	Future	**Future in the Past**
	(For negative, replace **ще** with **няма да**)	(For negative, replace **щях/щеше/щяхме/щяхте/щяха** with **нямаше**)
аз	ще оставам/остана	щях да оставам/остана
ти	ще оставаш/останеш	щеше да оставаш/останеш
той	ще остава/остане	щеше да остава/остане
ние	ще оставаме/останем	щяхме да оставаме/останем
вие	ще оставате/останете	щяхте да оставате/останете
те	ще остават/останат	щяха да остават/останат

Past Active Participles

M	**F**	**N**	**Pl**
оставал/останал	оставала/останала	оставало/останало	оставали/останали

	Present Perfect	**Past Perfect**
аз	съм оставал/останал	бях оставал/останал
ти	си оставал/останал	беше оставал/останал
той	е оставал/останал	беше оставал/останал
ние	сме оставали/останали	бяхме оставали/останали
вие	сте оставали/останали	бяхте оставали/останали
те	са оставали/останали	бяха оставали/останали

	Conditional Mood	**Imperative Mood**	
аз	бих оставал/останал	**Positive**	**Negative**
ти	би оставал/останал	оставай/остани	не оставай
той	би оставал/останал		
ние	бихме оставали/останали		
вие	бихте оставали/останали	оставайте/останете	не оставайте
те	биха оставали/останали		

Past Passive Participles

M	**F**	**N**	**PL**
N/A	N/A	N/A	N/A

134) **оставям/оставя;** *leave; abandon*

	Present	**Past Simple**	**Past Continuous**
аз	оставям	оставих	оставях
ти	оставяш	остави	оставяше
той	оставя	остави	оставяше
ние	оставяме	оставихме	оставяхме
вие	оставяте	оставихте	оставяхте
те	оставят	оставиха	оставяха

	Future	**Future in the Past**
	(For negative, replace **ще** with **няма да**)	(For negative, replace **щях/щеше/щяхме/щяхте/щяха** with **нямаше**)
аз	ще оставям/оставя	щях да оставям/оставя
ти	ще оставяш/оставиш	щеше да оставяш/оставиш
той	ще оставя/остави	щеше да оставя/остави
ние	ще оставяме/оставим	щяхме да оставяме/оставим
вие	ще оставяте/оставите	щяхте да оставяте/оставите
те	ще оставят/оставят	щяха да оставят/оставят

Past Active Participles

M	**F**	**N**	**Pl**
оставял/оставил	оставяла/оставила	оставяло/оставило	оставяли/оставили

	Present Perfect	**Past Perfect**
аз	съм оставял/оставил	бях оставял/оставил
ти	си оставял/оставил	беше оставял/оставил
той	е оставял/оставил	беше оставял/оставил
ние	сме оставяли/оставили	бяхме оставяли/оставили
вие	сте оставяли/оставили	бяхте оставяли/оставили
те	са оставяли/оставили	бяха оставяли/оставили

	Conditional Mood	**Imperative Mood**	
аз	бих оставял/оставил	**Positive**	**Negative**
ти	би оставял/оставил	оставяй/остави	не оставяй
той	би оставял/оставил		
ние	бихме оставяли/оставили		
вие	бихте оставяли/оставили	оставяйте/оставете	не оставяйте
те	биха оставяли/оставили		

Past Passive Participles

M	**F**	**N**	**Pl**
оставян/оставен	оставяна/оставена	оставяно/оставено	оставяни/оставени

135) **осъждам/осъдя;** *convict, blame*

	Present	**Past Simple**	**Past Continuous**
аз	осъждам	осъдих	осъждах
ти	осъждаш	осъди	осъждаше
той	осъжда	осъди	осъждаше
ние	осъждаме	осъдихме	осъждахме
вие	осъждате	осъдихте	осъждахте
те	осъждат	осъдиха	осъждаха

	Future	**Future in the Past**
	(For negative, replace **ще** with **няма да**)	(For negative, replace **щях/щеше/щяхме/щяхте/щяха** with **нямаше**)
аз	ще осъждам/осъдя	щях да осъждам/осъдя
ти	ще осъждаш/осъдиш	щеше да осъждаш/осъдиш
той	ще осъжда/осъди	щеше да осъжда/осъди
ние	ще осъждаме/осъдим	щяхме да осъждаме/осъдим
вие	ще осъждате/осъдите	щяхте да осъжате/осъдите
те	ще осъждат/осъдят	щяха да осъждат/осъдят

Past Active Participles

M	**F**	**N**	**Pl**
осъждал/осъдил	осъждала/осъдила	осъждало/осъдило	осъждали/осъдили

	Present Perfect	**Past Perfect**
аз	съм осъждал/осъдил	бях осъждал/осъдил
ти	си осъждал/осъдил	беше осъждал/осъдил
той	е осъждал/осъдил	беше осъждал/осъдил
ние	сме осъждали/осъдили	бяхме осъждали/осъдили
вие	сте осъждали/осъдили	бяхте осъждали/осъдили
те	са осъждали/осъдили	бяха осъждали/осъдили

	Conditional Mood	**Imperative Mood**	
аз	бих осъждал/осъдил	**Positive**	**Negative**
ти	би осъждал/осъдил	осъждай/осъди	не осъждай
той	би осъждал/осъдил		
ние	бихме осъждали/осъдили		
вие	бихте осъждали/осъдили	осъждайте/осъдете	не осъждайте
те	биха осъждали/осъдили		

Past Passive Participles

M	**F**	**N**	**Pl**
осъждан/осъден	осъждана/осъдена	осъждано/осъдено	осъждани/осъдени

136) **осъзнавам/осъзная;** *realize, become aware*

	Present	**Past Simple**	**Past Continuous**
аз	осъзнавам	осъзнах	осъзнавах
ти	осъзнаваш	осъзна	осъзнаваше
той	осъзнава	осъзна	осъзнаваше
ние	осъзнаваме	осъзнахме	осъзнавахме
вие	осъзнавате	осъзнахте	осъзнавахте
те	осъзнават	осъзнаха	осъзнаваха

	Future	**Future in the Past**
	(For negative, replace **ще** with **няма да**)	(For negative, replace **щях/щеше/щяхме/щяхте/щяха** with **нямаше**)
аз	ще осъзнавам/осъзная	щях да осъзнавам/осъзная
ти	ще осъзнаваш/осъзнаеш	щеше да осъзнаваш/осъзнаеш
той	ще осъзнава/осъзнае	щеше да осъзнава/осъзнае
ние	ще осъзнаваме/осъзнаем	щяхме да осъзнаваме/осъзнаем
вие	ще осъзнавате/осъзнаете	щяхте да осъзнавате/осъзнаете
те	ще осъзнават/осъзнаят	щяха да осъзнават/осъзнаят

Past Active Participles

M	**F**	**N**	**Pl**
осъзнавал/осъзнал	осъзнавала/осъзнала	осъзнавало/осъзнало	осъзнавали/осъзнали

	Present Perfect	**Past Perfect**
аз	съм осъзнавал/осъзнал	бях осъзнавал/осъзнал
ти	си осъзнавал/осъзнал	беше осъзнавал/осъзнал
той	е осъзнавал/осъзнал	беше осъзнавал/осъзнал
ние	сме осъзнавали/осъзнали	бяхме осъзнавали/осъзнали
вие	сте осъзнавали/осъзнали	бяхте осъзнавали/осъзнали
те	са осъзнавали/осъзнали	бяха осъзнавали/осъзнали

	Conditional Mood	**Imperative Mood**	
аз	бих осъзнавал/осъзнал	**Positive**	**Negative**
ти	би осъзнавал/осъзнал	осъзнавай/осъзнай	не осъзнавай
той	би осъзнавал/осъзнал		
ние	бихме осъзнавали/осъзнали		
вие	бихте осъзнавали/осъзнали	осъзнавайте/осъзнайте	не осъзнавайт
те	биха осъзнавали/осъзнали		

Past Passive Participles

M	**F**	**N**	**Pl**
осъзнаван/осъзнат	осъзнавана/осъзната	осъзнавано/осъзнато	осъзнавани/осъзнати

137) **отварям/отворя;** *open*

	Present	**Past Simple**	**Past Continuous**
аз	отварям	отворих	отварях
ти	отваряш	отвори	отваряше
той	отваря	отвори	отваряше
ние	отваряме	отворихме	отваряме
вие	отваряте	отворихте	отваряхте
те	отварят	отвориха	отваряха

	Future	**Future in the Past**
	(For negative, replace **ще** with **няма да**)	(For negative, replace **щях/щеше/щяхме/щяхте/щяха** with **нямаше**)
аз	ще отварям/отворя	щях да отварям/отворя
ти	ще отваряш/отвориш	щеше да отваряш/отвориш
той	ще отваря/отвори	щеше да отваря/отвори
ние	ще отваряме/отворим	щяхме да отваряме/отворим
вие	ще отваряте/отворите	щяхте да отваряте/отворите
те	ще отварят/отворят	щяха да отварят/отворят

Past Active Participles

M	**F**	**N**	**Pl**
отварял/отворил	отваряла/отворила	отваряло/отворило	отваряли/отворили

	Present Perfect	**Past Perfect**
аз	съм отварял/отворил	бях отварял/отворил
ти	си отварял/отворил	беше отварял/отворил
той	е отварял/отворил	беше отварял/отворил
ние	сме отваряли/отворили	бяхме отваряли/отворили
вие	сте отваряли/отворили	бяхте отваряли/отворили
те	са отваряли/отворили	бяха отваряли/отворили

	Conditional Mood	**Imperative Mood**	
аз	бих отварял/отворил	**Positive**	**Negative**
ти	би отварял/отворил	отваряй/отвори	не отваряй
той	би отварял/отворил		
ние	бихме отваряли/отворили		
вие	бихте отваряли/отворили	отваряйте/отворете	не отваряйте
те	биха отваряли/отворили		

Past Passive Participles

M	**F**	**N**	**Pl**
отварян/отворен	отваряна/отворена	отваряно/отворено	отваряни/отворени

138) **отговарям/отговоря;** *answer, reply* **отговарям;** *(only imperf) be responsible*

	Present	**Past Simple**	**Past Continuous**
аз	отговарям	отговорих	отговарях
ти	отговаряш	отговори	отговаряше
той	отговаря	отговори	отговаряше
ние	отговаряме	отговорихме	отговаряхме
вие	отговаряте	отговорихте	отговаряхте
те	отговарят	отговориха	отговаряха

	Future	**Future in the Past**
	(For negative, replace **ще** with **няма да**)	(For negative, replace **щях/щеше/щяхме/щяхте/щяха** with **нямаше**)
аз	ще отговарям/отговоря	щях да отговарям/отговоря
ти	ще отговаряш/отговориш	щеше да отговаряш/отговориш
той	ще отговаря/отговори	щеше да отговаря/отговори
ние	ще отговаряме/отговорим	щяхме да отговаряме/отговорим
вие	ще отговаряте/отговорите	щяхте да отговаряте/отговорите
те	ще отговарят/отговорят	щяха да отговарят/отговорят

Past Active Participles

M	**F**	**N**	**Pl**
отговарял/ отговорил	отговаряла/отговорила	отговаряло/отговорило	отговаряли/отговорили

	Present Perfect	**Past Perfect**
аз	съм отговарял/отговорил	бях отговарял/отговорил
ти	си отговарял/отговорил	беше отговарял/отговорил
той	е отговарял/отговорил	беше отговарял/отговорил
ние	сме отговаряли/отговорили	бяхме отговаряли/отговорили
вие	сте отговаряли/отговорили	бяхте отговаряли/отговорили
те	са отговаряли/отговорили	бяха отговаряли/отговорили

	Conditional Mood	**Imperative Mood**	
аз	бих отговарял/отговорил	**Positive**	**Negative**
ти	би отговарял/отговорил	отговаряй/отговори	не отговаряй
той	би отговарял/отговорил		
ние	бихме отговаряли/отговорили		
вие	бихте отговаряли/отговорили	отговаряйте/отговорете	не отговаряйте
те	биха отговаряли/отговорили		

Past Passive Participles

M	**F**	**N**	**Pl**
N/A	N/A	N/A	N/A

139) **отделям/отделя;** *separate; put aside*

	Present	**Past Simple**	**Past Continuous**
аз	отделям	отделих	отделях
ти	отделяш	отдели	отделяше
той	отделя	отдели	отделяше
ние	отделяме	отделихме	отделяхме
вие	отделяте	отделихте	отделяхте
те	отделят	отделиха	отделяха

	Future	**Future in the Past**
	(For negative, replace **ще** with **няма да**)	(For negative, replace **щях/щеше/щяхме/щяхте/щяха** with **нямаше**)
аз	ще отделям/отделя	щях да отделям/отделя
ти	ще отделяш/отделиш	щеше да отделяш/отделиш
той	ще отделя/отдели	щеше да отделя/отдели
ние	ще отделяме/отделим	щяхме да отделяме/отделим
вие	ще отделяте/отделите	щяхте да отделяте/отделите
те	ще отделят/отделят	щяха да отделят/отделят

Past Active Participles

M	F	N	Pl
отделял/отделил	отделяла/отделила	отделяло/отделило	отделяли/отделили

	Present Perfect	**Past Perfect**
аз	съм отделял/отделил	бях отделял/отделил
ти	си отделял/отделил	беше отделял/отделил
той	е отделял/отделил	беше отделял/отделил
ние	сме отделяли/отделили	бяхме отделяли/отделили
вие	сте отделяли/отделили	бяхте отделяли/отделили
те	са отделяли/отделили	бяха отделяли/отделили

	Conditional Mood	**Imperative Mood**	
аз	бих отделял/отделил	**Positive**	**Negative**
ти	би отделял/отделил	отделяй/отдели	не отделяй
той	би отделял/отделил		
ние	бихме отделяли/отделили		
вие	бихте отделяли/отделили	отделяйте/отделете	не отделяйте
те	биха отделяли/отделили		

Past Passive Participles

M	F	N	Pl
отделян/отделен	отделяна/отделена	отделяно/отделено	отделяни/отделени

140) **отивам/отида;** *go to, approach*

	Present	Past Simple	Past Continuous
аз	отивам	отидох	отивах
ти	отиваш	отиде	отиваше
той	отива	отиде	отиваше
ние	отиваме	отидохме	отивахме
вие	отивате	отидохте	отивахте
те	отиват	отидоха	отиваха

	Future	Future in the Past
	(For negative, replace **ще** with **няма да**)	(For negative, replace **щях/щеше/щяхме/щяхте/щяха** with **нямаше**)
аз	ще отивам/отида	щях да отивам/отида
ти	ще отиваш/отидеш	щеше да отиваш/отидеш
той	ще отива/отиде	щеше да отива/отиде
ние	ще отиваме/отидем	щяхме да отиваме/отидем
вие	ще отивате/отидете	щяхте да отивате/отидете
те	ще отиват/отидат	щяха да отиват/отидат

Past Active Participles

M	F	N	Pl
отивал/отишъл	отивала/отишла	отивало/отишло	отивали/отишли

	Present Perfect	Past Perfect
аз	съм отивал/отишъл	бях отивал/отишъл
ти	си отивал/отишъл	беше отивал/отишъл
той	е отивал/отишъл	беше отивал/отишъл
ние	сме отивали/отишли	бяхме отивали/отишли
вие	сте отивали/отишли	бяхте отивали/отишли
те	са отивали/отишли	бяха отивали/отишли

	Conditional Mood	Imperative Mood	
аз	бих отивал/отишъл	**Positive**	**Negative**
ти	би отивал/отишъл	отивай/отиди	не отивай
той	би отивал/отишъл	(иди)	
ние	бихме отивали/отишли		
вие	бихте отивали/отишли	отивайте/отидете	не отивайте
те	биха отивали/отишли	(идете)	

Past Passive Participles

M	F	N	Pl
N/A	N/A	N/A	N/A

141) **отключвам/отключа;** *unlock*

	Present	Past Simple	Past Continuous
аз	отключвам	отключих	отключвах
ти	отключваш	отключи	отключваше
той	отключва	отключи	отключваше
ние	отключваме	отключихме	отключвахме
вие	отключвате	отключихте	отключвахте
те	отключват	отключиха	отключваха

	Future	Future in the Past
	(For negative, replace **ще** with **няма да**)	(For negative, replace **щях/щеше/ щяхме/щяхте/щяха** with **нямаше**)
аз	ще отключвам/отключа	щях да отключвам/отключа
ти	ще отключваш/отключиш	щеше да отключмаш/отключиш
той	ще отключва/отключи	щеше да отключва/отключи
ние	ще отключваме/отключим	щяхме да отключваме/отключим
вие	ще отключвате/отключите	щяхте да отключвате/отключите
те	ще отключват/отключат	щяха да отключват/отключат

Past Active Participles

M	F	N	Pl
отключвал/ отключил	отключвала/ отключила	отключвало/ отключило	отключвали/ отключили

	Present Perfect	Past Perfect
аз	съм отключвал/отключил	бях отключвал/отключил
ти	си отключвал/отключил	беше отключвал/отключил
той	е отключвал/отключил	беше отключвал/отключил
ние	сме отключвали/отключили	бяхме отключвали/отключили
вие	сте отключвали/отключили	бяхте отключвали/отключили
те	са отключвали/отключили	бяха отключвали/отключили

	Conditional Mood	Imperative Mood	
аз	бих отключвал/отключил	**Positive**	**Negative**
ти	би отключвал/отключил	отключвай/отключи	не отключвай
той	би отключвал/отключил		
ние	бихме отключвали/отключили		
вие	бихте отключвали/отключили	отключвайте/отключете	не отключвайте
те	биха отключвали/отключили		

Past Passive Participles

M	F	N	Pl
отключван/ отключен	отключвана/отключена	отключвано/ отключено	отключвани/ отключени

142) **откривам/открия;** *discover, find out*

	Present	Past Simple	Past Continuous
аз	откривам	открих	откривах
ти	откриваш	откри	откриваше
той	открива	откри	откриваше
ние	откриваме	открихме	откривахме
вие	откривате	открихте	откривахте
те	откриват	откриха	откриваха

	Future	Future in the Past
	(For negative, replace **ще** with **няма да**)	(For negative, replace **щях/щеше/щяхме/щяхте/щяха** with **нямаше**)
аз	ще откривам/открия	щях да откривам/открия
ти	ще откриваш/откриеш	щеше да откриваш/откриеш
той	ще открива/открие	щеше да открива/открие
ние	ще откриваме/открием	щяхме да откриваме/открием
вие	ще откривате/откриете	щяхте да откривате/откриете
те	ще откриват/открият	щяха да откриват/открият

Past Active Participles

M	F	N	Pl
откривал/открил	откривала/открила	откривало/открило	откривали/открили

	Present Perfect	Past Perfect
аз	съм откривал/открил	бях откривал/открил
ти	си откривал/открил	беше откривал/открил
той	е откривал/открил	беше откривал/открил
ние	сме откривали/открили	бяхме откривали/открили
вие	сте откривали/открили	бяхте откривали/открили
те	са откривали/открили	бяха откривали/открили

	Conditional Mood	Imperative Mood	
аз	бих откривал/открил	**Positive**	**Negative**
ти	би откривал/открил	откривай/открий	не откривай
той	би откривал/открил		
ние	бихме откривали/открили		
вие	бихте откривали/открили	откривайте/открийте	не откривайте
те	биха откривали/открили		

Past Passive Participles

M	F	N	Pl
откриван/открит	откривана/открита	откривано/открито	откривани/открити

143) **отричам/отрека;** *refuse, decline, reject*

	Present	**Past Simple**	**Past Continuous**
аз	отричам	отрекох	отричах
ти	отричаш	отрече	отричаше
той	отрича	отрече	отричаше
ние	отричаме	отрекохме	отричахме
вие	отричате	отрекохте	отричахте
те	отричат	отрекоха	отричаха

	Future	**Future in the Past**
	(For negative, replace **ще** with **няма да**)	(For negative, replace **щях/щеше/щяхме/щяхте/щяха** with **нямаше**)
аз	ще отричам/отрека	щях да отричам/отрека
ти	ще отричаш/отречеш	щеше да отричаш/отречеш
той	ще отрича/отрече	щеше да отрича/отрече
ние	ще отричаме/отречем	щяхме да отричаме/отречем
вие	ще отричате/отречете	щяхте да отричате/отречете
те	ще отричат/отрекат	щяха да отричат/отрекат

Past Active Participles

M	**F**	**N**	**Pl**
отричал/отрекъл	отричала/отрекла	отричало/отрекло	отричали/отрекли

	Present Perfect	**Past Perfect**
аз	съм отричал/отрекъл	бях отричал/отрекъл
ти	си отричал/отрекъл	беше отричал/отрекъл
той	е отричал/отрекъл	беше отричал/отрекъл
ние	сме отричали/отрекли	бяхме отричали/отрекли
вие	сте отричали/отрекли	бяхте отричали/отрекли
те	са отричали/отрекли	бяха отричали/отрекли

	Conditional Mood	**Imperative Mood**	
аз	бих отричал/отрекъл	**Positive**	**Negative**
ти	би отричал/отрекъл	отричай/отречи	не отричай
той	би отричал/отрекъл		
ние	бихме отричали/отрекли		
вие	бихте отричали/отрекли	отричайте/отречете	не отричайте
те	биха отричали/отрекли		

Past Passive Participles

M	**F**	**N**	**Pl**
отричан/отречен	отричана/отречена	отричано/отречено	отричани/отречени

144) **отрязвам/отрежа;** *cut off, cut away, slice*

	Present	Past Simple	Past Continuous
аз	отрязвам	отрязах	отрязвах
ти	отрязваш	отряза	отрязваше
той	отрязва	отряза	отрязваше
ние	отрязваме	отрязахме	отрязвахме
вие	отрязвате	отрязахте	отрязвахте
те	отрязват	отрязаха	отрязваха

	Future	Future in the Past
	(For negative, replace **ще** with **няма да**)	(For negative, replace **щях/щеше/щяхме/щяхте/щяха** with **нямаше**)
аз	ще отрязвам/отрежа	щях да отрязвам/отрежа
ти	ще отрязваш/отрежеш	щеше да отрязваш/отрежеш
той	ще отрязва/отреже	щеше да отрязва/отреже
ние	ще отрязваме/отрежем	щяхме да отрязваме/отрежем
вие	ще отрязвате/отрежете	щяхте да отрязвате/отрежете
те	ще отрязват/отрежат	щяха да отрязват/отрежат

Past Active Participles

M	F	N	Pl
отрязвал/отрязал	отрязвала/отрязала	отрязвало/отрязало	отрязвали/отрязали

	Present Perfect	Past Perfect
аз	съм отрязвал/отрязал	бях отрязвал/отрязал
ти	си отрязвал/отрязал	беше отрязвал/отрязал
той	е отрязвал/отрязал	беше отрязвал/отрязал
ние	сме отрязвали/отрязали	бяхме отрязвали/отрязали
вие	сте отрязвали/отрязали	бяхте отрязвали/отрязали
те	са отрязвали/отрязали	бяха отрязвали/отрязали

	Conditional Mood	Imperative Mood	
		Positive	**Negative**
аз	бих отрязвал/отрязал		
ти	би отрязвал/отрязал	отрязвай/отрежи	не отрязвай
той	би отрязвал/отрязал		
ние	бихме отрязвали/отрязали		
вие	бихте отрязвали/отрязали	отрязвайте/отрежете	не отрязвайте
те	биха отрязвали/отрязали		

Past Passive Participles

M	F	N	Pl
отрязван/отрязан	отрязвана/отрязана	отрязвано/отрязано	отрязвани/отрязани

145) **отчайвам се/отчаям се;** *discourage, dispirit*

	Present	**Past Simple**	**Past Continuous**
аз	се отчайвам	се отчаях	се отчайвах
ти	се отчайваш	се отчая	се отчайваше
той	се отчайва	се отчая	се отчайваше
ние	се отчайваме	се отчаяхме	се отчайвахме
вие	се отчайвате	се отчаяхте	се отчайвахте
те	се отчайват	се отчаяха	се отчайваха

	Future	**Future in the Past**
	(For negative, replace **ще** with **няма да**)	(For negative, replace **щях/щеше/щяхме/щяхте/щяха** with **нямаше**)
аз	ще се отчайвам/отчаям	щях да се отчайвам/отчаям
ти	ще се отчайваш/отчаяш	щеше да се отчайваш/отчаяш
той	ще се отчайва/отчая	щеше да се отчайва/отчая
ние	ще се отчайваме/отчаяме	щяхме да се отчайваме/отчаяме
вие	ще се отчайвате/отчаяте	щяхте да се отчайвате/отчаяте
те	ще се отчайват/отчаят	щяха да се отчайват/отчаят

Past Active Participles

M	**F**	**N**	**Pl**
отчайвал/отчаял	отчайвала/отчаяла	отчайвало/отчаяло	Отчайвали/отчаяли

	Present Perfect	**Past Perfect**
аз	съм се отчайвал/отчаял	бях се отчайвал/отчаял
ти	си се отчайвал/отчаял	беше се отчайвал/отчаял
той	се е отчайвал/отчаял	беше се отчайвал/отчаял
ние	сме се отчайвали/отчаяли	бяхме се отчайвали/отчаяли
вие	сте се отчайвали/отчаяли	бяхте се отчайвали/отчаяли
те	са се отчайвали/отчаяли	бяха се отчайвали/отчаяли

	Conditional Mood	**Imperative Mood**	
аз	бих се отчайвал/отчаял	**Positive**	**Negative**
ти	би се отчайвал/отчаял	отчайвай се	не се отчайвай
той	би се отчайвал/отчаял		
ние	бихме се отчайвали/отчаяли		
вие	бихте се отчайвали/отчаяли	отчайвайте се	не се отчайвайте
те	биха се отчайвали/отчаяли		

Past Passive Participles

M	**F**	**N**	**Pl**
N/A	N/A	N/A	N/A

146) **оцелявам/оцелея;** *survive*

	Present	Past Simple	Past Continuous
аз	оцелявам	оцелях	оцелявах
ти	оцеляваш	оцеля	оцеляваше
той	оцелява	оцеля	оцеляваше
ние	оцеляваме	оцеляхме	оцелявахме
вие	оцелявате	оцеляхте	оцелявахте
те	оцеляват	оцеляха	оцеляваха

	Future	Future in the Past
	(For negative, replace **ще** with **няма да**)	(For negative, replace **щях/щеше/щяхме/щяхте/щяха** with **нямаше**)
аз	ще оцелявам/оцелея	щях да оцелявам/оцелея
ти	ще оцеляваш/оцелееш	щеше да оцеляваш/оцелееш
той	ще оцелява/оцелее	щеше да оцелява/оцелее
ние	ще оцеляваме/оцелеем	щяхме да оцеляваме/оцелеем
вие	ще оцелявате/оцелеете	щяхте да оцелявате/оцелеете
те	ще оцеляват/оцелеят	щяха да оцеляват/оцелеят

Past Active Participles

M	F	N	Pl
оцелявал/оцелял	оцелявала/оцеляла	оцелявало/оцеляло	оцелявали/оцелели

	Present Perfect	Past Perfect
аз	съм оцелявал/оцелял	бях оцелявал/оцелял
ти	си оцелявал/оцелял	беше оцелявал/оцелял
той	е оцелявал/оцелял	беше оцелявал/оцелял
ние	сме оцелявали/оцелели	бяхме оцелявали/оцелели
вие	сте оцелявали/оцелели	бяхте оцелявали/оцелели
те	са оцелявали/оцелели	бяха оцелявали/оцелели

	Conditional Mood	Imperative Mood	
		Positive	**Negative**
аз	бих оцелявал/оцелял		
ти	би оцелявал/оцелял	оцелявай/оцелей	не оцелявай
той	би оцелявал/оцелял		
ние	бихме оцелявали/оцелели		
вие	бихте оцелявали/оцелели	оцелявайте/оцелейте	не оцелявайте
те	биха оцелявали/оцелели		

Past Passive Participles

M	F	N	Pl
N/A	N/A	N/A	N/A

147) **падам/падна;** *fall, drop; reduce, decrease*

	Present	Past Simple	Past Continuous
аз	падам	паднах	падах
ти	падаш	падна	падаше
той	пада	падна	падаше
ние	падаме	паднахме	падахме
вие	падате	паднахте	падахте
те	падат	паднаха	падаха

	Future	Future in the Past
	(For negative, replace **ще** with **няма да**)	(For negative, replace **щях/щеше/щяхме/щяхте/щяха** with **нямаше**)
аз	ще падам/падна	щях да падам/падна
ти	ще падаш/паднеш	щеше да падаш/паднеш
той	ще пада/падне	щеше да пада/падне
ние	ще падаме/паднем	щяхме да падаме/паднем
вие	ще падате/паднете	щяхте да падате/паднете
те	ще падат/паднат	щяха да падат/паднат

Past Active Participles

M	F	N	Pl
падал/паднал	падала/паднала	падало/паднало	падали/паднали

	Present Perfect	Past Perfect
аз	съм падал/паднал	бях падал/паднал
ти	си падал/паднал	беше падал/паднал
той	е падал/паднал	беше падал/паднал
ние	сме падали/паднали	бяхме падали/паднали
вие	сте падали/паднали	бяхте падали/паднали
те	са падали/паднали	бяха падали/паднали

	Conditional Mood	Imperative Mood	
аз	бих падал/паднал	**Positive**	**Negative**
ти	би падал/паднал	падай/падни	не падай
той	би падал/паднал		
ние	бихме падали/паднали		
вие	бихте падали/паднали	падайте/паднете	не падайте
те	биха падали/паднали		

Past Passive Participles

M	F	N	Pl
N/A	N/A	N/A	N/A

148) **пазарувам;** *go shopping*

	Present	**Past Simple**	**Past Continuous**
аз	пазарувам	пазарувах	пазарувах
ти	пазаруваш	пазарува	пазаруваше
той	пазарува	пазарува	пазаруваше
ние	пазаруваме	пазарувахме	пазарувахме
вие	пазарувате	пазарувахте	пазарувахте
те	пазаруват	пазаруваха	пазаруваха

	Future	**Future in the Past**
	(For negative, replace **ще** with **няма да**)	(For negative, replace **щях/щеше/щяхме/щяхте/щяха** with **нямаше**)
аз	ще пазарувам	щях да пазарувам
ти	ще пазаруваш	щеше да пазаруваш
той	ще пазарува	щеше да пазарува
ние	ще пазаруваме	щяхме да пазаруваме
вие	ще пазарувате	щяхте да пазарувате
те	ще пазаруват	щяха да пазаруват

Past Active Participles

M	**F**	**N**	**Pl**
пазарувал	пазарувала	пазарувало	пазарували

	Present Perfect	**Past Perfect**
аз	съм пазарувал	бях пазарувал
ти	си пазарувал	беше пазарувал
той	е пазарувал	беше пазарувал
ние	сме пазарували	бяхме пазарували
вие	сте пазарували	бяхте пазарували
те	са пазарували	бяха пазарували

	Conditional Mood	**Imperative Mood**	
		Positive	**Negative**
аз	бих пазарувал		
ти	би пазарувал	пазарувай	не пазарувай
той	би пазарувал		
ние	бихме пазарували		
вие	бихте пазарували	пазарувай	не пазарувай
те	биха пазарували		

Past Passive Participles

M	**F**	**N**	**Pl**
N/A	N/A	N/A	N/A

149) **пазя;** *guard, protect, keep*

	Present	Past Simple	Past Continuous
аз	пазя	пазих	пазех
ти	пазиш	пази	пазеше
той	пази	пази	пазеше
ние	пазим	пазихме	пазехме
вие	пазите	пазихте	пазехте
те	пазят	пазиха	пазеха

	Future	Future in the Past
	(For negative, replace **ще** with **няма да**)	(For negative, replace **щях/щеше/щяхме/щяхте/щяха** with **нямаше**)
аз	ще пазя	щях да пазя
ти	ще пазиш	щеше да пазиш
той	ще пази	щеше да пази
ние	ще пазим	щяхме да пазим
вие	ще пазите	щяхте да пазите
те	ще пазят	щяха да пазят

Past Active Participles

M	F	N	Pl
пазил	пазила	пазило	пазили

	Present Perfect	Past Perfect
аз	съм пазил	бях пазил
ти	си пазил	беше пазил
той	е пазил	беше пазил
ние	сме пазили	бяхме пазили
вие	сте пазили	бяхте пазили
те	са пазили	бяха пазили

	Conditional Mood	Imperative Mood	
аз	бих пазил	**Positive**	**Negative**
ти	би пазил	пази	не пази
той	би пазил		
ние	бихме пазили		
вие	бихте пазили	пазете	не пазете
те	биха пазили		

Past Passive Participles

M	F	N	Pl
пазен	пазена	пазено	пазени

150) **пека;** *roast, bake*

	Present	**Past Simple**	**Past Continuous**
аз	пека	пекох	печах
ти	печеш	пече	печеше
той	пече	пече	печеше
ние	печем	пекохме	печахме
вие	печете	пекохте	печахте
те	пекат	пекоха	печаха

	Future	**Future in the Past**
	(For negative, replace **ще** with **няма да**)	(For negative, replace **щях/щеше/щяхме/щяхте/щяха** with **нямаше**)
аз	ще пека	щях да пека
ти	ще печеш	щеше да печеш
той	ще пече	щеше да пече
ние	ще печем	щяхме да печем
вие	ще печете	щяхте да печете
те	ще пекат	щяха да пекат

Past Active Participles

M	**F**	**N**	**Pl**
пекъл	пекла	пекло	пекли

	Present Perfect	**Past Perfect**
аз	съм пекъл	бях пекъл
ти	си пекъл	беше пекъл
той	е пекъл	беше пекъл
ние	сме пекли	бяхме пекли
вие	сте пекли	бяхте пекли
те	са пекли	бяха пекли

	Conditional Mood	**Imperative Mood**	
аз	бих пекъл	**Positive**	**Negative**
ти	би пекъл	печи	не печи
той	би пекъл		
ние	бихме пекли		
вие	бихте пекли	печете	не печете
те	биха пекли		

Past Passive Participles

M	**F**	**N**	**Pl**
печен	печена	печено	печени

151) **пера;** *wash, launder*

	Present	**Past Simple**	**Past Continuous**
аз	пера	прах	перях
ти	переш	пра	переше
той	пере	пра	переше
ние	перем	прахме	перяхме
вие	перете	прахте	перяхте
те	перат	праха	перяха

	Future	**Future in the Past**
	(For negative, replace **ще** with **няма да**)	(For negative, replace **щях/щеше/щяхме/щяхте/щяха** with **нямаше**)
аз	ще пера	щях да пера
ти	ще переш	щеше да переш
той	ще пере	щеше да пере
ние	ще перем	щяхме да перем
вие	ще перете	щяхте да перете
те	ще перат	щяха да перат

Past Active Participles

M	**F**	**N**	**Pl**
прал	прала	прало	прали

	Present Perfect	**Past Perfect**
аз	съм прал	бях прал
ти	си прал	беше прал
той	е прал	беше прал
ние	сме прали	бяхме прали
вие	сте прали	бяхте прали
те	са прали	бяха прали

	Conditional Mood	**Imperative Mood**	
аз	бих прал	**Positive**	**Negative**
ти	би прал	пери	не пери
той	би прал		
ние	бихме прали		
вие	бихте прали	перете	не перете
те	биха прали		

Past Passive Participles

M	**F**	**N**	**Pl**
пран	прана	прано	прани

152) **печеля;** *earn, gain; win*

	Present	**Past Simple**	**Past Continuous**
аз	печеля	печелих	печелех
ти	печелиш	печели	печелеше
той	печели	печели	печелеше
ние	печелим	печелихме	печелехме
вие	печелите	печелихте	печелехте
те	печелят	печелиха	печелеха

	Future	**Future in the Past**
	(For negative, replace **ще** with **няма да**)	(For negative, replace **щях/щеше/щяхме/щяхте/щяха** with **нямаше**)
аз	ще печеля	щях да печеля
ти	ще печелиш	щеше да печелиш
той	ще печели	щеше да печели
ние	ще печелим	щяхме да печелим
вие	ще печелите	щяхте да печелите
те	ще печелят	щяха да печелят

Past Active Participles

M	**F**	**N**	**Pl**
печелил	печелила	печелило	печелили

	Present Perfect	**Past Perfect**
аз	съм печелил	бях печелил
ти	си печелил	беше печелил
той	е печелил	беше печелил
ние	сме печелили	бяхме печелили
вие	сте печелили	бяхте печелили
те	са печелили	бяха печелили

	Conditional Mood	**Imperative Mood**	
аз	бих печелил	**Positive**	**Negative**
ти	би печелил	печели	не печели
той	би печелил		
ние	бихме печелили		
вие	бихте печелили	печелете	не печелете
те	биха печелили		

Past Passive Participles

M	**F**	**N**	**Pl**
печелен	печелена	печелено	печелени

153) **пея;** *sing*

	Present	**Past Simple**	**Past Continuous**
аз	пея	пях	пеех
ти	пееш	пя	пееше
той	пее	пя	пееше
ние	пеем	пяхме	пеехме
вие	пеете	пяхте	пеехте
те	пеят	пяха	пееха

	Future	**Future in the Past**
	(For negative, replace **ще** with **няма да**)	(For negative, replace **щях/щеше/щяхме/щяхте/щяха** with **нямаше**)
аз	ще пея	щях да пея
ти	ще пееш	щеше да пееш
той	ще пее	щеше да пее
ние	ще пеем	щяхме да пеем
вие	ще пеете	щяхте да пеете
те	ще пеят	щяха да пеят

Past Active Participles

M	**F**	**N**	**Pl**
пял	пяла	пяло	пели

	Present Perfect	**Past Perfect**
аз	съм пял	бях пял
ти	си пял	беше пял
той	е пял	беше пял
ние	сме пели	бяхме пели
вие	сте пели	бяхте пели
те	са пели	бяха пели

	Conditional Mood	**Imperative Mood**	
аз	бих пял	**Positive**	**Negative**
ти	би пял	пей	не пей
той	би пял		
ние	бихме пели		
вие	бихте пели	пейте	не пейте
те	биха пели		

Past Passive Participles

M	**F**	**N**	**Pl**
пян	пяна	пяно	пени

154) **питам/попитам;** *ask, inquire*

	Present	Past Simple	Past Continuous
аз	питам	попитах	питах
ти	питаш	попита	питаше
той	пита	попита	питаше
ние	питаме	попитахме	питахме
вие	питате	попитахте	питахте
те	питат	попитаха	питаха

	Future	Future in the Past
	(For negative, replace **ще** with **няма да**)	(For negative, replace **щях/щеше/щяхме/щяхте/щяха** with **нямаше**)
аз	ще питам/попитам	щях да питам/попитам
ти	ще питаш/попиташ	щеше да питаш/попиташ
той	ще пита/попита	щеше да пита/попита
ние	ще питаме/попитаме	щяхме да питаме/попитаме
вие	ще питате/попитате	щяхте да питате/попитате
те	ще питат/попитат	щяха да питат/попитат

Past Active Participles

M	F	N	Pl
питал/попитал	питала/попитала	питало/попитало	питали/попитали

	Present Perfect	Past Perfect
аз	съм питал/попитал	бях питал/попитал
ти	си питал/попитал	беше питал/попитал
той	е питал/попитал	беше питал/попитал
ние	сме питали/попитали	бяхме питали/попитали
вие	сте питали/попитали	бяхте питали/попитали
те	са питали/попитали	бяха питали/попитали

	Conditional Mood	Imperative Mood	
аз	бих питал/попитал	**Positive**	**Negative**
ти	би питал/попитал	питай/попитай	не питай
той	би питал/попитал		
ние	бихме питали/попитали		
вие	бихте питали/попитали	питайте/попитайте	не питайте
те	биха питали/попитали		

Past Passive Participles

M	F	N	Pl
питан/попитан	питана/попитана	питано/попитано	питани/попитани

155) **пиша;** *write*

	Present	**Past Simple**	**Past Continuous**
аз	пиша	писах	пишех
ти	пишеш	писа	пишеше
той	пише	писа	пишеше
ние	пишем	писахме	пишехме
вие	пишете	писахте	пишехте
те	пишат	писаха	пишеха

	Future	**Future in the Past**
	(For negative, replace **ще** with **няма да**)	(For negative, replace **щях/щеше/щяхме/щяхте/щяха** with **нямаше**)
аз	ще пиша	щях да пиша
ти	ще пишеш	щеше да пишеш
той	ще пише	щеше да пише
ние	ще пишем	щяхме да пишем
вие	ще пишете	щяхте да пишете
те	ще пишат	щяха да пишат

Past Active Participles

M	**F**	**N**	**Pl**
писал	Писала	писало	писали

	Present Perfect	**Past Perfect**
аз	съм писал	бях писал
ти	си писал	беше писал
той	е писал	беше писал
ние	сме писали	бяхме писали
вие	сте писали	бяхте писали
те	са писали	бяха писали

	Conditional Mood	**Imperative Mood**	
аз	бих писал	**Positive**	**Negative**
ти	би писал	Пиши	не пиши
той	би писал		
ние	бихме писали		
вие	бихте писали	пишете	не пишете
те	биха писали		

Past Passive Participles

M	**F**	**N**	**Pl**
писан	писана	писано	писани

156) **пия;** *drink, drink up*

	Present	**Past Simple**	**Past Continuous**
аз	пия	пих	пиех
ти	пиеш	пи	пиеше
той	пие	пи	пиеше
ние	пием	пихме	пиехме
вие	пиете	пихте	пиехте
те	пият	пиха	пиеха

	Future	**Future in the Past**
	(For negative, replace **ще** with **няма да**)	(For negative, replace **щях/щеше/щяхме/щяхте/щяха** with **нямаше**)
аз	ще пия	щях да пия
ти	ще пиеш	щеше да пиеш
той	ще пие	щеше да пие
ние	ще пием	щяхме да пием
вие	ще пиете	щяхте да пиете
те	ще пият	щяха да пият

Past Active Participles

M	**F**	**N**	**Pl**
пил	пила	пило	пили

	Present Perfect	**Past Perfect**
аз	съм пил	бях пил
ти	си пил	беше пил
той	е пил	беше пил
ние	сме пили	бяхме пили
вие	сте пили	бяхте пили
те	са пили	бяха пили

	Conditional Mood	**Imperative Mood**	
аз	бих пил	**Positive**	**Negative**
ти	би пил	пий	не пий
той	би пил		
ние	бихме пили		
вие	бихте пили	пийте	не пийте
те	биха пили		

Past Passive Participles

M	**F**	**N**	**Pl**
пит	пита	пито	пити

157) **плача;** *weep, cry*

	Present	**Past Simple**	**Past Continuous**
аз	плача	плаках	плачех
ти	плачеш	плака	плачеше
той	плаче	плака	плачеше
ние	плачем	плакахме	плачехме
вие	плачете	плакахте	плачехте
те	плачат	плакаха	плачеха

	Future	**Future in the Past**
	(For negative, replace **ще** with **няма да**)	(For negative, replace **щях/щеше/щяхме/щяхте/щяха** with **нямаше**)
аз	ще плача	щях да плача
ти	ще плачеш	щеше да плачеш
той	ще плаче	щеше да плаче
ние	ще плачем	щяхме да плачем
вие	ще плачете	щяхте да плачете
те	ще плачат	щяха да плачат

Past Active Participles

M	**F**	**N**	**Pl**
плакал	плакала	плакало	плакали

	Present Perfect	**Past Perfect**
аз	съм плакал	бях плакал
ти	си плакал	беше плакал
той	е плакал	беше плакал
ние	сме плакали	бяхме плакали
вие	сте плакали	бяхте плакали
те	са плакали	бяха плакали

	Conditional Mood	**Imperative Mood**	
аз	бих плакал	**Positive**	**Negative**
ти	би плакал	плачи	не плачи
той	би плакал		
ние	бихме плакали		
вие	бихте плакали	плачете	не плачете
те	биха плакали		

Past Passive Participles

M	**F**	**N**	**Pl**
N/A	N/A	N/A	N/A

158) **плащам/платя;** *pay, compensate, reimburse*

	Present	**Past Simple**	**Past Continuous**
аз	плащам	платих	плащах
ти	плащаш	плати	плащаше
той	плаща	плати	плащаше
ние	плащаме	плетихме	плащахме
вие	плащате	платихте	плащахте
те	плащат	платиха	плащаха

	Future	**Future in the Past**
	(For negative, replace **ще** with **няма да**)	(For negative, replace **щях/щеше/щяхме/щяхте/щяха** with **нямаше**)
аз	ще плащам/платя	щях да плащам/платя
ти	ще плащаш/платиш	щеше да плащаш/платиш
той	ще плаща/плати	щеше да плаща/плати
ние	ще плащаме/платим	щяхме да плащаме/платим
вие	ще плащате/платите	щяхте да плащате/платите
те	ще плащат/платят	щяха да плащат/платят

Past Active Participles

M	**F**	**N**	**Pl**
плащал/платил	плащала/платила	плащало/платило	плащали/платили

	Present Perfect	**Past Perfect**
аз	съм плащал/платил	бях плащал/платил
ти	си плащал/платил	беше плащал/платил
той	е плащал/платил	беше плащал/платил
ние	сме плащали/платили	бяхме плащали/платили
вие	сте плащали/платили	бяхте плащали/платили
те	са плащали/платили	бяха плащали/платили

	Conditional Mood	**Imperative Mood**	
аз	бих плащал/платил	**Positive**	**Negative**
ти	би плащал/платил	плащай/плати	не плащай
той	би плащал/платил		
ние	бихме плащали/платили		
вие	бихте плащали/платили	плащайте/платете	не плащайте
те	биха плащали/платили		

Past Passive Participles

M	**F**	**N**	**Pl**
плащан/платен	плащана/платена	плащано/платено	плащани/платени

159) **плувам;** *swim*

	Present	Past Simple	Past Continuous
аз	плувам	плувах	плувах
ти	плуваш	плува	плуваше
той	плува	плува	плуваше
ние	плуваме	плувахме	плувахме
вие	плувате	плувахте	плувахте
те	плуват	плуваха	плуваха

	Future	Future in the Past
	(For negative, replace **ще** with **няма да**)	(For negative, replace **щях/щеше/щяхме/щяхте/щяха** with **нямаше**)
аз	ще плувам	щях да плувам
ти	ще плуваш	щеше да плуваш
той	ще плува	щеше да плува
ние	ще плуваме	щяхме да плуваме
вие	ще плувате	щяхте да плувате
те	ще плуват	щяха да плуват

Past Active Participles

M	F	N	Pl
плувал	плувала	плувало	плували

	Present Perfect	Past Perfect
аз	съм плувал	бях плувал
ти	си плувал	беше плувал
той	е плувал	беше плувал
ние	сме плували	бяхме плували
вие	сте плували	бяхте плували
те	са плували	бяха плували

	Conditional Mood	Imperative Mood: Positive	Imperative Mood: Negative
аз	бих плувал		
ти	би плувал	плувай	не плувай
той	би плувал		
ние	бихме плували		
вие	бихте плували	плувайте	не плувайте
те	биха плували		

Past Passive Participles

M	F	N	Pl
N/A	N/A	N/A	N/A

160) **повтарям/повторя;** *repeat; recur*

	Present	Past Simple	Past Continuous
аз	повтарям	повторих	повтарях
ти	повтаряш	повтори	повтаряше
той	повтаря	повтори	повтаряше
ние	повтаряме	повторихме	повтаряхме
вие	повтаряте	повторихте	повтаряхте
те	повтарят	повториха	повтаряха

	Future	Future in the Past
	(For negative, replace **ще** with **няма да**)	(For negative, replace **щях/щеше/щяхме/щяхте/щяха** with **нямаше**)
аз	ще повтарям/повторя	щях да повтарям/повторя
ти	ще повтаряш/повториш	щеше да повтаряш/повториш
той	ще повтаря/повтори	щеше да павтаря/павтори
ние	ще повтаряме/повторим	щяхме да повтаряме/повторим
вие	ще повтаряте/повторите	щяхте да повтаряте/повторите
те	ще повтарят/повторят	щяха да повтарят/повторят

Past Active Participles

M	F	N	Pl
повтарял/повторил	повтаряла/повторила	повтаряло/повторило	повтаряли/повторили

	Present Perfect	Past Perfect
аз	съм повтарял/повторил	бях повтарял/повторил
ти	си повтарял/повторил	беше повтарял/повторил
той	е повтарял/повторил	беше повтарял/повторил
ние	сме повтаряли/повторили	бяхме повтаряли/повторили
вие	сте повтаряли/повторили	бяхте повтаряли/повторили
те	са повтаряли/повторили	бяха повтаряли/повторили

	Conditional Mood	Imperative Mood	
аз	бих повтарял/повторил	**Positive**	**Negative**
ти	би повтарял/повторил	повтаряй/повтори	не повтаряй
той	би повтарял/повторил		
ние	бихме повтаряли/повторили		
вие	бихте повтаряли/повторили	повтаряйте/повторете	не повтаряйте
те	биха повтаряли/повторили		

Past Passive Participles

M	F	N	Pl
повтарян/повторен	повтаряна/повторена	повтаряно/повторено	повтаряни/повторени

161) **подписвам/подпиша;** *sign*

	Present	Past Simple	Past Continuous
аз	подписвам	подписах	подписвах
ти	подписваш	подписа	подписваше
той	подписва	подписа	подписваше
ние	подписваме	подписахме	подписвахме
вие	подписвате	подписахте	подписвахте
те	подписват	подписаха	подписваха

	Future	Future in the Past
	(For negative, replace **ще** with **няма да**)	(For negative, replace **щях/щеше/щяхме/щяхте/щяха** with **нямаше**)
аз	ще подписвам/подпиша	щях да подписвам/подпиша
ти	ще подписваш/подпишеш	щеше да подписваш/подпишеш
той	ще подписва/подпише	щеше да подписва/подпише
ние	ще подписваме/подпишем	щяхме да подписваме/подпишем
вие	ще подписвате/подпишете	щяхте да подписвате/подпишете
те	ще подписват/подпишат	щяха да подписват/подпишат

Past Active Participles

M	F	N	Pl
подписвал/ подписал	подписвала/подписала	подписвало/подписало	подписвали/подписали

	Present Perfect	Past Perfect
аз	съм подписвал/подписал	бях подписвал/подписал
ти	си подписвал/подписал	беше подписвал/подписал
той	е подписвал/подписал	беше подписвал/подписал
ние	сме подписвали/подписали	бяхме подписвали/подписали
вие	сте подписвали/подписали	бяхте подписвали/подписали
те	са подписвали/подписали	бяха подписвали/подписали

	Conditional Mood	Imperative Mood	
аз	бих подписвал/подписал	**Positive**	**Negative**
ти	би подписвал/подписал	подписвай/подпиши	не подписвай
той	би подписвал/подписал		
ние	бихме подписвали/подписали		
вие	бихте подписвали/подписали	подписвайте/подпишете	не подписвайте
те	биха подписвали/подписали		

Past Passive Participles

M	F	N	Pl
подписван/ подписан	подписвана/подписана	подписвано/подписано	подписвани/подписани

162) **подстригвам/подстрижа;** *cut someone's hair*
подстригвам/подстрижа се; *have a haircut*

	Present	**Past Simple**	**Past Continuous**
аз	подстригвам	Подстригах	подстригвах
ти	подстригваш	подстрига	подстригваше
той	подстригва	подстрига	подстригваше
ние	подстригваме	подстригахме	подстригвахме
вие	подстригвате	подстригахте	подстригвахте
те	подстригват	подстригаха	подстригваха

	Future	**Future in the Past**
	(For negative, replace **ще** with **няма да**)	(For negative, replace **щях/щеше/щяхме/щяхте/щяха** with **нямаше**)
аз	ще подстригвам/подстрижа	щях да подстригвам/подстрижа
ти	ще подстригваш/подстрижеш	щеше да подстригваш/подстрижеш
той	ще подстригва/подстриже	щеше да подстригва/подстриже
ние	ще подстригваме/подстрижем	щяхме да подстригваме/подстрижем
вие	ще подстригвате/подстрижете	щяхте да подстригвате/подстрижете
те	ще подстригват/подстрижат	щяха да подстригват/подстрижат

Past Active Participles

M	**F**	**N**	**Pl**
подстригвал/ подстригал	подстригвала/ подстригала	подстригвало/ подстригало	подстригвали/ подстригали

	Present Perfect	**Past Perfect**
аз	съм подстригвал/подстригал	бях подстригвал/подстригал
ти	си подстригвал/подстригал	беше подстригвал/подстригал
той	е подстригвал/подстригал	беше подстригвал/подстригал
ние	сме подстригвали/подстригали	бяхме подстригвали/подстригали
вие	сте подстригвали/подстригали	бяхте подстригвали/подстригали
те	са подстригвали/подстригали	бяха подстригвали/подстригали

	Conditional Mood	**Imperative Mood**	
аз	бих подстригвал/подстригал	**Positive**	**Negative**
ти	би подстригвал/подстригал	подстригвай/подстрижи	не подстригвай
той	би подстригвал/подстригал		
ние	бихме подстригвали/подстригали		
вие	бихте подстригвали/подстригали	подстригвайте/подстрижете	не подстригвайте
те	биха подстригвали/подстригали		

Past Passive Participles

M	**F**	**N**	**Pl**
подстригван/ подстриган	подстригвана/ подстригана	подстригвано/ подстригано	подстригвани/ подстригани

163) **позволявам/позволя;** *allow, let* **позволявам/позволя си;** *dare*

	Present	Past Simple	Past Continuous
аз	позволявам	позволих	позволявах
ти	позволяваш	позволи	позволяваше
той	позволява	позволи	позволяваше
ние	позволяваме	позволихме	позволявахме
вие	позволявате	позволихте	позволявахте
те	позволяват	позволиха	позволяваха

	Future	Future in the Past
	(For negative, replace **ще** with **няма да**)	(For negative, replace **щях/щеше/щяхме/щяхте/щяха** with **нямаше**)
аз	ще позволявам/позволя	щях да позволявам/позволя
ти	ще позволяваш/позволиш	щеше да позволяваш/позволиш
той	ще позволява/позволи	щеше да позволява/позволи
ние	ще позволяваме/позволим	щяхме да позволяваме/позволим
вие	ще позволявате/позволите	щяхте да позволявате/позволите
те	ще позволяват/позволят	щяха да позволяват/позволят

Past Active Participles

M	F	N	Pl
позволявал/ позволил	позволявала/ позволила	позволявало/ позволило	позволявали/ позволили

	Present Perfect	Past Perfect
аз	съм позволявал/позволил	бях позволявал/позволил
ти	си позволявал/позволил	беше позволявал/позволил
той	е позволявал/позволил	беше позволявал/позволил
ние	сме позволявали/позволили	бяхме позволявали/позволили
вие	сте позволявали/позволили	бяхте позволявали/позволили
те	са позволявали/позволили	бяха позволявали/позволили

	Conditional Mood	Imperative Mood	
аз	бих позволявал/позволил	**Positive**	**Negative**
ти	би позволявал/позволил	позволявай/позволи	не позволявай
той	би позволявал/позволил		
ние	бихме позволявали/позволили		
вие	бихте позволявали/позволили	позволявайте/позволете	не позволявайте
те	биха позволявали/позволили		

Past Passive Participles

M	F	N	Pl
позволяван/ позволен	позволявана/ позволена	позволявано/позволено	позволявани/ позволени

164) **познавам/позная;** *know, be acquainted with*

	Present	**Past Simple**	**Past Continuous**
аз	познавам	познах	познавах
ти	познаваш	позна	познаваше
той	познава	позна	познаваше
ние	познаваме	познахме	познавахме
вие	познавате	познахте	познавахте
те	познават	познаха	познаваха

	Future	**Future in the Past**
	(For negative, replace **ще** with **няма да**)	(For negative, replace **щях/щеше/щяхме/щяхте/щяха** with **нямаше**)
аз	ще познавам/позная	щях да познавам/позная
ти	ще познаваш/познаеш	щеше да познаваш/познаеш
той	ще познава/познае	щеше да познава/познае
ние	ще познаваме/познаем	щяхме да познаваме/познаем
вие	ще познавате/познаете	щяхте да познавате/познаете
те	ще познават/познаят	щяха да познават/познаят

Past Active Participles

M	**F**	**N**	**Pl**
познавал/познал	познавала/познала	познавало/познало	познавали/познали

	Present Perfect	**Past Perfect**
аз	съм познавал/познал	бях познавал/познал
ти	си познавал/познал	беше познавал/познал
той	е познавал/познал	беше познавал/познал
ние	сме познавали/познали	бяхме познавали/познали
вие	сте познавали/познали	бяхте познавали/познали
те	са познавали/познали	бяха познавали/познали

	Conditional Mood	**Imperative Mood**	
аз	бих познавал/познал	**Positive**	**Negative**
ти	би познавал/познал	познавай/познай	не познавай
той	би познавал/познал		
ние	бихме познавали/познали		
вие	бихте познавали/познали	познавайте/познайте	не познавайте
те	биха познавали/познали		

Past Passive Participles

M	**F**	**N**	**Pl**
познат	позната	познато	познати

165) **получавам/получа;** *receive, obtain; accept*

	Present	**Past Simple**	**Past Continuous**
аз	получавам	получих	получавах
ти	получаваш	получи	получаваше
той	получава	получи	получаваше
ние	получаваме	получихме	получавахме
вие	получавате	получихте	получавахте
те	получават	получиха	получаваха

	Future	**Future in the Past**
	(For negative, replace **ще** with **няма да**)	(For negative, replace **щях/щеше/щяхме/щяхте/щяха** with **нямаше**)
аз	ще получавам/получа	щях да получавам/получа
ти	ще получаваш/получиш	щеше да получаваш/получиш
той	ще получава/получи	щеше да получава/получи
ние	ще получаваме/получим	щяхме да получаваме/получим
вие	ще получавате/получите	щяхте да получавате/получите
те	ще получават/получат	щяха да получават/получат

Past Active Participles

M	**F**	**N**	**Pl**
получавал/получил	получавала/получила	получавало/получило	получавали/получили

	Present Perfect	**Past Perfect**
аз	съм получавал/получил	бях получавал/получил
ти	си получавал/получил	беше получавал/получил
той	е получавал/получил	беше получавал/получил
ние	сме получавали/получили	бяхме получавали/получили
вие	сте получавали/получили	бяхте получавали/получили
те	са получавали/получили	бяха получавали/получили

	Conditional Mood	**Imperative Mood**	
аз	бих получавал/получил	**Positive**	**Negative**
ти	би получавал/получил	получавай/получи	не получавай
той	би получавал/получил		
ние	бихме получавали/получили		
вие	бихте получавали/получили	получавайте/получете	не получавайте
те	биха получавали/получили		

Past Passive Participles

M	**F**	**N**	**Pl**
получаван/получен	получавана/получена	получавано/получено	получавани/получен

166) **помагам/помогна;** *help, assist, aid*

	Present	**Past Simple**	**Past Continuous**
аз	помагам	помогнах	помагах
ти	помагаш	помогна	помагаше
той	помага	помогна	помагаше
ние	помагаме	помогнахме	помагахме
вие	помагате	помогнахте	помагахте
те	помагат	помогнаха	помагаха

	Future	**Future in the Past**
	(For negative, replace **ще** with **няма да**)	(For negative, replace **щях/щеше/щяхме/щяхте/щяха** with **нямаше**)
аз	ще помагам/помогна	щях да помагам/помогна
ти	ще помагаш/помогнеш	щеше да помагаш/помогнеш
той	ще помага/помогне	щеше да помага/помогне
ние	ще помагаме/помогнем	щяхме да помагаме/помогнем
вие	ще помагате/помогнете	щяхте да помагате/помогнете
те	ще помагат/помогнат	щяха да помагат/помогнат

Past Active Participles

M	**F**	**N**	**Pl**
помагал/помогнал	помагала/помогнала	помагало/помогнало	помагали/помогнали

	Present Perfect	**Past Perfect**
аз	съм помагал/помогнал	бях помагал/помогнал
ти	си помагал/помогнал	беше помагал/помогнал
той	е помагал/помогнал	беше помагал/помогнал
ние	сме помагали/помогнали	бяхме помагали/помогнали
вие	сте помагали/помогнали	бяхте помагали/помогнали
те	са помагали/помогнали	бяха помагали/помогнали

	Conditional Mood	**Imperative Mood**	
аз	бих помагал/помогнал	**Positive**	**Negative**
ти	би помагал/помогнал	помагай/помогни	не помагай
той	би помагал/помогнал		
ние	бихме помагали/помогнали		
вие	бихте помагали/помогнали	помагайте/помогнете	не помагайте
те	бих помагал/помогнал		

Past Passive Participles

M	**F**	**N**	**Pl**
N/A	N/A	N/A	N/A

167) **помня/запомня;** *remember, memorize*

	Present	**Past Simple**	**Past Continuous**
аз	помня	запомних	помнех
ти	помниш	запомни	помнеше
той	помни	запомни	помнеше
ние	помним	запомнихме	помнехме
вие	помните	запомнихте	помнехте
те	помнят	запомниха	помнеха

	Future	**Future in the Past**
	(For negative, replace **ще** with **няма да**)	(For negative, replace **щях/щеше/щяхме/щяхте/щяха** with **нямаше**)
аз	ще помня/запомня	щях да помня/запомня
ти	ще помниш/запомниш	щеше да помниш/запомниш
той	ще помни/запомни	щеше да помни/запомни
ние	ще помним/запомним	щяхме да помним/запомним
вие	ще помните/запомните	щяхте да помните/запомните
те	ще помнят/запомнят	щяха да помнят/запомнят

Past Active Participles

M	**F**	**N**	**Pl**
помнил/запомнил	помнила/запомнила	помнило/запомнило	помнили/запомнили

	Present Perfect	**Past Perfect**
аз	съм помнил/запомнил	бях помнил/запомнил
ти	си помнил/запомнил	беше помнил/запомнил
той	е помнил/запомнил	беше помнил/запомнил
ние	сме помнили/запомнили	бяхме помнили/запомнили
вие	сте помнили/запомнили	бяхте помнили/запомнили
те	са помнили/запомнили	бяха помнили/запомнили

	Conditional Mood	**Imperative Mood**	
аз	бих помнил/запомнил	**Positive**	**Negative**
ти	би помнил/запомнил	помни/запомни	не помни
той	би помнил/запомнил		
ние	бихме помнили/запомнили		
вие	бихте помнили/запомнили	помнете/запомнете	не помнете
те	биха помнили/запомнили		

Past Passive Participles

M	**F**	**N**	**Pl**
помнен/запомнен	помнена/запомнена	помнено/запомнено	помнени/запомнени

168) **поръчвам/поръчам;** *order, place an order; ask; tell*

	Present	Past Simple	Past Continuous
аз	поръчвам	поръчах	поръчвах
ти	поръчваш	поръча	поръчваше
той	поръчва	поръча	поръчваше
ние	поръчваме	поръчахме	поръчвахме
вие	поръчвате	поръчахте	поръчвахте
те	поръчват	поръчаха	поръчваха

	Future	Future in the Past
	(For negative, replace **ще** with **няма да**)	(For negative, replace **щях/щеше/щяхме/щяхте/щяха** with **нямаше**)
аз	ще поръчвам/поръчам	щях да поръчвам/поръчам
ти	ще поръчваш/поръчаш	щеше да поръчваш/поръчаш
той	ще поръчва/поръча	щеше да поръчва/поръча
ние	ще поръчваме/поръчаме	щяхме да поръчваме/поръчаме
вие	ще паръчвате/поръчате	щяхте да поръчвате/поръчате
те	ще поръчват/поръчат	щяха да поръчват/поръчат

Past Active Participles

M	F	N	Pl
поръчвал/поръчал	поръчвала/поръчала	поръчвало/поръчало	поръчвали/поръчали

	Present Perfect	Past Perfect
аз	съм поръчвал/поръчал	бях поръчвал/поръчал
ти	си поръчвал/поръчал	беше поръчвал/поръчал
той	е поръчвал/поръчал	беше поръчвал/поръчал
ние	сме поръчвали/поръчали	бяхме поръчвали/поръчали
вие	сте поръчвали/поръчали	бяхте поръчвали/поръчали
те	са поръчвали/поръчали	бяха поръчвали/поръчали

	Conditional Mood	Imperative Mood	
аз	бих поръчвал/поръчал	**Positive**	**Negative**
ти	би поръчвал/поръчал	поръчвай/поръчай	не поръчвай
той	би поръчвал/поръчал		
ние	бихме поръчвали/поръчали		
вие	бихте поръчвали/поръчали	поръчвайте/поръчайте	не поръчвайте
те	биха поръчвали/поръчали		

Past Passive Participles

M	F	N	Pl
поръчван/поръчан	поръчвана/поръчана	поръчвано/поръчано	поръчвани/поръчани

169) **посещавам/посетя;** *visit, pay a visit; attend*

	Present	Past Simple	Past Continuous
аз	посещавам	посетих	посещавах
ти	посещаваш	посети	посещаваше
той	посещава	посети	посещаваше
ние	посещаваме	посетихме	посещавахме
вие	посещавате	посетихте	посещавахте
те	посещават	посетиха	посещаваха

	Future	Future in the Past
	(For negative, replace **ще** with **няма да**)	(For negative, replace **щях/щеше/щяхме/щяхте/щяха** with **нямаше**)
аз	ще посещавам/посетя	щях да посещавам/посетя
ти	ще посещаваш/посетиш	щеше да посещаваш/посетиш
той	ще посещава/посети	щеше да посещава/посети
ние	ще посещаваме/посетим	щяхме да посещаваме/посетим
вие	ще посещавате/посетите	щяхте да посещавате/посетите
те	ще посещават/посетят	щяха да посещават/посетят

Past Active Participles

M	F	N	Pl
посещавал/посетил	посещавала/посетила	посещавало/посетило	посещавали/посетили

	Present Perfect	Past Perfect
аз	съм посещавал/посетил	бях посещавал/посетил
ти	си посещавал/посетил	беше посещавал/посетил
той	е посещавал/посетил	беше посещавал/посетил
ние	сме посещавали/посетили	бяхме посещавали/посетили
вие	сте посещавали/посетили	бяхте посещавали/посетили
те	са посещавали/посетили	бяха посещавали/посетили

	Conditional Mood	Imperative Mood	
аз	бих посещавал/посетил	**Positive**	**Negative**
ти	би посещавал/посетил	посещавай/посети	не посещавай
той	би посещавал/посетил		
ние	бихме посещавали/посетили		
вие	бихте посещавали/посетили	посещавайте/посетете	не посещавайте
те	биха посещавали/посетили		

Past Passive Participles

M	F	N	Pl
посещаван/посетен	посещавана/посетена	посещавано/посетено	посещавани/посетени

170) потвърждавам/потвърдя; *confirm, verify*

	Present	**Past Simple**	**Past Continuous**
аз	потвърждавам	потвърдих	потвърждавах
ти	потвърждаваш	потвърди	потвърждаваше
той	потвърждава	потвърди	потвърждаваше
ние	потвърждаваме	потвърдихме	потвърждавахме
вие	потвърждавате	потвърдихте	потвърждавахте
те	потвърждават	потвърдиха	потвърждаваха

	Future	**Future in the Past**
	(For negative, replace **ще** with **няма да**)	(For negative, replace **щях/щеше/щяхме/щяхте/щяха** with **нямаше**)
аз	ще потвърждавам/потвърдя	щях да потвърждавам/потвърдя
ти	ще потвърждаваш/потвърдиш	щеше да потвърждаваш/потвърдиш
той	ще потвърждава/потвърди	щеше да потвърждава/потвърди
ние	ще потвърждаваме/потвърдим	щяхме да потвърждаваме/потвърдим
вие	ще потвърждавате/потвърдите	щяхте да потвърждавате/потвърдите
те	ще потвърждават/потвърдят	щяха да потвърждават/потвърдят

Past Active Participles

M	**F**	**N**	**Pl**
потвърждавал/ потвърдил	потвърждавала/потвърдила	потвърждавало/потвърдило	потвърждавали/ потвърдили

	Present Perfect	**Past Perfect**
аз	съм потвърждавал/потвърдил	бях потвърждавал/потвърдил
ти	си потвърждавал/потвърдил	беше потвърждавал/потвърдил
той	е потвърждавал/потвърдил	беше потвърждавал/потвърдил
ние	сме потвърждавали/потвърдили	бяхме потвърждавали/потвърдили
вие	сте потвърждавали/потвърдили	бяхте потвърждавали/потвърдили
те	са потвърждавали/потвърдили	бяха потвърждавали/потвърдили

	Conditional Mood	**Imperative Mood**	
аз	бих потвърждавал/потвърдил	**Positive**	**Negative**
ти	би потвърждавал/потвърдил	потвърждавай/потвърди	не потвърждавай
той	би потвърждавал/потвърдил		
ние	бихме потвърждавали/потвърдили		
вие	бихте потвърждавали/ потвърдили	потвърждавайте/ потвърдете	не потвърждавайте
те	биха потвърждавали/ потвърдили		

Past Passive Participles

M	**F**	**N**	**Pl**
потвърждаван/ потвърден	потвърждавана/ потвърдена	потвърждавано/ потвърдено	потвърждавани/потвърдени

171) **почивам/почина;** *rest, relax* **почина;** *(only perf) pass away*

	Present	Past Simple	Past Continuous
аз	почивам	почината	почивах
ти	почиваш	почина	почиваше
той	почива	почина	почиваше
ние	почиваме	починахме	почивахме
вие	почивате	починахте	почивахте
те	почиват	починаха	почиваха

	Future	Future in the Past
	(For negative, replace **ще** with **няма да**)	(For negative, replace **щях/щеше/щяхме/щяхте/щяха** with **нямаше**)
аз	ще почивам/почина	щях да почивам/почина
ти	ще почиваш/починеш	щеше да почиваш/починеш
той	ще почива/почине	щеше да почива/почине
ние	ще почиваме/починем	щяхме да почиваме/починем
вие	ще почивате/починете	щяхте да почивате/починете
те	ще почиват/починат	щяха да почиват/починат

Past Active Participles

M	F	N	Pl
почивал/починал	почивала/починала	почивало/починало	почивали/починали

	Present Perfect	Past Perfect
аз	съм почивал/починал	бях почивал/починал
ти	си почивал/починал	беше почивал/починал
той	е почивал/починал	беше почивал/починал
ние	сме почивали/починали	бяхме почивали/починали
вие	сте почивали/починали	бяхте почивали/починали
те	са почивали/починали	бяха почивали/починали

	Conditional Mood	Imperative Mood	
аз	бих почивал/починал	**Positive**	**Negative**
ти	би почивал/починал	почивай/почини	не почивай
той	би почивал/починал		
ние	бихме почивали/починали		
вие	бихте почивали/починали	почивайте/починете	не почивайте
те	биха почивали/починали		

Past Passive Participles

M	F	N	Pl
N/A	N/A	N/A	N/A

172) **правя/направя;** *make, do*

	Present	**Past Simple**	**Past Continuous**
аз	правя	направих	правех
ти	правиш	направи	правеше
той	прави	направи	правеше
ние	правим	направихме	правехме
вие	правите	направихте	правехте
те	правят	направиха	правеха

	Future	**Future in the Past**
	(For negative, replace **ще** with **няма да**)	(For negative, replace **щях/щеше/щяхме/щяхте/щяха** with **нямаше**)
аз	ще правя/направя	щях да правя/направя
ти	ще правиш/направиш	щеше да правиш/направиш
той	ще прави/направи	щеше да прави/направи
ние	ще правим/направим	щяхме да правим/направим
вие	ще правите/направите	щяхте да правите/направите
те	ще правят/направят	щяха да правят/направят

Past Active Participles

M	**F**	**N**	**Pl**
правил/направил	правила/направила	правило/направило	правили/направили

	Present Perfect	**Past Perfect**
аз	съм правил/направил	бях правил/направил
ти	си правил/направил	беше правил/направил
той	е правил/направил	беше правил/направил
ние	сме правили/направили	бяхме правили/направили
вие	сте правили/направили	бяхте правили/направили
те	са правили/направили	бяха правили/направили

	Conditional Mood	**Imperative Mood**	
		Positive	**Negative**
аз	бих правил/направил		
ти	би правил/направил	прави/направи	не прави
той	би правил/направил		
ние	бихме правили/направили		
вие	бихте правили/направили	правете/направете	не правете
те	биха правили/направили		

Past Passive Participles

M	**F**	**N**	**Pl**
правен/направен	правена/направена	правено/направено	правени/направени

173) **превеждам/преведа;** *translate, interpret*

	Present	**Past Simple**	**Past Continuous**
аз	превеждам	преведох	превеждах
ти	превеждаш	преведе	превеждаше
той	превежда	преведе	превеждаше
ние	превеждаме	преведохме	превеждахме
вие	превеждате	преведохте	превеждахте
те	превеждат	преведоха	превеждаха

	Future	**Future in the Past**
	(For negative, replace **ще** with **няма да**)	(For negative, replace **щях/щеше/щяхме/щяхте/щяха** with **нямаше**)
аз	ще превеждам/преведа	щях да превеждам/преведа
ти	ще превеждаш/преведеш	щеше да превеждаш/преведеш
той	ще превежда/преведе	щеше да превежда/преведе
ние	ще превеждаме/преведем	щяхме да превеждаме/преведем
вие	ще превеждате/преведете	щяхте да превеждате/преведете
те	ще превеждат/преведат	щяха да превеждат/преведат

Past Active Participles

M	**F**	**N**	**Pl**
превеждал/превел	превеждала/превела	превеждало/превело	превеждали/превели

	Present Perfect	**Past Perfect**
аз	съм превеждал/превел	бях превеждал/превел
ти	си превеждал/превел	беше превеждал/превел
той	е превеждал/превел	беше превеждал/превел
ние	сме превеждали/превели	бяхме превеждали/превели
вие	сте превеждали/превели	бяхте превеждали/превели
те	са превеждали/превели	бяха превеждали/превели

	Conditional Mood	**Imperative Mood**	
		Positive	**Negative**
аз	бих превеждал/превел		
ти	би превеждал/превел	превеждай/преведи	не превеждай
той	би превеждал/превел		
ние	бихме превеждали/превели		
вие	бихте превеждали/превели	превеждайте/преведете	не преве
те	биха превеждали/превели		

Past Passive Participles

M	**F**	**N**	**Pl**
превеждан/преведен	превеждана/преведена	превеждано/преведено	превеждани/преведени

174) **преглеждам/прегледам;** *look through; examine, check, inspect*

	Present	**Past Simple**	**Past Continuous**
аз	преглеждам	прегледах	преглеждах
ти	преглеждаш	прегледа	преглеждаше
той	преглежда	прегледа	преглеждаше
ние	преглеждаме	прегледахме	преглеждахме
вие	преглеждате	прегледахте	преглеждахте
те	преглеждат	прегледаха	преглеждаха

	Future	**Future in the Past**
	(For negative, replace **ще** with **няма да**)	(For negative, replace **щях/щеше/щяхме/щяхте/щяха** with **нямаше**)
аз	ще преглеждам/прегледам	щях да преглеждам/прегледам
ти	ще преглеждаш/прегледаш	щеше да преглеждаш/прегледаш
той	ще преглежда/прегледа	щеше да преглежда/прегледа
ние	ще преглеждаме/прегледаме	щяхме да преглеждаме/прегледаме
вие	ще преглеждате/прегледате	щяхте да преглеждате/прегледате
те	ще преглеждат/прегледат	щяха да преглеждат/прегледат

Past Active Participles

M	**F**	**N**	**Pl**
преглеждал/ прегледал	преглеждала/ прегледала	преглеждало/ прегледало	преглеждали/ прегледали

	Present Perfect	**Past Perfect**
аз	съм преглеждал/прегледал	бях преглеждал/прегледал
ти	си преглеждал/прегледал	беше преглеждал/прегледал
той	е преглеждал/прегледал	беше преглеждал/прегледал
ние	сме преглеждали/прегледали	бяхме преглеждали/прегледали
вие	сте преглеждали/прегледали	бяхте преглеждали/прегледали
те	са преглеждали/прегледали	бяха преглеждали/прегледали

	Conditional Mood	**Imperative Mood**	
аз	бих преглеждал/прегледал	**Positive**	**Negative**
ти	би преглеждал/прегледал	преглеждай/прегледай	не преглеждай
той	би преглеждал/прегледал		
ние	бихме преглеждали/прегледали		
вие	бихте преглеждали/прегледали	преглеждайте/прегледайте	не преглеждайте
те	биха преглеждали/прегледали		

Past Passive Participles

M	**F**	**N**	**Pl**
преглеждан/ прегледан	преглеждана/прегледана	преглеждано/ прегледано	преглеждани/прегледани

175) **предлагам/предложа;** *offer, propose, suggest*

	Present	**Past Simple**	**Past Continuous**
аз	предлагам	предложих	предлагах
ти	предлагаш	предложи	предлагаше
той	предлага	предложи	предлагаше
ние	предлагаме	предложихме	предлагахме
вие	предлагате	предложихте	предлагахте
те	предлагат	предложиха	предлагаха

	Future	**Future in the Past**
	(For negative, replace **ще** with **няма да**)	(For negative, replace **щях/щеше/щяхме/щяхте/щяха** with **нямаше**)
аз	ще предлагам/предложа	щях да предлагам/предложа
ти	ще предлагаш/предложиш	щеше да предлагаш/предложиш
той	ще предлага/предложи	щеше да предлага/предложи
ние	ще предлагаме/предложим	щяхме да предлагаме/предложим
вие	ще предлагате/предложите	щяхте да предлагате/предложите
те	ще предлагат/предложат	щяха да предлагат/предложат

Past Active Participles

M	**F**	**N**	**Pl**
предлагал/предложил	предлагала/предложила	предлагало/предложило	предлагали/предложили

	Present Perfect	**Past Perfect**
аз	съм предлагал/предложил	бях предлагал/предложил
ти	си предлагал/предложил	беше предлагал/предложил
той	е предлагал/предложил	беше предлагал/предложил
ние	сме предлагали/предложили	бяхме предлагали/предложили
вие	сте предлагали/предложили	бяхте предлагали/предложили
те	са предлагали/предложили	бяха предлагали/предложили

	Conditional Mood	**Imperative Mood**	
аз	бих предлагал/предложил	**Positive**	**Negative**
ти	би предлагал/предложил	предлагай/предложи	не предлагай
той	би предлагал/предложил		
ние	бихме предлагали/предложили		
вие	бихте предлагали/предложили	предлагайте/предложете	не предлагайте
те	биха предлагали/предложили		

Past Passive Participles

M	**F**	**N**	**Pl**
предлаган/предложен	предлагана/предложена	предлагано/предложено	предлагани/предложени

176) **предпочитам/предпочета;** *prefer*

	Present	**Past Simple**	**Past Continuous**
аз	предпочитам	предпочетох	предпочитах
ти	предпочиташ	предпочете	предпочиташе
той	предпочита	предпочете	предпочиташе
ние	предпочитаме	предпочетохме	предпочитахме
вие	предпочитате	предпочетохте	предпочитахте
те	предпочитат	предпочетоха	предпочитаха

	Future	**Future in the Past**
	(For negative, replace **ще** with **няма да**)	(For negative, replace **щях/щеше/щяхме/щяхте/щяха** with **нямаше**)
аз	ще предпочитам/предпочета	щях да предпочитам/предпочета
ти	ще предпочиташ/предпочетеш	щеше да предпочиташ/предпочетеш
той	ще предпочита/предпочете	щеше да предпочита/предпочете
ние	ще предпочитаме/предпочетем	щяхме да предпочитаме/предпочетем
вие	ще предпочитате/предпочетете	щяхте да предпочитате/предпочетете
те	ще предпочитат/предпочетат	щяха да предпочитат/предпочетат

Past Active Participles

M	**F**	**N**	**Pl**
предпочитал/ предпочел	предпочитала/предпочела	предпочитало/предпочело	предпочитали/ предпочели

	Present Perfect	**Past Perfect**
аз	съм предпочитал/предпочел	бях предпочитал/предпочел
ти	си предпочитал/предпочел	беше предпочитал/предпочел
той	е предпочитал/предпочел	беше предпочитал/предпочел
ние	сме предпочитали/предпочели	бяхме предпочитали/предпочели
вие	сте предпочитали/предпочели	бяхте предпочитали/предпочели
те	са предпочитали/предпочели	бяха предпочитали/предпочели

	Conditional Mood	**Imperative Mood**	
аз	бих предпочитал/предпочел	**Positive**	**Negative**
ти	би предпочитал/предпочел	предпочитай/предпочети	не предпочитай
той	би предпочитал/предпочел		
ние	бихме предпочитали/предпочели		
вие	бихте предпочитали/предпочели	предпочитайте/предпочетете	не предпочитайте
те	биха предпочитали/предпочели		

Past Passive Participles

M	**F**	**N**	**Pl**
предпочитан/ предпочетен	предпочитана/ предпочетена	предпочитано/предпочетено	предпочитани/ предпочетени

177) **представям/представя;** *present; introduce; produce* **представям/представя си;** *imagine*

	Present	Past Simple	Past Continuous
аз	представям	представих	представях
ти	представяш	представи	представяше
той	представя	представи	представяше
ние	представяме	представихме	представяхме
вие	представяте	представихте	представяхте
те	представят	представиха	представяха

	Future	Future in the Past
	(For negative, replace **ще** with **няма да**)	(For negative, replace **щях/щеше/щяхме/щяхте/щяха** with **нямаше**)
аз	ще представям/представя	щях да представям/представя
ти	ще представяш/представиш	щеше да представяш/представиш
той	ще представя/представи	щеше да представя/представи
ние	ще представяме/представим	щяхме да представяме/представим
вие	ще представяте/представите	щяхте да представяте/представите
те	ще представят/представят	щяха да представят/представят

Past Active Participles

M	F	N	Pl
представял/ представил	представяла/представила	представяло/представило	представяли/представили

	Present Perfect	Past Perfect
аз	съм представял/представил	бях представял/представил
ти	си представял/представил	беше представял/представил
той	е представял/представил	беше представял/представил
ние	сме представяли/представили	бяхме представяли/представили
вие	сте представяли/представили	бяхте представяли/представили
те	са представяли/представили	бяха представяли/представили

	Conditional Mood	Imperative Mood	
		Positive	**Negative**
аз	бих представял/представил		
ти	би представял/представил	представяй/представи	не представяй
той	би представял/представил		
ние	бихме представяли/представили		
вие	бихте представяли/представили	представяйте/представете	не представяйте
те	биха представяли/представили		

Past Passive Participles

M	F	N	Pl
представян/ представен	представяна/представена	представяно/ представено	представяни/ представени

178) **прекарвам/прекарам;** *carry, transport; pass, drive; spend time*

	Present	Past Simple	Past Continuous
аз	прекарвам	прекарах	прекарвах
ти	прекарваш	прекара	прекарваше
той	прекарва	прекара	прекарваше
ние	прекарваме	прекарахме	прекарвахме
вие	прекарвате	прекарахте	прекарвахте
те	прекарват	прекараха	прекарваха

	Future	Future in the Past
	(For negative, replace **ще** with **няма да**)	(For negative, replace **щях/щеше/щяхме/щяхте/щяха** with **нямаше**)
аз	ще прекарвам/прекарам	щях да прекарвам/прекарам
ти	ще прекарваш/прекараш	щеше да прекарваш/прекараш
той	ще прекарва/прекара	щеше да прекарва/прекара
ние	ще прекарваме/прекараме	щяхме да прекарваме/прекараме
вие	ще прекарвате/прекарате	щяхте да прекарвате/прекарате
те	ще прекарват/прекарат	щяха да прекарват/прекарат

Past Active Participles

M	F	N	Pl
прекарвал/прекарал	прекарвала/прекарала	прекарвало/прекарало	прекарвали/прекарали

	Present Perfect	Past Perfect
аз	съм прекарвал/прекарал	бях прекарвал/прекарал
ти	си прекарвал/прекарал	беше прекарвал/прекарал
той	е прекарвал/прекарал	беше прекарвал/прекарал
ние	сме прекарвали/прекарали	бяхме прекарвали/прекарали
вие	сте прекарвали/прекарали	бяхте прекарвали/прекарали
те	са прекарвали/прекарали	бяха прекарвали/прекарали

	Conditional Mood	Imperative Mood	
аз	бих прекарвал/прекарал	**Positive**	**Negative**
ти	би прекарвал/прекарал	прекарвай/прекарай	не прекарвай
той	би прекарвал/прекарал		
ние	бихме прекарвали/прекарали		
вие	бихте прекарвали/прекарали	прекарвайте/прекарайте	не прекарвайте
те	биха прекарвали/прекарали		

Past Passive Participles

M	F	N	Pl
прекарван/прекаран	прекарвана/прекарана	прекарвано/прекарано	прекарвани/прекарани

179) **премествам/преместя;** *move, shift*

	Present	**Past Simple**	**Past Continuous**
аз	премествам	преместих	премествах
ти	преместваш	премести	местваше
той	премества	премести	премества ше
ние	преместваме	преместихме	премествахме
вие	премествате	преместихте	премествахте
те	преместват	преместиха	премествахa

	Future	**Future in the Past**
	(For negative, replace **ще** with **няма да**)	(For negative, replace **щях/щеше/щяхме/щяхте/щяха** with **нямаше**)
аз	ще премествам/преместя	щях да премествам/преместя
ти	ще преместваш/преместиш	щеше да преместваш/преместиш
той	ще премества/премести	щеше да премества/премести
ние	ще преместваме/преместим	щяхме да преместваме/преместим
вие	ще премествате/преместите	щяхте да премествате/преместите
те	ще преместват/преместят	щяха да преместват/преместят

Past Active Participles

M	**F**	**N**	**Pl**
премествал/ преместил	преместваla/преместила	преместваlo/преместило	премествали/преместили

	Present Perfect	**Past Perfect**
аз	съм премествал/преместил	бях премествал/преместил
ти	си премествал/преместил	беше премествал/преместил
той	е премествал/преместил	беше премествал/преместил
ние	сме премествали/преместили	бяхме премествали/преместили
вие	сте премествали/преместили	бяхте премествали/преместили
те	са премествали/преместили	бяха премествали/преместили

	Conditional Mood	**Imperative Mood**	
		Positive	**Negative**
аз	бих премествал/преместил		
ти	би премествал/преместил	премествай/премести	не премествай
той	би премествал/преместил		
ние	бихме премествали/преместили		
вие	бихте премествали/преместили	премествайте/преместете	не премествайте
те	биха премествали/преместили		

Past Passive Participles

M	**F**	**N**	**Pl**
преместван/ преместен	премествана/преместена	преместванo/ преместено	премествани/преместени

180) **пресичам/пресека;** *cut, cut off; cross, go across*

	Present	**Past Simple**	**Past Continuous**
аз	пресичам	пресякох	пресичах
ти	пресичаш	пресече	пресичаше
той	пресича	пресече	пресичаше
ние	пресичаме	пресякохме	пресичахме
вие	пресичате	пресякохте	пресичахте
те	пресичат	пресякоха	пресичаха

	Future	**Future in the Past**
	(For negative, replace **ще** with **няма да**)	(For negative, replace **щях/щеше/щяхме/щяхте/щяха** with **нямаше**)
аз	ще пресичам/пресека	щях да пресичам/пресека
ти	ще пресичаш/пресечеш	щеше да пресичаш/пресечеш
той	ще пресича/пресече	щеше да пресича/пресече
ние	ще пресичаме/пресечем	щяхме да пресичаме/пресечем
вие	ще пресичате/пресечете	щяхте да пресичате/пресечете
те	ще пресичат/пресекат	щяха да пресичат/пресекат

Past Active Participles

M	**F**	**N**	**Pl**
пресичал/ пресякъл	пресичала/пресякла	пресичало/пресякло	пресичали/ пресекли

	Present Perfect	**Past Perfect**
аз	съм пресичал/пресякъл	бях пресичал/пресякъл
ти	си пресичал/пресякъл	беше пресичал/пресякъл
той	е пресичал/пресякъл	беше пресичал/пресякъл
ние	сме пресичали/пресекли	бяхме пресичали/пресекли
вие	сте пресичали/пресекли	бяхте пресичали/пресекли
те	са пресичали/пресекли	бяха пресичали/пресекли

	Conditional Mood	**Imperative Mood**	
аз	бих пресичал/пресякъл	**Positive**	**Negative**
ти	би пресичал/пресякъл	пресичай/пресечи	не пресичай
той	би пресичал/пресякъл		
ние	бихме пресичали/пресекли		
вие	бихте пресичали/пресекли	пресичайте/пресечете	не пресичайте
те	биха пресичали/пресекли		

Past Passive Participles

M	**F**	**N**	**Pl**
пресичан/ пресечен	пресичана/ пресечена	пресичано/ пресечено	пресичани/ пресечени

181) **преценявам/преценя;** *appraise, assess, estimate, judge*

	Present	Past Simple	Past Continuous
аз	преценявам	преценних	преценявах
ти	преценяваш	прецени	преценяваше
той	преценява	прецени	преценяваше
ние	преценяваме	преценихме	преценявахме
вие	преценявате	преценихте	преценявахте
те	преценяват	прецениха	преценяваха

	Future	Future in the Past
	(For negative, replace **ще** with **няма да**)	(For negative, replace **щях/щеше/щяхме/щяхте/щяха** with **нямаше**)
аз	ще преценявам/преценя	щях да преценявам/преценя
ти	ще преценяваш/прецениш	щеше да преценяваш/прецениш
той	ще преценява/прецени	щеше да преценява/прецени
ние	ще преценяваме/преценим	щяхме да преценяваме/преценим
вие	ще преценявате/прецените	щяхте да преценявате/прецените
те	ще преценяват/преценят	щяха да преценяват/преценят

Past Active Participles

M	F	N	Pl
преценявал/ преценил	преценявала/ преценила	преценявало/ преценило	преценявали/ преценили

	Present Perfect	Past Perfect
аз	съм преценявал/преценил	бях преценявал/преценил
ти	си преценявал/преценил	беше преценявал/преценил
той	е преценявал/преценил	беше преценявал/преценил
ние	сме преценявали/преценили	бяхме преценявали/преценили
вие	сте преценявали/преценили	бяхте преценявали/преценили
те	са преценявали/преценили	бяха преценявали/преценили

	Conditional Mood	Imperative Mood	
аз	бих преценявал/преценил	**Positive**	**Negative**
ти	би преценявал/преценил	преценявай/прецени	не преценявай
той	би преценявал/преценил		
ние	бихме преценявали/преценили		
вие	бихте преценявали/преценили	преценявайте/преценете	не преценявайте
те	биха преценявали/преценили		

Past Passive Participles

M	F	N	Pl
преценяван/ преценен	преценявана/ преценена	преценявано/ преценено	преценявани/ преценени

182) **приготвям/приготвя;** *prepare; cook* **приготвям/приготвя се;** *get ready*

	Present	Past Simple	Past Continuous
аз	приготвям	приготвих	приготвях
ти	приготвяш	приготви	приготвяше
той	приготвя	приготви	приготвяше
ние	приготвяме	приготвихме	приготвяхме
вие	приготвяте	приготвихте	приготвяхте
те	приготвят	приготвиха	приготвяха

	Future	Future in the Past
	(For negative, replace **ще** with **няма да**)	(For negative, replace **щях/щеше/щяхме/щяхте/щяха** with **нямаше**)
аз	ще приготвям/приготвя	щях да приготвям/приготвя
ти	ще приготвяш/приготвиш	щеше да приготвяш/приготвиш
той	ще приготвя/приготви	щеше да приготвя/приготви
ние	ще приготвяме/приготвим	щяхме да приготвяме/приготвим
вие	ще приготвяте/приготвите	щяхте да приготвяте/приготвите
те	ще приготвят/приготвят	щяха да приготвят/приготвят

Past Active Participles

M	F	N	Pl
приготвял/ приготвил	приготвяла/ приготвила	приготвяло/ приготвило	приготвяли/ приготвили

	Present Perfect	Past Perfect
аз	съм приготвял/приготвил	бях приготвял/приготвил
ти	си приготвял/приготвил	беше приготвял/приготвил
той	е приготвял/приготвил	беше приготвял/приготвил
ние	сме приготвяли/приготвили	бяхме приготвяли/приготвили
вие	сте приготвяли/приготвили	бяхте приготвяли/приготвили
те	са приготвяли/приготвили	бяха приготвяли/приготвили

	Conditional Mood	Imperative Mood	
аз	бих приготвял/приготвил	**Positive**	**Negative**
ти	би приготвял/приготвил	приготвяй/приготви	не приготвяй
той	би приготвял/приготвил		
ние	бихме приготвяли/приготвили		
вие	бихте приготвяли/приготвили	приготвяйте/пригответе	не приготвяйте
те	биха приготвяли/приготвили		

Past Passive Participles

M	F	N	Pl
приготвян/ приготвен	приготвяна/ приготвена	приготвяно/ приготвено	приготвяни/ приготвени

183) **приемам/приема;** *accept, admit, acknowledge*

	Present	Past Simple	Past Continuous
аз	приемам	приех	приемах
ти	приемаш	прие	приемаше
той	приема	прие	приемаше
ние	приемаме	приехме	приемахме
вие	приемате	приехте	приемахте
те	приемат	приеха	приемаха

	Future	**Future in the Past**
	(For negative, replace **ще** with **няма да**)	(For negative, replace **щях/щеше/щяхме/щяхте/щяха** with **нямаше**)
аз	ще приемам/приема	щях да приемам/приема
ти	ще приемаш/приемеш	щеше да приемаш/приемеш
той	ще приема/приеме	щеше да приема/приеме
ние	ще приемаме/приемем	щяхме да приемаме/приемем
вие	ще приемате/приемете	щяхте да приемате/приемете
те	ще приемат/приемат	щяха да приемат/приемат

Past Active Participles

M	F	N	Pl
приемал/приел	приемала/приела	приемало/приело	приемали/приели

	Present Perfect	**Past Perfect**
аз	съм приемал/приел	бях приемал/приел
ти	си приемал/приел	беше приемал/приел
той	е приемал/приел	беше приемал/приел
ние	сме приемали/приели	бяхме приемали/приели
вие	сте приемали/приели	бяхте приемали/приели
те	са приемали/приели	бяха приемали/приели

	Conditional Mood	**Imperative Mood**	
аз	бих приемал/приел	**Positive**	**Negative**
ти	би приемал/приел	приемай/приеми	не приемай
той	би приемал/приел		
ние	бихме приемали/приели		
вие	бихте приемали/приели	приемайте/приемете	не приемайте
те	биха приемали/приели		

Past Passive Participles

M	F	N	Pl
приеман/приет	приемана/приета	приемано/прието	приемани/приети

184) **пристигам/пристигна;** *arrive*

	Present	Past Simple	Past Continuous
аз	пристигам	пристигнах	пристигах
ти	пристигаш	пристигна	пристигаше
той	пристига	пристигна	пристигаше
ние	пристигаме	пристигнахме	пристигахме
вие	пристигате	пристигнахте	пристигахте
те	пристигат	пристигнаха	пристигаха

	Future	**Future in the Past**
	(For negative, replace **ще** with **няма да**)	(For negative, replace **щях/щеше/щяхме/щяхте/щяха** with **нямаше**)
аз	ще пристигам/пристигна	щях да пристигам/пристигна
ти	ще пристигаш/пристигнеш	щеше да пристигаш/пристигнеш
той	ще пристига/пристигне	щеше да пристига/пристигне
ние	ще пристигаме/пристигнем	щяхме да пристигаме/пристигнем
вие	ще пристигате/пристигнете	щяхте да пристигате/пристигнете
те	ще пристигат/пристигнат	щяха да пристигат/пристигнат

Past Active Participles

M	F	N	Pl
пристигал/ пристигнал	пристигала/ пристигнала	пристигало/ пристигнало	пристигали/ пристигнали

	Present Perfect	**Past Perfect**
аз	съм пристигал/пристигнал	бях пристигал/пристигнал
ти	си пристигал/пристигнал	беше пристигал/пристигнал
той	е пристигал/пристигнал	беше пристигал/пристигнал
ние	сме пристигали/пристигнали	бяхме пристигали/пристигнали
вие	сте пристигали/пристигнали	бяхте пристигали/пристигнали
те	са пристигали/пристигнали	бяха пристигали/пристигнали

	Conditional Mood	**Imperative Mood**	
аз	бих пристигал/пристигнал	**Positive**	**Negative**
ти	би пристигал/пристигнал	пристигай/пристигни	не пристигай
той	би пристигал/пристигнал		
ние	бихме пристигали/пристигнали		
вие	бихте пристигали/пристигнали	пристигайте/пристигнете	не пристигайте
те	биха пристигали/пристигнали		

Past Passive Participles

M	F	N	Pl
N/A	N/A	N/A	N/A

185) **притеснявам/притесня;** *embarrass, make uneasy; rush*
притеснявам/притесня се; *worry*

	Present	Past Simple	Past Continuous
аз	притеснявам	притесних	притеснявах
ти	притесняваш	притесни	притесняваше
той	притеснява	притесни	притесняваше
ние	притесняваме	притеснихме	притеснявахме
вие	притеснявате	притеснихте	притеснявахте
те	притесняват	притесниха	притеснinfraваха

	Future	Future in the Past
	(For negative, replace **ще** with **няма да**)	(For negative, replace **щях/щеше/щяхме/щяхте/щяха** with **нямаше**)
аз	ще притеснявам/притесня	щях да притеснявам/притесня
ти	ще притесняваш/притесниш	щеше да притесняваш/притесниш
той	ще притеснява/притесни	щеше да притеснява/притесни
ние	ще притесняваме/притесним	щяхме да притесняваме/притесним
вие	ще притеснявате/притесните	щяхте да притеснявате/притесните
те	ще притесняват/притеснят	щяха да притесняват/притеснят

Past Active Participles

M	F	N	Pl
притеснявал/ притеснил	притсснявала/ притеснила	притеснявало/ притеснило	притеснявали/ притеснили

	Present Perfect	Past Perfect
аз	съм притеснявал/притеснил	бях притеснявал/притеснил
ти	си притеснявал/притеснил	беше притеснявал/притеснил
той	е притеснявал/притеснил	беше притеснявал/притеснил
ние	сме притеснявали/притеснили	бяхме притеснявали/притеснили
вие	сте притеснявали/притеснили	бяхте притеснявали/притеснили
те	са притеснявали/притеснили	бяха притеснявали/притеснили

	Conditional Mood	Imperative Mood	
аз	бих притеснявал/притеснил	**Positive**	**Negative**
ти	би притеснявал/притеснил	притеснявай/притесни	не притеснявай
той	би притеснявал/притеснил		
ние	бихме притеснявали/притеснили		
вие	бихте притеснявали/притеснили		
те	биха притеснявали/притеснили		

Past Passive Participles

M	F	N	Pl
притесняван/ притеснен	притеснявана/ притеснена	притеснявано/ притеснено	притеснявани/ притеснени

186) **проверявам/проверя;** *check, verify*

	Present	Past Simple	Past Continuous
аз	проверявам	проверих	проверявах
ти	проверяваш	провери	проверяваше
той	проверява	провери	проверяваше
ние	проверяваме	проверихме	проверявахме
вие	проверявате	проверихте	проверявахте
те	проверяват	провериха	проверяваха

	Future	**Future in the Past**
	(For negative, replace **ще** with **няма да**)	(For negative, replace **щях/щеше/щяхме/щяхте/щяха** with **нямаше**)
аз	ще проверявам/проверя	щях да проверявам/проверя
ти	ще проверяваш/провериш	щеше да проверяваш/провериш
той	ще проверява/провери	щеше да проверява/провери
ние	ще проверяваме/проверим	щяхме да проверяваме/проверим
вие	ще проверявате/проверите	щяхте да проверявате/проверите
те	ще проверяват/проверят	щяха да проверяват/проверят

Past Active Participles

M	F	N	Pl
проверявал/ проверил	проверявала/ проверила	проверявало/ проверило	проверявали/ проверили

	Present Perfect	**Past Perfect**
аз	съм проверявал/проверил	бях проверявал/проверил
ти	си проверявал/проверил	беше проверявал/проверил
той	е проверявал/проверил	беше проверявал/проверил
ние	сме проверявали/проверили	бяхме проверявали/проверили
вие	сте проверявали/проверили	бяхте проверявали/проверили
те	са проверявали/проверили	бяха проверявали/проверили

	Conditional Mood	**Imperative Mood**	
аз	бих проверявал/проверил	**Positive**	**Negative**
ти	би проверявал/проверил	проверявай/провери	не проверявай
той	би проверявал/проверил		
ние	бихме проверявали/проверили		
вие	бихте проверявали/проверили	проверявайте/проверете	не проверявайте
те	биха проверявали/проверили		

Past Passive Participles

M	F	N	Pl
проверяван/ проверен	проверявана/ проверена	проверявано/ проверено	проверявани/ проверени

187) **продавам/продам;** *sell, vend*

	Present	Past Simple	Past Continuous
аз	продавам	продадох	продавах
ти	продаваш	продаде	продаваше
той	продава	продаде	продаваше
ние	продаваме	продадохме	продавахме
вие	продавате	продадохте	продавахте
те	продават	продадоха	продаваха

	Future	**Future in the Past**
	(For negative, replace **ще** with **няма да**)	(For negative, replace **щях/щеше/щяхме/щяхте/щяха** with **нямаше**)
аз	ще продавам/продам	щях да продавам/ продам
ти	ще продаваш/продадеш	щеше да продаваш/ продадеш
той	ще продава/продаде	щеше да продава/ продаде
ние	ще продаваме/продадем	щяхме да продаваме/ продадем
вие	ще продавате/продадете	щяхте да продавате/ продадете
те	ще продават/продадат	щяха да продават/ продадат

Past Active Participles

M	F	N	Pl
продавал/продал	продавала/продала	продавало/продало	продавали/продали

	Present Perfect	**Past Perfect**
аз	съм продавал/продал	бях продавал/продал
ти	си продавал/продал	беше продавал/продал
той	е продавал/продал	беше продавал/продал
ние	сме продавали/продали	бяхме продавали/продали
вие	сте продавали/продали	бяхте продавали/продали
те	са продавали/продали	бяха продавали/продали

	Conditional Mood	**Imperative Mood**	
аз	бих продавал/продал	**Positive**	**Negative**
ти	би продавал/продал	продавай/продай	не продавай
той	би продавал/продал		
ние	бихме продавали/продали		
вие	бихте продавали/продали	продавайте/продайте	не продавайте
те	биха продавали/продали		

Past Passive Participles

M	F	N	Pl
продаван/продаден	продавана/продадена	продавано/продадено	продавани/продадени

188) **продължавам/продължа;** *continue, carry on; extend*

	Present	Past Simple	Past Continuous
аз	продължавам	продължих	продължавах
ти	продължаваш	продължи	продължаваше
той	продължава	продължи	продължаваше
ние	продължаваме	продължихме	продължавахме
вие	продължавате	продължихте	продължавахте
те	продължават	продължиха	продължаваха

	Future	**Future in the Past**
	(For negative, replace **ще** with **няма да**)	(For negative, replace **щях/щеше/щяхме/щяхте/щяха** with **нямаше**)
аз	ще продължавам/продължа	щях да продължавам/продължа
ти	ще продължаваш/продължиш	щеше да продължаваш/продължиш
той	ще продължава/продължи	щеше да продължава/продължи
ние	ще продължаваме/продължим	щяхме да продължаваме/продължим
вие	ще продължавате/продължите	щяхте да продължавате/продължите
те	ще продължават/продължат	щяха да продължават/продължат

Past Active Participles

M	F	N	Pl
продължавал/ продължил	продължавала/ продължила	продължавало/ продължило	продължавали/ продължили

	Present Perfect	**Past Perfect**
аз	съм продължавал/продължил	бях продължавал/продължил
ти	си продължавал/продължил	беше продължавал/продължил
той	е продължавал/продължил	беше продължавал/продължил
ние	сме продължавали/продължили	бяхме продължавали/продължили
вие	сте продължавали/продължили	бяхте продължавали/продължили
те	са продължавали/продължили	бяха продължавали/продължили

	Conditional Mood	**Imperative Mood**	
аз	бих продължавал/продължил	**Positive**	**Negative**
ти	би продължавал/продължил	продължавай/продължи	не продължавай
той	би продължавал/продължил		
ние	бихме продължавали/продължили		
вие	бихте продължавали/продължили	продължавайте/продължете	не продължавайте
те	биха продължавали/продължили		

Past Passive Participles

M	F	N	Pl
продължаван/ продължен	продължавано/ продължено	продължавана/ продължена	продължавани/ продължени

189) **пускам/пусна;** *release; drop*

	Present	**Past Simple**	**Past Continuous**
аз	пускам	пуснах	пусках
ти	пускаш	пусна	пускаше
той	пуска	пусна	пускаше
ние	пускаме	пуснахме	пускахме
вие	пускате	пуснахте	пускахте
те	пускат	пуснаха	пускаха

	Future	**Future in the Past**
	(For negative, replace **ще** with **няма да**)	(For negative, replace **щях/щеше/щяхме/щяхте/щяха** with **нямаше**)
аз	ще пускам/пусна	щях да пускам/пусна
ти	ще пускаш/пуснеш	щеше да пускаш/пуснеш
той	ще пуска/пусне	щеше да пуска/пусне
ние	ще пускаме/пуснем	щяхме да пускаме/пуснем
вие	ще пускате/пуснете	щяхте да пускате/пуснете
те	ще пускат/пуснат	щяха да пускат/пуснат

Past Active Participles

M	**F**	**N**	**Pl**
пускал/пуснал	пускала/пуснала	пускало/пуснало	пускали/пуснали

	Present Perfect	**Past Perfect**
аз	съм пускал/пуснал	бях пускал/пуснал
ти	си пускал/пуснал	беше пускал/пуснал
той	е пускал/пуснал	беше пускал/пуснал
ние	сме пускали/пуснали	бяхме пускали/пуснали
вие	сте пускали/пуснали	бяхте пускали/пуснали
те	са пускали/пуснали	бяха пускали/пуснали

	Conditional Mood	**Imperative Mood**	
аз	бих пускал/пуснал	**Positive**	**Negative**
ти	би пускал/пуснал	пускай/пусни	не пускай
той	би пускал/пуснал		
ние	бихме пускали/пуснали		
вие	бихте пускали/пуснали	пускайте/пуснете	не пускайте
те	биха пускали/пуснали		

Past Passive Participles

M	**F**	**N**	**Pl**
пускан/пуснат	пускана/пусната	пускано/пуснато	пускани/пуснати

190) **пуша;** *smoke*

	Present	**Past Simple**	**Past Continuous**
аз	пуша	пуших	пушех
ти	пушиш	пуши	пушеше
той	пуши	пуши	пушеше
ние	пушим	пушихме	пушехме
вие	пушите	пушихте	пушехте
те	пушат	пушиха	пушеха

	Future	**Future in the Past**
	(For negative, replace **ще** with **няма да**)	(For negative, replace **щях/щеше/щяхме/щяхте/щяха** with **нямаше**)
аз	ще пуша	щях да пуша
ти	ще пушиш	щеше да пушиш
той	ще пуши	щеше да пуши
ние	ще пушим	щяхме да пушим
вие	ще пушите	щяхте да пушите
те	ще пушат	щяха да пушат

Past Active Participles

M	**F**	**N**	**Pl**
пушил	пушила	пушило	пушили

	Present Perfect	**Past Perfect**
аз	съм пушил	бях пушил
ти	си пушил	беше пушил
той	е пушил	беше пушил
ние	сме пушили	бяхме пушили
вие	сте пушили	бяхте пушили
те	са пушили	бяха пушили

	Conditional Mood	**Imperative Mood**	
аз	бих пушил	**Positive**	**Negative**
ти	би пушил	Пуши	не пуши
той	би пушил		
ние	бихме пушили		
вие	бихте пушили	Пушете	не пушете
те	биха пушили		

Past Passive Participles

M	**F**	**N**	**Pl**
пушен	пушена	пушено	пушени

191) **пътувам;** *travel, journey*

	Present	Past Simple	Past Continuous
аз	пътувам	пътувах	пътувах
ти	пътуваш	пътува	пътуваше
той	пътува	пътува	пътуваше
ние	пътуваме	пътувахме	пътувахме
вие	пътувате	пътувахте	пътувахте
те	пътуват	пътуваха	пътуваха

	Future	Future in the Past
	(For negative, replace **ще** with **няма да**)	(For negative, replace **щях/щеше/щяхме/щяхте/щяха** with **нямаше**)
аз	ще пътувам	щях да пътувам
ти	ще пътуваш	щеше да пътуваш
той	ще пътува	щеше да пътува
ние	ще пътуваме	щяхме да пътуваме
вие	ще пътувате	щяхте да пътувате
те	ще пътуват	щяха да пътуват

Past Active Participles

M	F	N	Pl
пътувал	пътувала	пътувало	пътували

	Present Perfect	Past Perfect
аз	съм пътувал	бях пътувал
ти	си пътувал	беше пътувал
той	е пътувал	беше пътувал
ние	сме пътували	бяхме пътували
вие	сте пътували	бяхте пътували
те	са пътували	бяха пътували

	Conditional Mood	Imperative Mood	
аз	бих пътувал	**Positive**	**Negative**
ти	би пътувал	пътувай	не пътувай
той	би пътувал		
ние	бихме пътували		
вие	бихте пътували	пътувайте	не пътувайте
те	биха пътували		

Past Passive Participles

M	F	N	Pl
N/A	N/A	N/A	N/A

192) **работя;** *work; operate*

	Present	Past Simple	Past Continuous
аз	работя	работих	работех
ти	работиш	работи	работеше
той	работи	работи	работеше
ние	работим	работихме	работехме
вие	работите	работихте	работехте
те	работят	работиха	работеха

	Future	Future in the Past
	(For negative, replace **ще** with **няма да**)	(For negative, replace **щях/щеше/щяхме/щяхте/щяха** with **нямаше**)
аз	ще работя	щях да работя
ти	ще работиш	щеше да работиш
той	ще работи	щеше да работи
ние	ще работим	щяхме да работим
вие	ще работите	щяхте да работите
те	ще работят	щяха да работят

Past Active Participles

M	F	N	Pl
Работил	работила	работило	работили

	Present Perfect	Past Perfect
аз	съм работил	бях работил
ти	си работил	беше работил
той	е работил	беше работил
ние	сме работили	бяхме работили
вие	сте работили	бяхте работили
те	са работили	бяха работили

	Conditional Mood	Imperative Mood	
аз	бих работил	**Positive**	**Negative**
ти	би работил	работи	не работи
той	би работил		
ние	бихме работили		
вие	бихте работили	работете	не работете
те	биха работили		

Past Passive Participles

M	F	N	Pl
N/A	N/A	N/A	N/A

193) **раждам/родя;** *give birth* **раждам/родя се;** *be born*

	Present	**Past Simple**	**Past Continuous**
аз	раждам	родих	раждах
ти	раждаш	роди	раждаше
той	ражда	роди	раждаше
ние	раждаме	родихме	раждахме
вие	раждате	родихте	раждахте
те	раждат	родиха	раждаха

	Future	**Future in the Past**
	(For negative, replace **ще** with **няма да**)	(For negative, replace **щях/щеше/щяхме/щяхте/щяха** with **нямаше**)
аз	ще раждам/родя	щях да раждам/родя
ти	ще раждаш/родиш	щеше да раждаш/родиш
той	ще ражда/роди	щеше да ражда/роди
ние	ще раждаме/родим	щяхме да раждаме/родим
вие	ще раждате/родите	щяхте да раждате/родите
те	ще раждат/родят	щяха да раждат/родят

Past Active Participles

M	**F**	**N**	**Pl**
раждал/родил	раждала/родила	раждало/родило	раждали/родили

	Present Perfect	**Past Perfect**
аз	съм раждал/родил	бях раждал/родил
ти	си раждал/родил	беше раждал/родил
той	е раждал/родил	беше раждал/родил
ние	сме раждали/родили	бяхме раждали/родили
вие	сте раждали/родили	бяхте раждали/родили
те	са раждали/родили	бяха раждали/родили

	Conditional Mood	**Imperative Mood**	
аз	бих раждал/родил	**Positive**	**Negative**
ти	би раждал/родил	раждай/роди	не раждай
той	би раждал/родил		
ние	бихме раждали/родили		
вие	бихте раждали/родили	раждайте/родете	не раждайте
те	биха раждали/родили		

Past Passive Participles

M	**F**	**N**	**Pl**
раждан/роден	раждана/родена	раждано/родено	раждани/родени

194) **разбирам/разбера;** *understand* **разбирам/разбера се;** *get along with; resolve*

	Present	**Past Simple**	**Past Continuous**
аз	разбирам	разбрах	разбирах
ти	разбираш	разбра	разбираше
той	разбира	разбра	разбираше
ние	разбираме	разбрахме	разбирахме
вие	разбирате	разбрахте	разбирахте
те	разбират	разбраха	разбираха

	Future	**Future in the Past**
	(For negative, replace **ще** with **няма да**)	(For negative, replace **щях/щеше/щяхме/щяхте/щяха** with **нямаше**)
аз	ще разбирам/разбера	щях да разбирам/разбера
ти	ще разбираш/разбереш	щеше да разбираш/разбереш
той	ще разбира/разбере	щеше да разбира/разбере
ние	ще разбираме/разберем	щяхме да разбираме/разберем
вие	ще разбирате/разберете	щяхте да разбирате/разберете
те	ще разбират/разберат	щяха да разбират/разберат

Past Active Participles

M	**F**	**N**	**Pl**
разбирал/разбрал	разбирала/разбрала	разбирало/разбрало	разбирали/разбрали

	Present Perfect	**Past Perfect**
аз	съм разбирал/разбрал	бях разбирал/разбрал
ти	си разбирал/разбрал	беше разбирал/разбрал
той	е разбирал/разбрал	беше разбирал/разбрал
ние	сме разбирали/разбрали	бяхме разбирали/разбрали
вие	сте разбирали/разбрали	бяхте разбирали/разбрали
те	са разбирали/разбрали	бяха разбирали/разбрали

	Conditional Mood	**Imperative Mood**	
аз	бих разбирал/разбрал	**Positive**	**Negative**
ти	би разбирал/разбрал	разбирай/разбери	не разбирай
той	би разбирал/разбрал		
ние	бихме разбирали/разбрали		
вие	бихте разбирали/разбрали	разбирайте/разберете	не разбирайте
те	биха разбирали/разбрали		

Past Passive Participles

M	**F**	**N**	**Pl**
разбиран/разбран	разбирана/разбрана	разбирано/разбрано	разбирани/разбрани

195) **разболявам се/разболея се;** *get sick*

	Present	Past Simple	Past Continuous
аз	се разболявам	се разболях	се разболявах
ти	се разболяваш	се разболя	се разболяваше
той	се разболява	се разболя	се разболяваше
ние	се разболяваме	се разболяхме	се разболявахме
вие	се разболявате	се разболяхте	се разболявахте
те	се разболяват	се разболяха	се разболяваха

	Future	Future in the Past
	(For negative, replace **ще** with **няма да**)	(For negative, replace **щях/щеше/щяхме/щяхте/щяха** with **нямаше**)
аз	ще се разболявам/разболея	щях да се разболявам/разболея
ти	ще се разболяваш/разболееш	щеше да се разболяваш/разболееш
той	ще се разболява/разболее	щеше да се разболява/разболее
ние	ще се разболяваме/разболеем	щяхме да се разболяваме/разболеем
вие	ще се разболявате/разболеете	щяхте да се разболявате/разболеете
те	ще се разболяват/разболеят	щяха да се разболяват/разболеят

Past Active Participles

M	F	N	Pl
разболявал/ разболял	разболявала/ разболяла	разболявало/ разболяло	разболявали/ разболели

	Present Perfect	Past Perfect
аз	съм се разболявал/разболял	бях се разболявал/разболял
ти	си се разболявал/разболял	беше се разболявал/разболял
той	се е разболявал/разболял	беше се разболявал/разболял
ние	сме се разболявали/разболели	бяхме се разболявали/разболели
вие	сте се разболявали/разболели	бяхте се разболявали/разболели
те	са се разболявали/разболели	бяха се разболявали/разболели

	Conditional Mood	Imperative Mood	
аз	бих се разболявал/разболял	**Positive**	**Negative**
ти	би се разболявал/разболял	разболявай/разболей се	не се разболявай
той	би се разболявал/разболял		
ние	бихме се разболявали/разболели		
вие	бихте се разболявали/разболели	разболявайте/разболейте се	не се разболявайте
те	биха се разболявали/разболели		

Past Passive Participles

M	F	N	Pl
N/A	N/A	N/A	N/A

196) **развеждам/разведа;** *guide, give a tour* **развеждам/разведа се;** *get a divorce*

	Present	Past Simple	Past Continuous
аз	развеждам	разведох	развеждах
ти	развеждаш	разведе	развеждаше
той	развежда	разведе	развеждаше
ние	развеждаме	разведохме	развеждахме
вие	развеждате	разведохте	развеждахте
те	развеждат	разведоха	развеждаха

	Future	Future in the Past
	(For negative, replace **ще** with **няма да**)	(For negative, replace **щях/щеше/щяхме/щяхте/щяха** with **нямаше**)
аз	ще развеждам/разведа	щях да развеждам/разведа
ти	ще развеждаш/разведеш	щеше да развеждаш/разведеш
той	ще развежда/разведе	щеше да развежда/разведе
ние	ще развеждаме/разведем	щяхме да развеждаме/разведем
вие	ще развеждате/разведете	щяхте да развеждате/разведете
те	ще развеждат/разведат	щяха да развеждат/разведат

Past Active Participles

M	F	N	Pl
развеждал/ развел	развеждала/ развела	развеждало/ развело	развеждали/ развели

	Present Perfect	Past Perfect
аз	съм развеждал/развел	бях развеждал/развел
ти	си развеждал/развел	беше развеждал/развел
той	е развеждал/развел	беше развеждал/развел
ние	сме развеждали/развели	бяхме развеждали/развели
вие	сте развеждали/развели	бяхте развеждали/развели
те	са развеждали/развели	бяха развеждали/развели

	Conditional Mood	Imperative Mood Positive	Negative
аз	бих развеждал/развел		
ти	би развеждал/развел	развеждай/разведи	не развеждай
той	би развеждал/развел		
ние	бихме развеждали/развели		
вие	бихте развеждали/развели	развеждайте/разведете	не развеждайте
те	биха развеждали/развели		

Past Passive Participles

M	F	N	Pl
развеждан/ разведен	развеждана/ разведена	Развеждано /разведено	развеждани/ разведени

197) **разливам/разлея;** *spill, pour out, leak*

	Present	**Past Simple**	**Past Continuous**
аз	разливам	разлях	разливах
ти	разливаш	разля	разливаше
той	разлива	разля	разливаше
ние	разливаме	разляхме	разливахме
вие	разливате	разляхте	разливахте
те	разливат	разляха	разливаха

	Future	**Future in the Past**
	(For negative, replace **ще** with **няма да**)	(For negative, replace **щях/щеше/щяхме/щяхте/щяха** with **нямаше**)
аз	ще разливам/разлея	щях да разливам/разлея
ти	ще разливаш/разлееш	щеше да разливаш/разлееш
той	ще разлива/разлее	щеше да разлива/разлее
ние	ще разливаме/разлеем	щяхме да разливаме/разлеем
вие	ще разливате/разлеете	щяхте да разливате/разлеете
те	ще разливат/разлеят	щяха да разливат/разлеят

Past Active Participles

M	**F**	**N**	**Pl**
разливал/разлял	разливала/разляла	разливало/разляло	разливали/разлели

	Present Perfect	**Past Perfect**
аз	съм разливал/разлял	бях разливал/разлял
ти	си разливал/разлял	беше разливал/разлял
той	се е разливал/разлял	беше разливал/разлял
ние	сме разливали/разлели	бяхме разливали/разлели
вие	сте разливали/разлели	бяхте разливали/разлели
те	са разливали/разлели	бяха разливали/разлели

	Conditional Mood	**Imperative Mood**	
аз	бих разливал/разлял	**Positive**	**Negative**
ти	би разливал/разлял	разливай/разлей	не разливай
той	би разливал/разлял		
ние	бихме разливали/разлели		
вие	бихте разливали/разлели	разливайте/разлейте	не разливайте
те	биха разливали/разлели		

Past Passive Participles

M	**F**	**N**	**Pl**
разливан/разлят	разливана/разлята	разливано/разлято	разливани/разлети

198) **разхождам/разходя;** *take for a walk*

	Present	**Past Simple**	**Past Continuous**
аз	разхождам	разходих	разхождах
ти	разхождаш	разходи	разхождаше
той	разхожда	разходи	разхождаше
ние	разхождаме	разходихме	разхождахме
вие	разхождате	разходихте	разхождахте
те	разхождат	разходиха	разхождаха

	Future	**Future in the Past**
	(For negative, replace **ще** with **няма да**)	(For negative, replace **щях/щеше/щяхме/щяхте/щяха** with **нямаше**)
аз	ще разхождам/разходя	щях да разхождам/разходя
ти	ще разхождаш/разходиш	щеше да разхождаш/разходиш
той	ще разхожда/разходи	щеше да разхожда/разходи
ние	ще разхождаме/разходим	щяхме да разхождаме/разходим
вие	ще разхождате/разходите	щяхте да разхождате/разходите
те	ще разхождат/разходят	щяха да разхождат/разходят

Past Active Participles

M	**F**	**N**	**Pl**
разхождал/ разходил	разхождала/ разходила	разхождало/ разходило	разхождали/ разходили

	Present Perfect	**Past Perfect**
аз	съм разхождал/разходил	бях разхождал/разходил
ти	си разхождал/разходил	беше разхождал/разходил
той	е разхождал/разходил	беше разхождал/разходил
ние	сме разхождали/разходили	бяхме разхождали/разходили
вие	сте разхождали/разходили	бяхте разхождали/разходили
те	са разхождали/разходили	бяха разхождали/разходили

	Conditional Mood	**Imperative Mood**	
аз	бих разхождал/разходил	**Positive**	**Negative**
ти	би разхождал/разходил	разхождай/разходи	не разхождай
той	би разхождал/разходил		
ние	бихме разхождали/разходили		
вие	бихте разхождали/разходили	разхождайте/разходете	не разхождайте
те	биха разхождали/разходили		

Past Passive Participles

M	**F**	**N**	**Pl**
разхождан/ разходен	разхождана/ разходена	разхождано/ разходено	разхождани/ разходени

199) **ранявам/раня;** *hurt, injure*

	Present	**Past Simple**	**Past Continuous**
аз	ранявам	раних	ранявах
ти	раняваш	рани	раняваше
той	ранява	рани	раняваше
ние	раняваме	ранихме	ранявахме
вие	ранявате	ранихте	ранявахте
те	раняват	раниха	ранявaха

	Future	**Future in the Past**
	(For negative, replace **ще** with **няма да**)	(For negative, replace **щях/щеше/щяхме/щяхте/щяха** with **нямаше**)
аз	ще ранявам/раня	щях да ранявам/раня
ти	ще раняваш/раниш	щеше да раняваш/раниш
той	ще ранява/рани	щеше да ранява/рани
ние	ще раняваме/раним	щяхме да раняваме/раним
вие	ще ранявате/раните	щяхте да ранявате/раните
те	ще раняват/ранят	щяха да раняват/ранят

Past Active Participles

M	**F**	**N**	**Pl**
ранявал/ранил	ранявала/ранила	ранявало/ранило	ранявали/ранили

	Present Perfect	**Past Perfect**
аз	съм ранявал/ранил	бях ранявал/ранил
ти	си ранявал/ранил	беше ранявал/ранил
той	е ранявал/ранил	беше ранявал/ранил
ние	сме ранявали/ранили	бяхме ранявали/ранили
вие	сте ранявали/ранили	бяхте ранявали/ранили
те	са ранявали/ранили	бяха ранявали/ранили

	Conditional Mood	**Imperative Mood**	
аз	бих ранявал/ранил	**Positive**	**Negative**
ти	би ранявал/ранил	ранявай/рани	не ранявай
той	би ранявал/ранил		
ние	бихме ранявали/ранили		
вие	бихте ранявали/ранили	ранявайте/ранете	не ранявайте
те	биха ранявали/ранили		

Past Passive Participles

M	**F**	**N**	**Pl**
раняван/ранен	ранявана/ранена	ранявано/ранено	ранявани/ранени

200) **раста/порасна;** *grow up*

	Present	Past Simple	Past Continuous
аз	раста	пораснах	растях
ти	растеш	порасна	растеше
той	расте	порасна	растеше
ние	растем	пораснахме	растяхме
вие	растете	пораснахте	растяхте
те	растат	пораснаха	растяха

	Future	Future in the Past
	(For negative, replace **ще** with **няма да**)	(For negative, replace **щях/щеше/щяхме/щяхте/щяха** with **нямаше**)
аз	ще раста/порасна	щях да раста/порасна
ти	ще растеш/пораснеш	щеше да растеш/пораснеш
той	ще расте/порасне	щеше да расте/порасне
ние	ще растем/пораснем	щяхме да растем/пораснем
вие	ще растете/пораснете	щяхте да растете/пораснете
те	ще растат/пораснат	щяха да растат/пораснат

Past Active Participles

M	F	N	Pl
расъл/пораснал	расла/пораснала	расло/пораснало	расли/пораснали

	Present Perfect	Past Perfect
аз	съм расъл/пораснал	бях расъл/пораснал
ти	си расъл/пораснал	беше расъл/пораснал
той	е расъл/пораснал	беше расъл/пораснал
ние	сме расли/пораснали	бяхме расли/пораснали
вие	сте расли/пораснали	бяхте расли/пораснали
те	са расли/пораснали	бяха расли/пораснали

	Conditional Mood	Imperative Mood	
аз	бих расъл/пораснал	**Positive**	**Negative**
ти	би расъл/пораснал	расти/порасни	не расти
той	би расъл/пораснал		
ние	бихме расли/пораснали		
вие	бихте расли/пораснали	растете/пораснете	не растете
те	биха расли/пораснали		

Past Passive Participles

M	F	N	Pl
N/A	N/A	N/A	N/A

201) **решавам/реша;** *decide*

	Present	**Past Simple**	**Past Continuous**
аз	решавам	реших	решавах
ти	решаваш	реши	решаваше
той	решава	реши	решаваше
ние	решаваме	решихме	решавахме
вие	решавате	решихте	решавахте
те	решават	решиха	решаваха

	Future	**Future in the Past**
	(For negative, replace **ще** with **няма да**)	(For negative, replace **щях/щеше/щяхме/щяхте/щяха** with **нямаше**)
аз	ще решавам/реша	щях да решавам/реша
ти	ще решаваш/решиш	щеше да решаваш/решиш
той	ще решава/реши	щеше да решава/реши
ние	ще решаваме/решим	щяхме да решаваме/решим
вие	ще решавате/решите	щяхте да решавате/решите
те	ще решават/решат	щяха да решават/решат

Past Active Participles

M	**F**	**N**	**Pl**
решавал/решил	решавала/решила	решавало/решило	решавали/решили

	Present Perfect	**Past Perfect**
аз	съм решавал/решил	бях решавал/решил
ти	си решавал/решил	беше решавал/решил
той	е решавал/решил	беше решавал/решил
ние	сме решавали/решили	бяхме решавали/решили
вие	сте решавали/решили	бяхте решавали/решили
те	са решавали/решили	бяха решавали/решили

	Conditional Mood	**Imperative Mood**	
аз	бих решавал/решил	**Positive**	**Negative**
ти	би решавал/решил	решавай/реши	не решавай
той	би решавал/решил		
ние	бихме решавали/решили		
вие	бихте решавали/решили	решавайте/решете	не решавайте
те	биха решавали/решили		

Past Passive Participles

M	**F**	**N**	**Pl**
решаван/решен	решавана/решена	решавано/решено	решавани/решени

202) **свиря;** *play music*

	Present	**Past Simple**	**Past Continuous**
аз	свиря	свирих	свирех
ти	свириш	свири	свиреше
той	свири	свири	свиреше
ние	свирим	свирихме	свирехме
вие	свирите	свирихте	свирехте
те	свирят	свириха	свиреха

	Future	**Future in the Past**
	(For negative, replace **ще** with **няма да**)	(For negative, replace **щях/щеше/щяхме/щяхте/щяха** with **нямаше**)
аз	ще свиря	щях да свиря
ти	ще свириш	щеше да свириш
той	ще свири	щеше да свири
ние	ще свирим	щяхме да свирим
вие	ще свирите	щяхте да свирите
те	ще свирят	щяха да свирят

Past Active Participles

M	**F**	**N**	**Pl**
свирил	свирила	свирило	свирили

	Present Perfect	**Past Perfect**
аз	съм свирил	бях свирил
ти	си свирил	беше свирил
той	е свирил	беше свирил
ние	сме свирили	бяхме свирили
вие	сте свирили	бяхте свирили
те	са свирили	бяха свирили

	Conditional Mood	**Imperative Mood**	
аз	бих свирил	**Positive**	**Negative**
ти	би свирил	свири	не свири
той	би свирил		
ние	бихме свирили		
вие	бихте свирили	свирете	не свирете
те	биха свирили		

Past Passive Participles

M	**F**	**N**	**Pl**
свирен	свирена	свирено	свирени

203) **свързвам/свържа;** *bind, connect, link, associate*

	Present	**Past Simple**	**Past Continuous**
аз	свързвам	свързах	свързвах
ти	свързваш	свърза	свързваше
той	свързва	свърза	свързваше
ние	свързваме	свързахме	свързвахме
вие	свързвате	свързахте	свързвахте
те	свързват	свързаха	свързваха

	Future	**Future in the Past**
	(For negative, replace **ще** with **няма да**)	(For negative, replace **щях/щеше/щяхме/щяхте/щяха** with **нямаше**)
аз	ще свързвам/свържа	щях да свързвам/свържа
ти	ще свързваш/свържеш	щеше да свързваш/свържеш
той	ще свързва/свърже	щеше да свързва/свърже
ние	ще свързваме/свържем	щяхме да свързваме/свържем
вие	ще свързвате/свържете	щяхте да свързвате/свържете
те	ще свързват/свържат	щяха да свързват/свържат

Past Active Participles

M	**F**	**N**	**Pl**
свързвал/ свързал	свързвала/ свързала	свързвало/ свързало	свързвали/ свързали

	Present Perfect	**Past Perfect**
аз	съм свързвал/свързал	бях свързвал/свързал
ти	си свързвал/свързал	беше свързвал/свързал
той	е свързвал/свързал	беше свързвал/свързал
ние	сме свързвали/свързали	бяхме свързвали/свързали
вие	сте свързвали/свързали	бяхте свързвали/свързали
те	са свързвали/свързали	бяха свързвали/свързали

	Conditional Mood	**Imperative Mood**	
		Positive	**Negative**
аз	бих свързвал/свързал		
ти	би свързвал/свързал	свързвай/свържи	не свързвай
той	би свързвал/свързал		
ние	бихме свързвали/свързали		
вие	бихте свързвали/свързали	свързвайте/свържете	не свързвайте
те	биха свързвали/свързали		

Past Passive Participles

M	**F**	**N**	**Pl**
свързван/ свързан	свързвана/ свързана	свързвано/ свързано	свързвани/ свързани

204) **свършвам/свърша;** *finish, terminate*

	Present	Past Simple	Past Continuous
аз	свършвам	свърших	свършвах
ти	свършваш	свърши	свършваше
той	свършва	свърши	свършваше
ние	свършваме	свършихме	свършвахме
вие	свършвате	свършихте	свършвахте
те	свършват	свършиха	свършваха

	Future	Future in the Past
	(For negative, replace **ще** with **няма да**)	(For negative, replace **щях/щеше/щяхме/щяхте/щяха** with **нямаше**)
аз	щях да свършвам/свърша	щях да свършвам/свърша
ти	щеше да свършваш/свършиш	щеше да свършваш/свършиш
той	щеше да свършва/свърши	щеше да свършва/свърши
ние	щяхме да свършваме/свършим	щяхме да свършваме/свършим
вие	щяхте да свършвате/свършите	щяхте да свършвате/свършите
те	щяха да свършват/свършат	щяха да свършват/свършат

Past Active Participles

M	F	N	Pl
свършвал/ свършил	свършвала/ свършила	свършвало/ свършило	свършвали/ свършили

	Present Perfect	Past Perfect
аз	съм свършвал/свършил	бях свършвал/свършил
ти	си свършвал/свършил	беше свършвал/свършил
той	е свършвал/свършил	беше свършвал/свършил
ние	сме свършвали/свършили	бяхме свършвали/свършили
вие	сте свършвали/свършили	бяхте свършвали/свършили
те	са свършвали/свършили	бяха свършвали/свършили

	Conditional Mood	Imperative Mood	
аз	бих свършвал/свършил	**Positive**	**Negative**
ти	би свършвал/свършил	свършвай/свърши	не свършвай
той	би свършвал/свършил		
ние	бихме свършвали/свършили		
вие	бихте свършвали/свършили	свършвайте/свършете	не свършвайте
те	биха свършвали/свършили		

Past Passive Participles

M	F	N	Pl
свършван/ свършен	свършвана/ свършена	свършвано/ свършено	свършвани/ свършени

205) **слагам/сложа;** *put, place, set, position*

	Present	**Past Simple**	**Past Continuous**
аз	слагам	сложих	слагах
ти	слагаш	сложи	слагаше
той	слага	сложи	слагаше
ние	слагаме	сложихме	слагахме
вие	слагате	сложихте	слагахте
те	слагат	сложиха	слагаха

	Future	**Future in the Past**
	(For negative, replace **ще** with **няма да**)	(For negative, replace **щях/щеше/щяхме/щяхте/щяха** with **нямаше**)
аз	ще слагам/сложа	щях да слагам/сложа
ти	ще слагаш/сложиш	щеше да слагаш/сложиш
той	ще слага/сложи	щеше да слага/сложи
ние	ще слагаме/сложим	щяхме да слагаме/сложим
вие	ще слагате/сложите	щяхте да слагате/сложите
те	ще слагат/сложат	щяха да слагат/сложат

Past Active Participles

M	**F**	**N**	**Pl**
слагал/сложил	слагала/сложила	слагало/сложило	слагали/сложили

	Present Perfect	**Past Perfect**
аз	съм слагал/сложил	бях слагал/сложил
ти	си слагал/сложил	беше слагал/сложил
той	е слагал/сложил	беше слагал/сложил
ние	сме слагали/сложили	бяхме слагали/сложили
вие	сте слагали/сложили	бяхте слагали/сложили
те	са слагали/сложили	бяха слагали/сложили

	Conditional Mood	**Imperative Mood**	
аз	бих слагал/сложил	**Positive**	**Negative**
ти	би слагал/сложил	слагай/сложи	не слагай
той	би слагал/сложил		
ние	бихме слагали/сложили		
вие	бихте слагали/сложили	слагайте/сложете	не слагайте
те	биха слагали/сложили		

Past Passive Participles

M	**F**	**N**	**Pl**
слаган/сложен	слагана/сложена	слагано/сложено	слагани/сложени

206) **следвам;** *follow, come after; study at a university*

	Present	**Past Simple**	**Past Continuous**
аз	следвам	следвах	
ти	следваш	следва	следваше
той	следва	следва	следваше
ние	следваме	следвахме	следвахме
вие	следвате	следвахте	следвахте
те	следват	следваха	следваха

	Future	**Future in the Past**
	(For negative, replace **ще** with **няма да**)	(For negative, replace **щях/щеше/щяхме/щяхте/щяха** with **нямаше**)
аз	ще следвам	щях да следвам
ти	ще следваш	щеше да следваш
той	ще следва	щеше да следва
ние	ще следваме	щяхме да следваме
вие	ще следвате	щяхте да следвате
те	ще следват	щяха да следват

Past Active Participles

M	**F**	**N**	**Pl**
следвал	следвала	следвало	следвали

	Present Perfect	**Past Perfect**
аз	съм следвал	бях следвал
ти	си следвал	беше следвал
той	е следвал	беше следвал
ние	сме следвали	бяхме следвали
вие	сте следвали	бяхте следвали
те	са следвали	бяха следвали

	Conditional Mood	**Imperative Mood**	
аз	бих следвал	**Positive**	**Negative**
ти	би следвал	следвай	не следвай
той	би следвал		
ние	бихме следвали		
вие	бихте следвали	следвайте	не следвайте
те	биха следвали		

Past Passive Participles

M	**F**	**N**	**Pl**
следван	следвана	следвано	следвани

207) **слушам;** *listen, pay attention*

	Present	Past Simple	Past Continuous
аз	слушам	слушах	слушах
ти	слушаш	слуша	слушаше
той	слуша	слуша	слушаше
ние	слушаме	слушахме	слушахме
вие	слушате	слушахте	слушахте
те	слушат	слушаха	слушаха

	Future	Future in the Past
	(For negative, replace **ще** with **няма да**)	(For negative, replace **щях/щеше/щяхме/щяхте/щяха** with **нямаше**)
аз	ще слушам	щях да слушам
ти	ще слушаш	щеше да слушаш
той	ще слуша	щеше да слуша
ние	ще слушаме	щяхме да слушаме
вие	ще слушате	щяхте да слушате
те	ще слушат	щяха да слушат

Past Active Participles

M	F	N	Pl
слушал	слушала	слушало	слушали

	Present Perfect	Past Perfect
аз	съм слушал	бях слушал
ти	си слушал	беше слушал
той	е слушал	беше слушал
ние	сме слушали	бяхме слушали
вие	сте слушали	бяхте слушали
те	са слушали	бяха слушали

	Conditional Mood	Imperative Mood	
аз	бих слушал	**Positive**	**Negative**
ти	би слушал	слушай	не слушай
той	би слушал		
ние	бихме слушали		
вие	бихте слушали	слушайте	не слушайте
те	биха слушали		

Past Passive Participles

M	F	N	Pl
слушан	слушана	слушано	слушани

208) **сменям/сменя;** *change, transform, convert*

	Present	**Past Simple**	**Past Continuous**
аз	сменям	смених	сменях
ти	сменяш	смени	сменяше
той	сменя	смени	сменяше
ние	сменяме	сменихме	сменяхме
вие	сменяте	сменихте	сменяхте
те	сменят	смениха	сменяха

	Future	**Future in the Past**
	(For negative, replace **ще** with **няма да**)	(For negative, replace **щях/щеше/щяхме/щяхте/щяха** with **нямаше**)
аз	ще сменям/сменя	щях да сменям/сменя
ти	ще сменяш/смениш	щеше да сменяш/смениш
той	ще сменя/смени	щеше да сменя/смени
ние	ще сменяме/сменим	щяхме да сменяме/сменим
вие	ще сменяте/смените	щяхте да сменяте/смените
те	ще сменят/сменят	щяха да сменят/сменят

Past Active Participles

M	**F**	**N**	**Pl**
сменял/сменил	сменяла/сменила	сменяло/сменило	сменяли/сменили

	Present Perfect	**Past Perfect**
аз	съм сменял/сменил	бях сменял/сменил
ти	си сменял/сменил	беше сменял/сменил
той	е сменял/сменил	беше сменял/сменил
ние	сме сменяли/сменили	бяхме сменяли/сменили
вие	сте сменяли/сменили	бяхте сменяли/сменили
те	са сменяли/сменили	бяха сменяли/сменили

	Conditional Mood	**Imperative Mood**	
аз	бих сменял/сменил	**Positive**	**Negative**
ти	би сменял/сменил	сменяй/смени	не сменяй
той	би сменял/сменил		
ние	бихме сменяли/сменили		
вие	бихте сменяли/сменили	сменяйте/сменете	не сменяйте
те	биха сменяли/сменили		

Past Passive Participles

M	**F**	**N**	**Pl**
сменян/сменен	сменяна/сменена	сменяно/сменено	сменяни/сменени

209) **смея;** *dare* **смея се;** *laugh*

	Present	Past Simple	Past Continuous
аз	смея	смях	смеех
ти	смееш	смя	смееше
той	смее	смя	смееше
ние	смеем	смяхме	смеехме
вие	смеете	смяхте	смеехте
те	смеят	смяха	смееха

	Future	Future in the Past
	(For negative, replace **ще** with **няма да**)	(For negative, replace **щях/щеше/щяхме/щяхте/щяха** with **нямаше**)
аз	ще смея	щях да смея
ти	ще смееш	щеше да смееш
той	ще смее	щеше да смее
ние	ще смеем	щяхме да смеем
вие	ще смеете	щяхте да смеете
те	ще смеят	щяха да смеят

Past Active Participles

M	F	N	Pl
смял	смяла	смяло	смели

	Present Perfect	Past Perfect
аз	съм смял	бях смял
ти	си смял	беше смял
той	е смял	беше смял
ние	сме смели	бяхме смели
вие	сте смели	бяхте смели
те	са смели	бяха смели

	Conditional Mood	Imperative Mood Positive	Negative
аз	бих смял		
ти	би смял	смей	не смей
той	би смял		
ние	бихме смели		
вие	бихте смели	смейте	не смейте
те	биха смели		

Past Passive Participles

M	F	N	Pl
N/A	N/A	N/A	N/A

210) **спестявам/спестя;** *save, economize*

	Present	**Past Simple**	**Past Continuous**
аз	спестявам	спестих	спестявах
ти	спестяваш	спести	спестяваше
той	спестява	спести	спестяваше
ние	спестяваме	спестихме	спестявахме
вие	спестявате	спестихте	спестявахте
те	спестяват	спестиха	спестяваха

	Future	**Future in the Past**
	(For negative, replace **ще** with **няма да**)	(For negative, replace **щях/щеше/щяхме/щяхте/щяха** with **нямаше**)
аз	ще спестявам/спестя	щях да спестявам/спестя
ти	ще спестяваш/спестиш	щеше да спестяваш/спестиш
той	ще спестява/спести	щеше да спестява/спести
ние	ще спестяваме/спестим	щяхме да спестяваме/спестим
вие	ще спестявате/спестите	щяхте да спестявате/спестите
те	ще спестяват/спестят	щяха да спестяват/спестят

Past Active Participles

M	**F**	**N**	**Pl**
спестявал/ спестил	спестявала/спестила	спестявало/спестило	спестявали/спестили

	Present Perfect	**Past Perfect**
аз	съм спестявал/спестил	бях спестявал/спестил
ти	си спестявал/спестил	беше спестявал/спестил
той	е спестявал/спестил	беше спестявал/спестил
ние	сме спестявали/спестили	бяхме спестявали/спестили
вие	сте спестявали/спестили	бяхте спестявали/спестили
те	са спестявали/спестили	бяха спестявали/спестили

	Conditional Mood	**Imperative Mood**	
		Positive	**Negative**
аз	бих спестявал/спестил		
ти	би спестявал/спестил	спестявай/спести	не спестявай
той	би спестявал/спестил		
ние	бихме спестявали/спестили		
вие	бихте спестявали/спестили	спестявайте/спестете	не спестявайте
те	биха спестявали/спестили		

Past Passive Participles

M	**F**	**N**	**Pl**
спестяван/ спестен	спестявана/спестена	спестявано/спестено	спестявани/спестени

211) **спирам/спра;** *stop, discontinue*

	Present	Past Simple	Past Continuous
аз	спирам	спрях	спирах
ти	спираш	спря	спираше
той	спира	спря	спираше
ние	спираме	спряхме	спирахме
вие	спирате	спряхте	спирахте
те	спират	спряха	спираха

	Future	Future in the Past
	(For negative, replace **ще** with **няма да**)	(For negative, replace **щях/щеше/щяхме/щяхте/щяха** with **нямаше**)
аз	ще спирам/спра	щях да спирам/спра
ти	ще спираш/спреш	щеше да спираш/спреш
той	ще спира/спре	щеше да спира/спре
ние	ще спираме/спрем	щяхме да спираме/спрем
вие	ще спирате/спрете	щяхте да спирате/спрете
те	ще спират/спрат	щяха да спират/спрат

Past Active Participles

M	F	N	Pl
спирал/спрял	спирала/спряла	спирало/спряло	спирали/спрели

	Present Perfect	Past Perfect
аз	съм спирал/спрял	бях спирал/спрял
ти	си спирал/спрял	беше спирал/спрял
той	е спирал/спрял	беше спирал/спрял
ние	сме спирали/спрели	бяхме спирали/спрели
вие	сте спирали/спрели	бяхте спирали/спрели
те	са спирали/спрели	бяха спирали/спрели

	Conditional Mood	Imperative Mood	
аз	бих спирал/спрял	**Positive**	**Negative**
ти	би спирал/спрял	спирай/спри	не спирай
той	би спирал/спрял		
ние	бихме спирали/спрели		
вие	бихте спирали/спрели	спирайте/спрете	не спирайте
те	биха спирали/спрели		

Past Passive Participles

M	F	N	Pl
спиран/спрян	спирана/спряна	спирано/спряно	спирани/спрени

212) **спомням си/спомня си;** *remember, recall*

	Present	Past Simple	Past Continuous
аз	си спомням	си спомних	си спомнях
ти	си спомняш	си спомни	си спомняше
той	си спомня	си спомни	си спомняше
ние	си спомняме	си спомнихме	си спомняхме
вие	си спомняте	си спомнихте	си спомняхте
те	си спомнят	си спомниха	си спомняха

	Future	Future in the Past
	(For negative, replace **ще** with **няма да**)	(For negative, replace **щях/щеше/щяхме/щяхте/щяха** with **нямаше**)
аз	ще си спомням/спомня	щях да си спомням/спомня
ти	ще си спомняш/спомниш	щеше да си спомняш/спомниш
той	ще си спомня/спомни	щеше да си спомня/спомни
ние	ще си спомняме/спомним	щяхме да си спомняме/спомним
вие	ще си спомняте/спомните	щяхте да си спомняте/спомните
те	ще си спомнят/спомнят	щяха да си спомнят/спомнят

Past Active Participles

M	F	N	Pl
спомнял/ спомнил	спомняла/спомнила	спомняло/спомнило	спомняли/ спомнили

	Present Perfect	Past Perfect
аз	съм си спомнял/спомнил	бях си спомнял/спомнил
ти	си си спомнял/спомнил	беше си спомнял/спомнил
той	си е спомнял/спомнил	беше си спомнял/спомнил
ние	сме си спомняли/спомнили	бяхме си спомняли/спомнили
вие	сте си спомняли/спомнили	бяхте си спомняли/спомнили
те	са си спомняли/спомнили	бяха си спомняли/спомнили

	Conditional Mood	Imperative Mood	
аз	бих си спомнял/спомнил	**Positive**	**Negative**
ти	би си спомнял/спомнил	спомняй/спомни си	не си спомняй
той	би си спомнял/спомнил		
ние	бихме си спомняли/спомнили		
вие	бихте си спомняли/спомнили	спомняйте/спомнете си	не си спомняйте
те	биха си спомняли/спомнили		

Past Passive Participles

M	F	N	Pl
N/A	N/A	N/A	N/A

213) **справям се/справя се;** *manage, handle, cope*

	Present	Past Simple	Past Continuous
аз	се справям	се справих	се справях
ти	се справяш	се справи	се справяше
той	се справя	се справи	се справяше
ние	се справяме	се справихме	се справяхме
вие	се справяте	се справихте	се справяхте
те	се справят	се справиха	се справяха

	Future	Future in the Past
	(For negative, replace **ще** with **няма да**)	(For negative, replace **щях/щеше/щяхме/щяхте/щяха** with **нямаше**)
аз	ще се справям/справя	щях да се справям/справя
ти	ще се справяш/справиш	щеше да се справяш/справиш
той	ще се справя/справи	щеше да се справя/справи
ние	ще се справяме/справим	щяхме да се справяме/справим
вие	ще се справяте/справите	щяхте да се справяте/справите
те	ще се справят/справят	щяха да се справят/справят

Past Active Participles

M	F	N	Pl
справял/ справил	справяла/справила	справяло/справило	справяли/справили

	Present Perfect	Past Perfect
аз	съм се справял/справил	бях се справял/справил
ти	си се справял/справил	беше се справял/справил
той	се е справял/справил	беше се справял/справил
ние	сме се справяли/справили	бяхме се справяли/справили
вие	сте се справяли/справили	бяхте се справяли/справили
те	са се справяли/справили	бяха се справяли/справили

	Conditional Mood	Imperative Mood	
аз	бих се справял/справил	**Positive**	**Negative**
ти	би се справял/справил	справяй/справи се	не се справяй
той	би се справял/справил		
ние	бихме се справяли/справили		
вие	бихте се справяли/справили	справяйте/справете се	не се справяйте
те	биха се справяли/справили		

Past Passive Participles

M	F	N	Pl
N/A	N/A	N/A	N/A

214) **спя;** *sleep*

	Present	**Past Simple**	**Past Continuous**
аз	спя	спах	спях
ти	спиш	спа	спеше
той	спи	спа	спеше
ние	спим	спахме	спяхме
вие	спите	спахте	спяхте
те	спят	спаха	спяха

	Future	**Future in the Past**
	(For negative, replace **ще** with **няма да**)	(For negative, replace **щях/щеше/щяхме/щяхте/щяха** with **нямаше**)
аз	ще спя	щях да спя
ти	ще спиш	щеше да спиш
той	ще спи	щеше да спи
ние	ще спим	щяхме да спим
вие	ще спите	щяхте да спите
те	ще спят	щяха да спят

Past Active Participles

M	**F**	**N**	**Pl**
спал	спала	спало	спали

	Present Perfect	**Past Perfect**
аз	съм спал	бях спал
ти	си спал	беше спал
той	е спал	беше спал
ние	сме спали	бяхме спали
вие	сте спали	бяхте спали
те	са спали	бяха спали

	Conditional Mood	**Imperative Mood**	
аз	бих спал	**Positive**	**Negative**
ти	би спал	спи	не спи
той	би спал		
ние	бихме спали		
вие	бихте спали	спете	не спете
те	биха спали		

Past Passive Participles

M	**F**	**N**	**Pl**
N/A	N/A	N/A	N/A

215) **срещам/срещна;** *meet, get together, encounter*

	Present	Past Simple	Past Continuous
аз	срещам	срещнах	срещах
ти	срещаш	срещна	срещаше
той	среща	срещна	срещаше
ние	срещаме	срещнахме	срещахме
вие	срещате	срещнахте	срещахте
те	срещат	срещнаха	срещаха

	Future	Future in the Past
	(For negative, replace **ще** with **няма да**)	(For negative, replace **щях/щеше/щяхме/щяхте/щяха** with **нямаше**)
аз	ще срещам/срещна	щях да срещам/срещна
ти	ще срещаш/срещнеш	щеше да срещаш/срещнеш
той	ще среща/срещне	щеше да среща/срещне
ние	ще срещаме/срещнем	щяхме да срещаме/срещнем
вие	ще срещате/срещнете	щяхте да срещате/срещнете
те	ще срещат/срещнат	щяха да срещат/срещнат

Past Active Participles

M	F	N	Pl
срещал/ срещнал	срещала/срещнала	срещало/срещнало	срещали/ срещнали

	Present Perfect	Past Perfect
аз	съм срещал/срещнал	бях срещал/срещнал
ти	си срещал/срещнал	беше срещал/срещнал
той	е срещал/срещнал	беше срещал/срещнал
ние	сме срещали/срещнали	бяхме срещали/срещнали
вие	сте срещали/срещнали	бяхте срещали/срещнали
те	са срещали/срещнали	бяха срещали/срещнали

	Conditional Mood	Imperative Mood	
аз	бих срещал/срещнал	**Positive**	**Negative**
ти	би срещал/срещнал	срещай/срещни	не срещай
той	би срещал/срещнал		
ние	бихме срещали/срещнали		
вие	бихте срещали/срещнали	срещайте/срещнете	не срещайте
те	биха срещали/срещнали		

Past Passive Participles

M	F	N	Pl
срещан/ срещнат	срещана/срещната	срещано/срещнато	срещани/срещнати

216) **ставам/стана;** *get up, wake up; become; happen*

	Present	Past Simple	Past Continuous
аз	ставам	станах	ставах
ти	ставаш	стана	ставаше
той	става	стана	ставаше
ние	ставаме	станахме	ставахме
вие	ставате	станахте	ставахте
те	стават	станаха	ставаха

	Future	Future in the Past
	(For negative, replace **ще** with **няма да**)	(For negative, replace **щях/щеше/щяхме/щяхте/щяха** with **нямаше**)
аз	ще ставам/стана	щях да ставам/стана
ти	ще ставаш/станеш	щеше да ставаш/станеш
той	ще става/стане	щеше да става/стане
ние	ще ставаме/станем	щяхме да ставаме/станем
вие	ще ставате/станете	щяхте да ставате/станете
те	ще стават/станат	щяха да стават/станат

Past Active Participles

M	F	N	Pl
ставал/ станал	ставала/станала	ставало/станало	ставали/станали

	Present Perfect	Past Perfect
аз	съм ставал/станал	бях ставал/станал
ти	си ставал/станал	беше ставал/станал
той	е ставал/станал	беше ставал/станал
ние	сме ставали/станали	бяхме ставали/станали
вие	сте ставали/станали	бяхте ставали/станали
те	са ставали/станали	бяха ставали/станали

	Conditional Mood	Imperative Mood	
аз	бих ставал/станал	**Positive**	**Negative**
ти	би ставал/станал	ставай/стани	не ставай
той	би ставал/станал		
ние	бихме ставали/станали		
вие	бихте ставали/станали	ставайте/станете	не ставайте
те	биха ставали/станали		

Past Passive Participles

M	F	N	Pl
N/A	N/A	N/A	N/A

217) **стигам/стигна;** *reach, arrive at, get to*

	Present	**Past Simple**	**Past Continuous**
аз	стигам	стигнах	стигах
ти	стигаш	стигна	стигаше
той	стига	стигна	стигаше
ние	стигаме	стигнахме	стигахме
вие	стигате	стигнахте	стигахте
те	стигат	стигнаха	стигаха

	Future	**Future in the Past**
	(For negative, replace **ще** with **няма да**)	(For negative, replace **щях/щеше/щяхме/щяхте/щяха** with **нямаше**)
аз	ще стигам/стигна	щях да стигам/стигна
ти	ще стигаш/стигнеш	щеше да стигаш/стигнеш
той	ще стига/стигне	щеше да стига/стигне
ние	ще стигаме/стигнем	щяхме да стигаме/стигнем
вие	ще стигате/стигнете	щяхте да стигате/стигнете
те	ще стигат/стигнат	щяха да стигат/стигнат

Past Active Participles

M	**F**	**N**	**Pl**
стигал/ стигнал	стигала/стигнала	стигало/стигнало	стигали/стигнали

	Present Perfect	**Past Perfect**
аз	съм стигал/стигнал	бях стигал/стигнал
ти	си стигал/стигнал	беше стигал/стигнал
той	е стигал/стигнал	беше стигал/стигнал
ние	сме стигали/стигнали	бяхме стигали/стигнали
вие	сте стигали/стигнали	бяхте стигали/стигнали
те	са стигали/стигнали	бяха стигали/стигнали

	Conditional Mood	**Imperative Mood**	
аз	бих стигал/стигнал	**Positive**	**Negative**
ти	би стигал/стигнал	стигай/стигни	не стигай
той	би стигал/стигнал		
ние	бихме стигали/стигнали		
вие	бихте стигали/стигнали	стигайте/стигнете	не стигайте
те	биха стигали/стигнали		

Past Passive Participles

M	**F**	**N**	**Pl**
N/A	N/A	N/A	N/A

218) **стоя;** *stay, wait; reside*

	Present	**Past Simple**	**Past Continuous**
аз	стоя	стоях	стоях
ти	стоиш	стоя	стоеше
той	стои	стоя	стоеше
ние	стоим	стояхме	стояхме
вие	стоите	стояхте	стояхте
те	стоят	стояха	стояха

	Future	**Future in the Past**
	(For negative, replace **ще** with **няма да**)	(For negative, replace **щях/щеше/щяхме/щяхте/щяха** with **нямаше**)
аз	ще стоя	щях да стоя
ти	ще стоиш	щеше да стоиш
той	ще стои	щеше да стои
ние	ще стоим	щяхме да стоим
вие	ще стоите	щяхте да стоите
те	ще стоят	щяха да стоят

Past Active Participles

M	**F**	**N**	**Pl**
стоял	стояла	стояло	стояли

	Present Perfect	**Past Perfect**
аз	съм стоял	бях стоял
ти	си стоял	беше стоял
той	е стоял	беше стоял
ние	сме стояли	бяхме стояли
вие	сте стояли	бяхте стояли
те	са стояли	бяха стояли

	Conditional Mood	**Imperative Mood**	
аз	бих стоял	**Positive**	**Negative**
ти	би стоял	стой	не стой
той	би стоял		
ние	бихме стояли		
вие	бихте стояли	стойте	не стойте
те	биха стояли		

Past Passive Participles

M	**F**	**N**	**Pl**
N/A	N/A	N/A	N/A

219) **събуждам/събудя;** *wake, awaken, arouse*
събуждам/събудя се; *wake up, get up*

	Present	Past Simple	Past Continuous
аз	събуждам	събудих	събуждах
ти	събуждаш	събуди	събуждаше
той	събужда	събуди	събуждаше
ние	събуждаме	събудихме	събуждахме
вие	събуждате	събудихте	събуждахте
те	събуждат	събудиха	събуждаха

	Future	Future in the Past
	(For negative, replace **ще** with **няма да**)	(For negative, replace **щях/щеше/щяхме/щяхте/щяха** with **нямаше**)
аз	ще събуждам/събудя	щях да събуждам/събудя
ти	ще събуждаш/събудиш	щеше да събуждаш/събудиш
той	ще събужда/събуди	щеше да събужда/събуди
ние	ще събуждаме/събудим	щяхме да събуждаме/събудим
вие	ще събуждате/събудите	щяхте да събуждате/събудите
те	ще събуждат/събудят	щяха да събуждат/събудят

Past Active Participles

M	F	N	Pl
събуждал/ събудил	събуждала/събудила	събуждало/събудило	събуждали/събудили

	Present Perfect	Past Perfect
аз	съм събуждал/събудил	бях събуждал/събудил
ти	си събуждал/събудил	беше събуждал/събудил
той	е събуждал/събудил	беше събуждал/събудил
ние	сме събуждали/събудили	бяхме събуждали/събудили
вие	сте събуждали/събудили	бяхте събуждали/събудили
те	са събуждали/събудили	бяха събуждали/събудили

		Imperative Mood	
аз	бих събуждал/събудил	**Positive**	**Negative**
ти	би събуждал/събудил	събуждай/събуди	не събуждай
той	би събуждал/събудил		
ние	бихме събуждали/събудили		
вие	бихте събуждали/събудили	събуждайте/събудете	не събуждайте
те	биха събуждали/събудили		

Past Passive Participles

M	F	N	Pl
събуждан/ събуден	събуждана/събудена	събуждано/събудено	събуждани/събудени

220) **съжалявам/съжаля;** *feel sorry, regret*

	Present	**Past Simple**	**Past Continuous**
аз	съжалявам	съжалих	съжалявах
ти	съжаляваш	съжали	съжаляваше
той	съжалява	съжали	съжаляваше
ние	съжаляваме	съжалихме	съжалявахме
вие	съжалявате	съжалихте	съжалявахте
те	съжаляват	съжалиха	съжаляваха

	Future	**Future in the Past**
	(For negative, replace **ще** with **няма да**)	(For negative, replace **щях/щеше/щяхме/щяхте/щяха** with **нямаше**)
аз	ще съжалявам/съжаля	щях да съжалявам/съжаля
ти	ще съжаляваш/съжалиш	щеше да съжаляваш/съжалиш
той	ще съжалява/съжали	щеше да съжалява/съжали
ние	ще съжаляваме/съжалим	щяхме да съжаляваме/съжалим
вие	ще съжалявате/съжалите	щяхте да съжалявате/съжалите
те	ще съжаляват/съжалят	щяха да съжаляват/съжалят

Past Active Participles

M	**F**	**N**	**Pl**
съжалявал/ съжалил	съжалявала/съжалила	съжалявало/съжалило	съжалявали/съжалили

	Present Perfect	**Past Perfect**
аз	съм съжалявал/съжалил	бях съжалявал/съжалил
ти	си съжалявал/съжалил	беше съжалявал/съжалил
той	е съжалявал/съжалил	беше съжалявал/съжалил
ние	сме съжалявали/съжалили	бяхме съжалявали/съжалили
вие	сте съжалявали/съжалили	бяхте съжалявали/съжалили
те	са съжалявали/съжалили	бяха съжалявали/съжалили

	Conditional Mood	**Imperative Mood**	
		Positive	**Negative**
аз	бих съжалявал/съжалил		
ти	би съжалявал/съжалил	съжалявай/съжали	не съжалявай
той	би съжалявал/съжалил		
ние	бихме съжалявали/съжалили		
вие	бихте съжалявали/съжалили	съжалявайте/съжалете	не съжалявайте
те	биха съжалявали/съжалили		

Past Passive Participles

M	**F**	**N**	**Pl**
съжаляван/ съжален	съжалявана/съжалена	съжалявано/съжалено	съжалявани/съжалени

221) **съм;** *be*

	Present	Past Simple = Past Continuous
аз	съм	бях
ти	си	беше
той	е	беше
ние	сме	бяхме
вие	сте	бяхте
те	са	бяха

	Future	Future in the Past
	(For negative, replace **ще** with **няма да**)	(For negative, replace **щях/щеше/щяхме/щяхте/щяха** with **нямаше**)
аз	ще бъда/съм	щях да бъда/съм
ти	ще бъдеш/си	щеше да бъдеш/си
той	ще бъде/е	щеше да бъде/е
ние	ще бъдем/сме	щяхме да бъдем/сме
вие	ще бъдете/сте	щяхте да бъдете/сте
те	ще бъдат/са	щяха да бъдат/са

Past Active Participles

M	F	N	Pl
бил	била	било	били

	Present Perfect	Past Perfect
аз	съм бил	N/A
ти	си бил	N/A
той	е бил	N/A
ние	сме били	N/A
вие	сте били	N/A
те	са били	N/A

	Conditional Mood	Imperative Mood	
аз	бих бил	**Positive**	**Negative**
ти	би бил	Бъди	не бъди
той	би бил		
ние	бихме били		
вие	бихте били	бъдете	не бъдете
те	биха били		

Past Passive Participles

M	F	N	Pl
N/A	N/A	N/A	N/A

222) **съобщавам/съобщя;** *announce, declare*

	Present	**Past Simple**	**Past Continuous**
аз	съобщавам	съобщих	съобщавах
ти	съобщаваш	съобщи	съобщаваше
той	съобщава	съобщи	съобщаваше
ние	съобщаваме	съобщихме	съобщавахме
вие	съобщавате	съобщихте	съобщавахте
те	съобщават	съобщиха	съобщаваха

	Future	**Future in the Past**
	(For negative, replace **ще** with **няма да**)	(For negative, replace **щях/щеше/щяхме/щяхте/щяха** with **нямаше**)
аз	ще съобщавам/съобщя	щях да съобщавам/съобщя
ти	ще съобщаваш/съобщиш	щеше да съобщаваш/съобщиш
той	ще съобщава/съобщи	щеше да съобщава/съобщи
ние	ще съобщаваме/съобщим	щяхме да съобщаваме/съобщим
вие	ще съобщавате/съобщите	щяхте да съобщавате/съобщите
те	ще съобщават/съобщят	щяха да съобщават/съобщят

Past Active Participles

M	**F**	**N**	**Pl**
съобщавал/ съобщил	съобщавала/ съобщила	съобщавало/ съобщило	съобщавали/ съобщили

	Present Perfect	**Past Perfect**
аз	съм съобщавал/съобщил	бях съобщавал/съобщил
ти	си съобщавал/съобщил	беше съобщавал/съобщил
той	е съобщавал/съобщил	беше съобщавал/съобщил
ние	сме съобщавали/съобщили	бяхме съобщавали/съобщили
вие	сте съобщавали/съобщили	бяхте съобщавали/съобщили
те	са съобщавали/съобщили	бяха съобщавали/съобщили

	Conditional Mood	**Imperative Mood**	
аз	бих съобщавал/съобщил	**Positive**	**Negative**
ти	би съобщавал/съобщил	съобщавай/съобщи	не съобщавай
той	би съобщавал/съобщил		
ние	бихме съобщавали/съобщили		
вие	бихте съобщавали/съобщили	съобщавайте/съобщете	не съобщавайте
те	биха съобщавали/съобщили		

Past Passive Participles

M	**F**	**N**	**Pl**
съобщаван/ съобщен	съобщавана/ съобщена	съобщавано/ съобщено	съобщавани/ съобщени

223) **сядам/седна;** *sit, take a seat*

	Present	Past Simple	Past Continuous
аз	сядам	седнах	сядах
ти	сядаш	седна	сядаше
той	сяда	седна	сядаше
ние	сядаме	седнахме	сядахме
вие	сядате	седнахте	сядахте
те	сядат	седнаха	сядаха

	Future	Future in the Past
	(For negative, replace **ще** with **няма да**)	(For negative, replace **щях/щеше/щяхме/щяхте/щяха** with **нямаше**)
аз	ще сядам/седна	щях да сядам/седна
ти	ще сядаш/седнеш	щеше да сядаш/седнеш
той	ще сяда/седне	щеше да сяда/седне
ние	ще сядаме/седнем	щяхме да сядаме/седнем
вие	ще сядате/седнете	щяхте да сядате/седнете
те	ще сядат/седнат	щяха да сядат/седнат

Past Active Participles

M	F	N	Pl
сядал/седнал	сядала/седнала	сядало/седнало	сядали/седнали

	Present Perfect	Past Perfect
аз	съм сядал/седнал	бях сядал/седнал
ти	си сядал/седнал	беше сядал/седнал
той	е сядал/седнал	беше сядал/седнал
ние	сме сядали/седнали	бяхме сядали/седнали
вие	сте сядали/седнали	бяхте сядали/седнали
те	са сядали/седнали	бяха сядали/седнали

	Conditional Mood	Imperative Mood	
аз	бих сядал/седнал	**Positive**	**Negative**
ти	би сядал/седнал	сядай/седни	не сядай
той	би сядал/седнал		
ние	бихме сядали/седнали		
вие	бихте сядали/седнали	сядайте/седнете	не сядайте
те	биха сядали/седнали		

Past Passive Participles

M	F	N	Pl
N/A	N/A	N/A	N/A

224) **тръгвам/тръгна;** *leave, depart*

	Present	Past Simple	Past Continuous
аз	тръгвам	тръгнах	тръгвах
ти	тръгваш	тръгна	тръгваше
той	тръгва	тръгна	тръгваше
ние	тръгваме	тръгнахме	тръгвахме
вие	тръгвате	тръгнахте	тръгвахте
те	тръгват	тръгнаха	тръгваха

	Future	Future in the Past
	(For negative, replace **ще** with **няма да**)	(For negative, replace **щях/щеше/щяхме/щяхте/щяха** with **нямаше**)
аз	ще тръгвам/тръгна	щях да тръгвам/тръгна
ти	ще тръгваш/тръгнеш	щеше да тръгваш/тръгнеш
той	ще тръгва/тръгне	щеше да тръгва/тръгне
ние	ще тръгваме/тръгнем	щяхме да тръгваме/тръгнем
вие	ще тръгвате/тръгнете	щяхте да тръгвате/тръгнете
те	ще тръгват/тръгнат	щяха да тръгват/тръгнат

Past Active Participles

M	F	N	Pl
тръгвал/тръгнал	тръгвала/тръгнала	тръгвало/тръгнало	тръгвали/тръгнали

	Present Perfect	Past Perfect
аз	съм тръгвал/тръгнал	бях тръгвал/тръгнал
ти	си тръгвал/тръгнал	беше тръгвал/тръгнал
той	е тръгвал/тръгнал	беше тръгвал/тръгнал
ние	сме тръгвали/тръгнали	бяхме тръгвали/тръгнали
вие	сте тръгвали/тръгнали	бяхте тръгвали/тръгнали
те	са тръгвали/тръгнали	бяха тръгвали/тръгнали

	Conditional Mood	Imperative Mood	
аз	бих тръгвал/тръгнал	**Positive**	**Negative**
ти	би тръгвал/тръгнал	тръгвай/тръгни	не тръгвай
той	би тръгвал/тръгнал		
ние	бихме тръгвали/тръгнали		
вие	бихте тръгвали/тръгнали	тръгвайте/тръгнете	не тръгвайте
те	биха тръгвали/тръгнали		

Past Passive Participles

M	F	N	Pl
N/A	N/A	N/A	N/A

225) **търся;** *look for, search, seek*

	Present	**Past Simple**	**Past Continuous**
аз	търся	търсих	търсех
ти	търсиш	търси	търсеше
той	търси	търси	търсеше
ние	търсим	търсихме	търсехме
вие	търсите	търсихте	търсехте
те	търсят	търсиха	търсеха

	Future	**Future in the Past**
	(For negative, replace **ще** with **няма да**)	(For negative, replace **щях/щеше/щяхме/щяхте/щяха** with **нямаше**)
аз	ще търся	щях да търся
ти	ще търсиш	щеше да търсиш
той	ще търси	щеше да търси
ние	ще търсим	щяхме да търсим
вие	ще търсите	щяхте да търсите
те	ще търсят	щяха да търсят

Past Active Participles

M	**F**	**N**	**Pl**
търсил	търсила	търсило	търсили

	Present Perfect	**Past Perfect**
аз	съм търсил	бях търсил
ти	си търсил	беше търсил
той	е търсил	беше търсил
ние	сме търсили	бяхме търсили
вие	сте търсили	бяхте търсили
те	са търсили	бяха търсили

	Conditional Mood	**Imperative Mood**	
аз	бих търсил	**Positive**	**Negative**
ти	би търсил	търси	не търси
той	би търсил		
ние	бихме търсили		
вие	бихте търсили	търсете	не търсете
те	биха търсили		

Past Passive Participles

M	**F**	**N**	**Pl**
търсен	търсена	търсено	търсени

226) **убивам/убия;** *kill, murder*

	Present	**Past Simple**	**Past Continuous**
аз	убивам	убих	убивах
ти	убиваш	уби	убиваше
той	убива	уби	убиваше
ние	убиваме	убихме	убивахме
вие	убивате	убихте	убивахте
те	убиват	убиха	убиваха

	Future	**Future in the Past**
	(For negative, replace **ще** with **няма да**)	(For negative, replace **щях/щеше/щяхме/щяхте/щяха** with **нямаше**)
аз	ще убивам/убия	щях да убивам/убия
ти	ще убиваш/убиеш	щеше да убиваш/убиеш
той	ще убива/убие	щеше да убива/убие
ние	ще убиваме/убием	щяхме да убиваме/убием
вие	ще убивате/убиете	щяхте да убивате/убиете
те	ще убиват/убият	щяха да убиват/убият

Past Active Participles

M	**F**	**N**	**Pl**
убивал/убил	убивала/убила	убивало/убило	убивали/убили

	Present Perfect	**Past Perfect**
аз	съм убивал/убил	бях убивал/убил
ти	си убивал/убил	беше убивал/убил
той	е убивал/убил	беше убивал/убил
ние	сме убивали/убили	бяхме убивали/убили
вие	сте убивали/убили	бяхте убивали/убили
те	са убивали/убили	бяха убивали/убили

	Conditional Mood	**Imperative Mood**	
аз	бих убивал/убил	**Positive**	**Negative**
ти	би убивал/убил	убивай/убий	не убивай
той	би убивал/убил		
ние	бихме убивали/убили		
вие	бихте убивали/убили	убивайте/убийте	не убивайте
те	биха убивали/убили		

Past Passive Participles

M	**F**	**N**	**Pl**
убиван/убит	убивана/убита	убивано/убито	убивани/убити

227) **увеличавам/увелича;** *increase, enlarge, raise*

	Present	Past Simple	Past Continuous
аз	увеличавам	увеличих	увеличавах
ти	увеличаваш	увеличи	увеличаваше
той	увеличава	увеличи	увеличаваше
ние	увеличаваме	увеличихме	увеличавахме
вие	увеличавате	увеличихте	увеличавахте
те	увеличават	увеличиха	увеличаваха

	Future	Future in the Past
	(For negative, replace **ще** with **няма да**)	(For negative, replace **щях/щеше/щяхме/щяхте/щяха** with **нямаше**)
аз	ще увеличавам/увелича	щях да увеличавам/увелича
ти	ще увеличаваш/увеличиш	щеше да увеличаваш/увеличиш
той	ще увеличава/увеличи	щеше да увеличава/увеличи
ние	ще увеличаваме/увеличим	щяхме да увеличаваме/увеличим
вие	ще увеличавате/увеличите	щяхте да увеличавате/увеличите
те	ще увеличават/увеличат	щяха да увеличават/увеличат

Past Active Participles

M	F	N	Pl
увеличавал/ увеличил	увеличавала/ увеличила	увеличавало/ увеличило	увеличавали/ увеличили

	Present Perfect	Past Perfect
аз	съм увеличавал/увеличил	бях увеличавал/увеличил
ти	си увеличавал/увеличил	беше увеличавал/увеличил
той	е увеличавал/увеличил	беше увеличавал/увеличил
ние	сме увеличавали/увеличили	бяхме увеличавали/увеличили
вие	сте увеличавали/увеличили	бяхте увеличавали/увеличили
те	са увеличавали/увеличили	бяха увеличавали/увеличили

	Conditional Mood	Imperative Mood	
аз	бих увеличавал/увеличил	**Positive**	**Negative**
ти	би увеличавал/увеличил	увеличавай/увеличи	не увеличавай
той	би увеличавал/увеличил		
ние	бихме увеличавали/увеличили		
вие	бихте увеличавали/увеличили	увеличавайте/увеличете	не увеличавайте
те	биха увеличавали/увеличили		

Past Passive Participles

M	F	N	Pl
увеличаван/ увеличен	увеличавана/ увеличена	увеличавано/ увеличено	увеличавани/ увеличени

228) **умирам/умра;** *die, pass away*

	Present	**Past Simple**	**Past Continuous**
аз	умирам	умрях	умирах
ти	умираш	умря	умираше
той	умира	умря	умираше
ние	умираме	умряхме	умирахме
вие	умирате	умряхте	умирахте
те	умират	умряха	умираха

	Future	**Future in the Past**
	(For negative, replace **ще** with **няма да**)	(For negative, replace **щях/щеше/щяхме/щяхте/щяха** with **нямаше**)
аз	ще умирам/умра	щях да умирам/умра
ти	ще умираш/умреш	щеше да умираш/умреш
той	ще умира/умре	щеше да умира/умре
ние	ще умираме/умрем	щяхме да умираме/умрем
вие	ще умирате/умрете	щяхте да умирате/умрете
те	ще умират/умрат	щяха да умират/умрат

Past Active Participles

M	**F**	**N**	**Pl**
умирал/умрял	умирала/умряла	умирало/умряло	умирали/умрели

	Present Perfect	**Past Perfect**
аз	съм умирал/умрял	бях умирал/умрял
ти	си умирал/умрял	беше умирал/умрял
той	е умирал/умрял	беше умирал/умрял
ние	сме умирали/умрели	бяхме умирали/умрели
вие	сте умирали/умрели	бяхте умирали/умрели
те	са умирали/умрели	бяха умирали/умрели

	Conditional Mood	**Imperative Mood**	
аз	бих умирал/умрял	**Positive**	**Negative**
ти	би умирал/умрял	умирай/умри	не умирай
той	би умирал/умрял		
ние	бихме умирали/умрели		
вие	бихте умирали/умрели	умирайте/умрете	не умирайте
те	биха умирали/умрели		

Past Passive Participles

M	**F**	**N**	**Pl**
N/A	N/A	N/A	N/A

229) **употребявам/употребя;** *use, employ*

	Present	Past Simple	Past Continuous
аз	употребявам	употребих	употребих
ти	употребяваш	употреби	употреби
той	употребява	употреби	употреби
ние	употребяваме	употребихме	употребихме
вие	употребявате	употребихте	употребихте
те	употребяват	употребиха	употребиха

	Future	Future in the Past
	(For negative, replace **ще** with **няма да**)	(For negative, replace **щях/щеше/щяхме/щяхте/щяха** with **нямаше**)
аз	ще употребявам/употребя	щях да употребявам/употребя
ти	ще употребяваш/употребиш	щеше да употребяваш/употребиш
той	ще употребява/употреби	щеше да употребява/употреби
ние	ще употребяваме/употребим	щяхме да употребяваме/употребим
вие	ще употребявате/употребите	щяхте да употребявате/употребите
те	ще употребяват/употребят	щяха да употребяват/употребят

Past Active Participles

M	F	N	Pl
употребявал/ употребил	употребявала/ употребила	употребявало/ употребило	употребявали/ употребили

	Present Perfect	Past Perfect
аз	съм употребявал/употребил	бях употребявал/употребил
ти	си употребявал/употребил	беше употребявал/употребил
той	е употребявал/употребил	беше употребявал/употребил
ние	сме употребявали/употребили	бяхме употребявали/употребили
вие	сте употребявали/употребили	бяхте употребявали/употребили
те	са употребявали/употребили	бяха употребявали/употребили

	Conditional Mood	Imperative Mood	
аз	бих употребявал/употребил	**Positive**	**Negative**
ти	би употребявал/употребил	употребявай/употреби	не употребявай
той	би употребявал/употребил		
ние	бихме употребявали/употребили		
вие	бихте употребявали/употребили	употребявайте/употребете	не употребявайте
те	биха употребявали/употребили		

Past Passive Participles

M	F	N	Pl
употребяван/ употребен	употребявана/ употребена	употребявано/ употребено	употребявани/ употребени

230) **уреждам/уредя;** *arrange, settle*

	Present	**Past Simple**	**Past Continuous**
аз	уреждам	уредих	уреждах
ти	уреждаш	уреди	уреждаше
той	урежда	уреди	уреждаше
ние	уреждаме	уредихме	уреждахме
вие	уреждате	уредихте	уреждахте
те	уреждат	уредиха	уреждаха

	Future	**Future in the Past**
	(For negative, replace **ще** with **няма да**)	(For negative, replace **щях/щеше/щяхме/щяхте/щяха** with **нямаше**)
аз	ще уреждам/уредя	щях да уреждам/уредя
ти	ще уреждаш/уредиш	щеше да уреждаш/уредиш
той	ще урежда/уреди	щеше да урежда/уреди
ние	ще уреждаме/уредим	щяхме да уреждаме/уредим
вие	ще уреждате/уредите	щяхте да уреждате/уредите
те	ще уреждат/уредят	щяха да уреждат/уредят

Past Active Participles

M	**F**	**N**	**Pl**
уреждал/уредил	уреждала/уредила	уреждало/уредило	уреждали/уредили

	Present Perfect	**Past Perfect**
аз	съм уреждал/уредил	бях уреждал/уредил
ти	си уреждал/уредил	беше уреждал/уредил
той	е уреждал/уредил	беше уреждал/уредил
ние	сме уреждали/уредили	бяхме уреждали/уредили
вие	сте уреждали/уредили	бяхте уреждали/уредили
те	са уреждали/уредили	бяха уреждали/уредили

	Conditional Mood	**Imperative Mood**	
аз	бих уреждал/уредил	**Positive**	**Negative**
ти	би уреждал/уредил	уреждай/уреди	не уреждай
той	би уреждал/уредил		
ние	бихме уреждали/уредили		
вие	бихте уреждали/уредили	уреждайте/уредете	не уреждайте
те	биха уреждали/уредили		

Past Passive Participles

M	**F**	**N**	**Pl**
уреждан/уреден	уреждана/уредена	уреждано/уредено	уреждани/уредени

231) **усмихвам се/усмихна се;** *smile*

	Present	Past Simple	Past Continuous
аз	се усмихвам	се усмихнах	се усмихвах
ти	се усмихваш	се усмихна	се усмихваше
той	се усмихва	се усмихна	се усмихваше
ние	се усмихваме	се усмихнахме	се усмихвахме
вие	се усмихвате	се усмихнахте	се усмихвахте
те	се усмихват	се усмихнаха	се усмихваха

	Future	Future in the Past
	(For negative, replace **ще** with **няма да**)	(For negative, replace **щях/щеше/щяхме/щяхте/щяха** with **нямаше**)
аз	ще се усмихвам/усмихна	щях да се усмихвам/усмихна
ти	ще се усмихваш/усмихнеш	щеше да се усмихваш/усмихнеш
той	ще се усмихва/усмихне	щеше да се усмихва/усмихне
ние	ще се усмихваме/усмихнем	щяхме да се усмихваме/усмихнем
вие	ще се усмихвате/усмихнете	щяхте да се усмихвате/усмихнете
те	ще се усмихват/усмихнат	щяха да се усмихват/усмихнат

Past Active Participles

M	F	N	Pl
усмихвал/ усмихнал	усмихвала/ усмихнала	усмихвало/ усмихнало	усмихвали/ усмихнали

	Present Perfect	Past Perfect
аз	съм се усмихвал/усмихнал	бях се усмихвал/усмихнал
ти	си се усмихвал/усмихнал	беше се усмихвал/усмихнал
той	се е усмихвал/усмихнал	беше се усмихвал/усмихнал
ние	сме се усмихвали/усмихнали	бяхме се усмихвали/усмихнали
вие	сте се усмихвали/усмихнали	бяхте се усмихвали/усмихнали
те	са се усмихвали/усмихнали	бяха се усмихвали/усмихнали

	Conditional Mood	Imperative Mood	
		Positive	**Negative**
аз	бих се усмихвал/усмихнал		
ти	би се усмихвал/усмихнал	усмихвай/усмихни се	не се усмихвай
той	би се усмихвал/усмихнал		
ние	бихме се усмихвали/усмихнали		
вие	бихте се усмихвали/усмихнали	усмихвайте/усмихнете се	не се усмихвайте
те	биха се усмихвали/усмихнали		

Past Passive Participles

M	F	N	Pl
N/A	N/A	N/A	N/A

232) **успокоявам/успокоя;** *calm down, relax*

	Present	**Past Simple**	**Past Continuous**
аз	успокоявам	успокоих	успокоявах
ти	успокояваш	успокои	успокояваше
той	успокоява	успокои	успокояваше
ние	успокояваме	успокоихме	успокоявахме
вие	успокоявате	успокоихте	успокоявахте
те	успокояват	успокоиха	успокояваха

	Future	**Future in the Past**
	(For negative, replace **ще** with **няма да**)	(For negative, replace **щях/щеше/щяхме/щяхте/щяха** with **нямаше**)
аз	ще успокоявам/успокоя	щях да успокоявам/успокоя
ти	ще успокояваш/успокоиш	щеше да успокояваш/успокоиш
той	ще успокоява/успокои	щеше да успокоява/успокои
ние	ще успокояваме/успокоим	щяхме да успокояваме/успокоим
вие	ще успокоявате/успокоите	щяхте да успокоявате/успокоите
те	ще успокояват/успокоят	щяха да успокояват/успокоят

Past Active Participles

M	**F**	**N**	**Pl**
успокоявал/ успокоил	успокоявала/ успокоила	успокоявало/ успокоило	успокоявали/ успокоили

	Present Perfect	**Past Perfect**
аз	съм успокоявал/успокоил	бях успокоявал/успокоил
ти	си успокоявал/успокоил	беше успокоявал/успокоил
той	е успокоявал/успокоил	беше успокоявал/успокоил
ние	сме успокоявали/успокоили	бяхме успокоявали/успокоили
вие	сте успокоявали/успокоили	бяхте успокоявали/успокоили
те	са успокоявали/успокоили	бяха успокоявали/успокоили

	Conditional Mood	**Imperative Mood**	
аз	бих успокоявал/успокоил	**Positive**	**Negative**
ти	би успокоявал/успокоил	успокоявай/успокой	не успокоявай
той	би успокоявал/успокоил		
ние	бихме успокоявали/успокоили		
вие	бихте успокоявали/успокоили	успокоявайте/успокойте	не успокоявайте
те	биха успокоявали/успокоили		

Past Passive Participles

M	**F**	**N**	**Pl**
успокояван/ успокоен	успокоявана/ успокоена	успокоявано/ успокоено	успокоявани/ успокоени

233) **успявам/успея;** *succeed, achieve, accomplish*

	Present	**Past Simple**	**Past Continuous**
аз	успявам	успях	успявах
ти	успяваш	успя	успяваше
той	успява	успя	успяваше
ние	успяваме	успяхме	успявахме
вие	успявате	успяхте	успявахте
те	успяват	успяха	успяваха

	Future	**Future in the Past**
	(For negative, replace **ще** with **няма да**)	(For negative, replace **щях/щеше/щяхме/щяхте/щяха** with **нямаше**)
аз	ще успявам/успея	щях да успявам/успея
ти	ще успяваш/успееш	щеше да успяваш/успееш
той	ще успява/успее	щеше да успява/успее
ние	ще успяваме/успеем	щяхме да успяваме/успеем
вие	ще успявате/успеете	щяхте да успявате/успеете
те	ще успяват/успеят	щяха да успяват/успеят

Past Active Participles

M	**F**	**N**	**Pl**
успявал/успял	успявала/успяла	успявало/успяло	успявали/успели

	Present Perfect	**Past Perfect**
аз	съм успявал/успял	бях успявал/успял
ти	си успявал/успял	беше успявал/успял
той	е успявал/успял	беше успявал/успял
ние	сме успявали/успели	бяхме успявали/успели
вие	сте успявали/успели	бяхте успявали/успели
те	са успявали/успели	бяха успявали/успели

	Conditional Mood	**Imperative Mood**	
аз	бих успявал/успял	**Positive**	**Negative**
ти	би успявал/успял	успявай/успей	не успявай
той	би успявал/успял		
ние	бихме успявали/успели		
вие	бихте успявали/успели	успявайте/успейте	не успявайте
те	биха успявали/успели		

Past Passive Participles

M	**F**	**N**	**Pl**
N/A	N/A	N/A	N/A

234) **уча;** *study, learn*

	Present	**Past Simple**	**Past Continuous**
аз	уча	учих	учех
ти	учиш	учи	учеше
той	учи	учи	учеше
ние	учим	учихме	учехме
вие	учите	учихте	учехте
те	учат	учиха	учеха

	Future	**Future in the Past**
	(For negative, replace **ще** with **няма да**)	(For negative, replace **щях/щеше/щяхме/щяхте/щяха** with **нямаше**)
аз	ще уча	щях да уча
ти	ще учиш	щеше да учиш
той	ще учи	щеше да учи
ние	ще учим	щяхме да учим
вие	ще учите	щяхте да учите
те	ще учат	щяха да учат

Past Active Participles

M	**F**	**N**	**Pl**
учил	учила	учило	учили

	Present Perfect	**Past Perfect**
аз	съм учил	бях учил
ти	си учил	беше учил
той	е учил	беше учил
ние	сме учили	бяхме учили
вие	сте учили	бяхте учили
те	са учили	бяха учили

	Conditional Mood	**Imperative Mood**	
аз	бих учил	**Positive**	**Negative**
ти	би учил	учи	не учи
той	би учил		
ние	бихме учили		
вие	бихте учили	учете	не учете
те	биха учили		

Past Passive Participles

M	**F**	**N**	**Pl**
учен	учена	учено	учени

235) **харесвам/харесам;** *like, love, adore*

	Present	**Past Simple**	**Past Continuous**
аз	харесвам	харесах	харесвах
ти	харесваш	хареса	харесваше
той	харесва	хареса	харесваше
ние	харесваме	харесахме	харесвахме
вие	харесвате	харесахте	харесвахте
те	харесват	харесаха	харесваха

	Future	**Future in the Past**
	(For negative, replace **ще** with **няма да**)	(For negative, replace **щях/щеше/щяхме/щяхте/щяха** with **нямаше**)
аз	ще харесвам/харесам	щях да харесвам/харесам
ти	ще харесваш/харесаш	щеше да харесваш/харесаш
той	ще харесва/хареса	щеше да харесва/хареса
ние	ще харесваме/харесаме	щяхме да харесваме/харесаме
вие	ще харесвате/харесате	щяхте да харесвате/харесате
те	ще харесват/харесат	щяха да харесват/харесат

Past Active Participles

M	**F**	**N**	**Pl**
харесвал/ харесал	харесвала/харесала	харесвало/харесало	харесвали/харесали

	Present Perfect	**Past Perfect**
аз	съм харесвал/харесал	бях харесвал/харесал
ти	си харесвал/харесал	беше харесвал/харесал
той	е харесвал/харесал	беше харесвал/харесал
ние	сме харесвали/харесали	бяхме харесвали/харесали
вие	сте харесвали/харесали	бяхте харесвали/харесали
те	са харесвали/харесали	бяха харесвали/харесали

	Conditional Mood	**Imperative Mood**	
аз	бих харесвал/харесал	**Positive**	**Negative**
ти	би харесвал/харесал	харесвай/харесай	не харесвай
той	би харесвал/харесал		
ние	бихме харесвали/харесали		
вие	бихте харесвали/харесали	харесвайте/харесайте	не харесвайте
те	биха харесвали/харесали		

Past Passive Participles

M	**F**	**N**	**Pl**
харесван/ харесан	харесвана/ харесана	харесвано/ харесано	харесвани/ харесани

236) **хващам/хвана;** *catch, grab, take*

	Present	**Past Simple**	**Past Continuous**
аз	хващам	хванах	хващах
ти	хващаш	хвана	хващаше
той	хваща	хвана	хващаше
ние	хващаме	хванахме	хващахме
вие	хващате	хванахте	хващахте
те	хващат	хванаха	хващаха

	Future	**Future in the Past**
	(For negative, replace **ще** with **няма да**)	(For negative, replace **щях/щеше/щяхме/щяхте/щяха** with **нямаше**)
аз	ще хващам/хвана	щях да хващам/хвана
ти	ще хващаш/хванеш	щеше да хващаш/хванеш
той	ще хваща/хване	щеше да хваща/хване
ние	ще хващаме/хванем	щяхме да хващаме/хванем
вие	ще хващате/хванете	щяхте да хващате/хванете
те	ще хващат/хванат	щяха да хващат/хванат

Past Active Participles

M	**F**	**N**	**Pl**
хващал/хванал	хващала/хванала	хващало/хванало	хващали/хванали

	Present Perfect	**Past Perfect**
аз	съм хващал/хванал	бях хващал/хванал
ти	си хващал/хванал	беше хващал/хванал
той	е хващал/хванал	беше хващал/хванал
ние	сме хващали/хванали	бяхме хващали/хванали
вие	сте хващали/хванали	бяхте хващали/хванали
те	са хващали/хванали	бяха хващали/хванали

	Conditional Mood	**Imperative Mood**	
аз	бих хващал/хванал	**Positive**	**Negative**
ти	би хващал/хванал	хващай/хвани	не хващай
той	би хващал/хванал		
ние	бихме хващали/хванали		
вие	бихте хващали/хванали	хващайте/хванете	не хващайте
те	биха хващали/хванали		

Past Passive Participles

M	**F**	**N**	**Pl**
хващан/хванат	хващана/хваната	хващано/хванато	хващани/хванати

237) **хвърлям/хвърля;** *throw, toss*

	Present	**Past Simple**	**Past Continuous**
аз	хвърлям	хвърлих	хвърлях
ти	хвърляш	хвърли	хвърляше
той	хвърля	хвърли	хвърляше
ние	хвърляме	хвърлихме	хвърляхме
вие	хвърляте	хвърлихте	хвърляхте
те	хвърлят	хвърлиха	хвърляха

	Future	**Future in the Past**
	(For negative, replace **ще** with **няма да**)	(For negative, replace **щях/щеше/щяхме/щяхте/щяха** with **нямаше**)
аз	ще хвърлям/хвърля	щях да хвърлям/хвърля
ти	ще хвърляш/хвърлиш	щеше да хвърляш/хвърлиш
той	ще хвърля/хвърли	щеше да хвърля/хвърли
ние	ще хвърляме/хвърлим	щяхме да хвърляме/хвърлим
вие	ще хвърляте/хвърлите	щяхте да хвърляте/хвърлите
те	ще хвърлят/хвърлят	щяха да хвърлят/хвърлят

Past Active Participles

M	**F**	**N**	**Pl**
хвърлял/ хвърлил	хвърляла/хвърлила	хвърляло/хвърлило	хвърляли/хвърлили

	Present Perfect	**Past Perfect**
аз	съм хвърлял/хвърлил	бях хвърлял/хвърлил
ти	си хвърлял/хвърлил	беше хвърлял/хвърлил
той	е хвърлял/хвърлил	беше хвърлял/хвърлил
ние	сме хвърляли/хвърлили	бяхме хвърляли/хвърлили
вие	сте хвърляли/хвърлили	бяхте хвърляли/хвърлили
те	са хвърляли/хвърлили	бяха хвърляли/хвърлили

	Conditional Mood	**Imperative Mood**	
аз	бих хвърлял/хвърлил	**Positive**	**Negative**
ти	би хвърлял/хвърлил	хвърляй/хвърли	не хвърляй
той	би хвърлял/хвърлил		
ние	бихме хвърляли/хвърлили		
вие	бихте хвърляли/хвърлили	хвърляйте/хвърлете	не хвърляйте
те	биха хвърляли/хвърлили		

Past Passive Participles

M	**F**	**N**	**Pl**
хвърлян/хвърлен	хвърляна/хвърлена	хвърляно/хвърлено	хвърляни/хвърлени

238) **ходя;** *go, walk, hike*

	Present	**Past Simple**	**Past Continuous**
аз	ходя	ходих	ходех
ти	ходиш	ходи	ходеше
той	ходи	ходи	ходеше
ние	ходим	ходихме	ходехме
вие	ходите	ходихте	ходехте
те	ходят	ходиха	ходеха

	Future	**Future in the Past**
	(For negative, replace **ще** with **няма да**)	(For negative, replace **щях/щеше/щяхме/щяхте/щяха** with **нямаше**)
аз	ще ходя	щях да ходя
ти	ще ходиш	щеше да ходиш
той	ще ходи	щеше да ходи
ние	ще ходим	щяхме да ходим
вие	ще ходите	щяхте да ходите
те	ще ходят	щяха да ходят

Past Active Participles

M	**F**	**N**	**Pl**
ходил	ходила	ходило	ходили

	Present Perfect	**Past Perfect**
аз	съм ходил	бях ходил
ти	си ходил	беше ходил
той	е ходил	беше ходил
ние	сме ходили	бяхме ходили
вие	сте ходили	бяхте ходили
те	са ходили	бяха ходили

	Conditional Mood	**Imperative Mood**	
аз	бих ходил	**Positive**	**Negative**
ти	би ходил	ходи	не ходи
той	би ходил		
ние	бихме ходили		
вие	бихте ходили	ходете	не ходете
те	биха ходили		

Past Passive Participles

M	**F**	**N**	**Pl**
N/A	N/A	N/A	N/A

239) **храня;** *feed, nurse* **храня се;** *eat, consume, have meals*

	Present	Past Simple	Past Continuous
аз	храня	храних	Хранех
ти	храниш	храни	хранеше
той	храни	храни	хранеше
ние	храним	хранихме	хранехме
вие	храните	хранихте	хранехте
те	хранят	храниха	хранеха

	Future	Future in the Past
	(For negative, replace **ще** with **няма да**)	(For negative, replace **щях/щеше/щяхме/щяхте/щяха** with **нямаше**)
аз	ще храня	щях да храня
ти	ще храниш	щеше да храниш
той	ще храни	щеше да храни
ние	ще храним	щяхме да храним
вие	ще храните	щяхте да храните
те	ще хранят	щяха да хранят

Past Active Participles

M	F	N	Pl
хранил	хранила	хранило	хранили

	Present Perfect	Past Perfect
аз	съм хранил	бях хранил
ти	си хранил	беше хранил
той	е хранил	беше хранил
ние	сме хранили	бяхме хранили
вие	сте хранили	бяхте хранили
те	са хранили	бяха хранили

	Conditional Mood	Imperative Mood	
аз	бих хранил	**Positive**	**Negative**
ти	би хранил	храни	не храни
той	би хранил		
ние	бихме хранили		
вие	бихте хранили	хранете	не хранете
те	биха хранили		

Past Passive Participles

M	F	N	Pl
хранен	хранена	хранено	хранени

240) **целувам/целуна;** *kiss*

	Present	**Past Simple**	**Past Continuous**
аз	целувам	целунах	целувах
ти	целуваш	целуна	целуваше
той	целува	целуна	целуваше
ние	целуваме	целунахме	целувахме
вие	целувате	целунахте	целувахте
те	целуват	целунаха	целуваха

	Future	**Future in the Past**
	(For negative, replace **ще** with **няма да**)	(For negative, replace **щях/щеше/щяхме/щяхте/щяха** with **нямаше**)
аз	ще целувам/целуна	щях да целувам/целуна
ти	ще целуваш/целунеш	щеше да целуваш/целунеш
той	ще целува/целуне	щеше да целува/целуне
ние	ще целуваме/целунем	щяхме да целуваме/целунем
вие	ще целувате/целунете	щяхте да целувате/целунете
те	ще целуват/целунат	щяха да целуват/целунат

Past Active Participles

M	**F**	**N**	**Pl**
целувал/ целунал	целувала/целунала	целувало/целунало	целували/целунали

	Present Perfect	**Past Perfect**
аз	съм целувал/целунал	бях целувал/целунал
ти	си целувал/целунал	беше целувал/целунал
той	е целувал/целунал	беше целувал/целунал
ние	сме целували/целунали	бяхме целували/целунали
вие	сте целували/целунали	бяхте целували/целунали
те	са целували/целунали	

	Conditional Mood	**Imperative Mood**	
		Positive	**Negative**
аз	бих целувал/целунал		
ти	би целувал/целунал	целувай/целуни	не целувай
той	би целувал/целунал		
ние	бихме целували/целунали		
вие	бихте целували/целунали	целувайте/целунете	не целувайте
те	биха целували/целунали		

Past Passive Participles

M	**F**	**N**	**Pl**
целуван/ целунат	целувана/целуната	целувано/целунато	целувани/целунати

241) **чакам;** *wait, stop*

	Present	**Past Simple**	**Past Continuous**
аз	чакам	чаках	чаках
ти	чакаш	чака	чакаше
той	чака	чака	чакаше
ние	чакаме	чакахме	чакахме
вие	чакате	чакахте	чакахте
те	чакат	чакаха	чакаха

	Future	**Future in the Past**
	(For negative, replace **ще** with **няма да**)	(For negative, replace **щях/щеше/щяхме/щяхте/щяха** with **нямаше**)
аз	ще чакам	щях да чакам
ти	ще чакаш	щеше да чакаш
той	ще чака	щеше да чака
ние	ще чакаме	щяхме да чакаме
вие	ще чакате	щяхте да чакате
те	ще чакат	щяха да чакат

Past Active Participles

M	**F**	**N**	**Pl**
чакал	чакала	чакало	чакали

	Present Perfect	**Past Perfect**
аз	съм чакал	бях чакал
ти	си чакал	беше чакал
той	е чакал	беше чакал
ние	сме чакали	бяхме чакали
вие	сте чакали	бяхте чакали
те	са чакали	бяха чакали

	Conditional Mood	**Imperative Mood**	
		Positive	**Negative**
аз	бих чакал		
ти	би чакал	чакай	не чакай
той	би чакал		
ние	бихме чакали		
вие	бихте чакали	чакайте	не чакайте
те	биха чакали		

Past Passive Participles

M	**F**	**N**	**Pl**
чакан	чакана	чакано	чакани

242) **чета;** *read, study*

	Present	**Past Simple**	**Past Continuous**
аз	чета	четох	четях
ти	четеш	чете	четеше
той	чете	чете	четеше
ние	четем	четохме	четяхме
вие	четете	четохте	четяхте
те	четат	четоха	четяха

	Future	**Future in the Past**
	(For negative, replace **ще** with **няма да**)	(For negative, replace **щях/щеше/щяхме/щяхте/щяха** with **нямаше**)
аз	ще чета	щях да чета
ти	ще четеш	щеше да четеш
той	ще чете	щеше да чете
ние	ще четем	щяхме да четем
вие	ще четете	щяхте да четете
те	ще четат	щяха да четат

Past Active Participles

M	**F**	**N**	**Pl**
чел	чела	чело	чели

	Present Perfect	**Past Perfect**
аз	съм чел	бях чел
ти	си чел	беше чел
той	е чел	беше чел
ние	сме чели	бяхме чели
вие	сте чели	бяхте чели
те	са чели	бяха чели

	Conditional Mood	**Imperative Mood**	
аз	бих чел	**Positive**	**Negative**
ти	би чел	чети	не чети
той	би чел		
ние	бихме чели		
вие	бихте чели	четете	не четете
те	биха чели		

Past Passive Participles

M	**F**	**N**	**Pl**
четен	четена	четено	четени

243) **чистя;** *clean, cleanse, dust*

	Present	**Past Simple**	**Past Continuous**
аз	чистя	чистих	чистех
ти	чистиш	чисти	чистеше
той	чисти	чисти	чистеше
ние	чистим	чистихме	чистехме
вие	чистите	чистихте	чистехте
те	чистят	чистиха	чистеха

	Future	**Future in the Past**
	(For negative, replace **ще** with **няма да**)	(For negative, replace **щях/щеше/щяхме/щяхте/щяха** with **нямаше**)
аз	ще чистя	щях да чистя
ти	ще чистиш	щеше да чистиш
той	ще чисти	щеше да чисти
ние	ще чистим	щяхме да чистим
вие	ще чистите	щяхте да чистите
те	ще чистят	щяха да чистят

Past Active Participles

M	**F**	**N**	**Pl**
чистил	чистила	чистило	чистили

	Present Perfect	**Past Perfect**
аз	съм чистил	бях чистил
ти	си чистил	беше чистил
той	е чистил	беше чистил
ние	сме чистили	бяхме чистили
вие	сте чистили	бяхте чистили
те	са чистили	бяха чистили

	Conditional Mood	**Imperative Mood**	
аз	бих чистил	**Positive**	**Negative**
ти	би чистил	чисти	не чисти
той	би чистил		
ние	бихме чистили		
вие	бихте чистили	чистете	не чистете
те	биха чистили		

Past Passive Participles

M	**F**	**N**	**Pl**
чистен	чистена	чистено	чистени

244) **чувам/чуя;** *hear, listen*

	Present	**Past Simple**	**Past Continuous**
аз	чувам	чух	чувах
ти	чуваш	чу	чуваше
той	чува	чу	чуваше
ние	чуваме	чухме	чувахме
вие	чувате	чухте	чувахте
те	чуват	чуха	чуваха

	Future	**Future in the Past**
	(For negative, replace **ще** with **няма да**)	(For negative, replace **щях/щеше/щяхме/щяхте/щяха** with **нямаше**)
аз	ще чувам/чуя	щях да чувам/чуя
ти	ще чуваш/чуеш	щеше да чуваш/чуеш
той	ще чува/чуе	щеше да чува/чуе
ние	ще чуваме/чуем	щяхме да чуваме/чуем
вие	ще чувате/чуете	щяхте да чувате/чуете
те	ще чуват/чут	щяха да чуват/чут

Past Active Participles

M	**F**	**N**	**Pl**
чувал/чул	чувала/чула	чувало/чуло	чували/чули

	Present Perfect	**Past Perfect**
аз	съм чувал/чул	бях чувал/чул
ти	си чувал/чул	беше чувал/чул
той	е чувал/чул	беше чувал/чул
ние	сме чували/чули	бяхме чували/чули
вие	сте чували/чули	бяхте чували/чули
те	са чували/чули	бяха чували/чули

	Conditional Mood	**Imperative Mood**	
аз	бих чувал/чул	**Positive**	**Negative**
ти	би чувал/чул	чувай/чуй	не чувай
той	би чувал/чул		
ние	бихме чували/чули		
вие	бихте чували/чули	чувайте/чуйте	не чувайте
те	биха чували/чули		

Past Passive Participles

M	**F**	**N**	**Pl**
чут	чута	чуто	чути

245) **чупя/счупя;** *break, crack, fracture*

	Present	**Past Simple**	**Past Continuous**
аз	чупя	счупих	чупех
ти	чупиш	счупи	чупеше
той	чупи	счупи	чупеше
ние	чупим	счупихме	чупехме
вие	чупите	счупихте	чупехте
те	чупят	счупиха	чупеха

	Future	**Future in the Past**
	(For negative, replace **ще** with **няма да**)	(For negative, replace **щях/щеше/щяхме/щяхте/щяха** with **нямаше**)
аз	ще чупя/счупя	щях да чупя/счупя
ти	ще чупиш/счупиш	щеше да чупиш/счупиш
той	ще чупи/счупи	щеше да чупи/счупи
ние	ще чупим/счупим	щяхме да чупим/счупим
вие	ще чупите/счупите	щяхте да чупите/счупите
те	ще чупят/счупят	щяха да чупят/счупят

Past Active Participles

M	**F**	**N**	**Pl**
чупил/счупил	чупила/счупила	чупило/счупило	чупили/счупили

	Present Perfect	**Past Perfect**
аз	съм чупил/счупил	бях чупил/счупил
ти	си чупил/счупил	беше чупил/счупил
той	е чупил/счупил	беше чупил/счупил
ние	сме чупили/счупили	бяхме чупили/счупили
вие	сте чупили/счупили	бяхте чупили/счупили
те	са чупили/счупили	бяха чупили/счупили

	Conditional Mood	**Imperative Mood**	
аз	бих чупил/счупил	**Positive**	**Negative**
ти	би чупил/счупил	чупи/счупи	не чупи
той	би чупил/счупил		
ние	бихме чупили/счупили		
вие	бихте чупили/счупили	чупете/счупете	не чупете
те	биха чупили/счупили		

Past Passive Participles

M	**F**	**N**	**Pl**
чупен/счупен	чупена/счупена	чупено/счупено	чупени/счупени

246) **шегувам се;** *joke, tease, mock*

	Present	**Past Simple**	**Past Continuous**
аз	се шегувам	се шегувах	се шегувах
ти	се шегуваш	се шегува	се шегуваше
той	се шегува	се шегува	се шегуваше
ние	се шегуваме	се шегувахме	се шегувахме
вие	се шегувате	се шегувахте	се шегувахте
те	се шегуват	се шегуваха	се шегуваха

	Future	**Future in the Past**
	(For negative, replace **ще** with **няма да**)	(For negative, replace **щях/щеше/щяхме/щяхте/щяха** with **нямаше**)
аз	ще се шегувам	щях да се шегувам
ти	ще се шегуваш	щеше да се шегуваш
той	ще се шегува	щеше да се шегува
ние	ще се шегуваме	щяхме да се шегуваме
вие	ще се шегувате	щяхте да се шегувате
те	ще се шегуват	щяха да се шегуват

Past Active Participles

M	**F**	**N**	**Pl**
шегувал	шегувала	шегувало	шегували

	Present Perfect	**Past Perfect**
аз	съм се шегувал	бях се шегувал
ти	си се шегувал	беше се шегувал
той	се е шегувал	беше се шегувал
ние	сме се шегували	бяхме се шегували
вие	сте се шегували	бяхте се шегували
те	са се шегували	бяха се шегували

	Conditional Mood	**Imperative Mood**	
аз	бих се шегувал	**Positive**	**Negative**
ти	би се шегувал	шегувай се	не се шегувай
той	би се шегувал		
ние	бихме се шегували		
вие	бихте се шегували	шегувайте се	не се шегувайте
те	биха се шегували		

Past Passive Participles

M	**F**	**N**	**Pl**
N/A	N/A	N/A	N/A

247) **шия;** *sew, stitch*

	Present	Past Simple	Past Continuous
аз	шия	ших	шиех
ти	шиеш	ши	шиеше
той	шие	ши	шиеше
ние	шием	шихме	шиехме
вие	шиете	шихте	шиехте
те	шият	шиха	шиеха

	Future	Future in the Past
	(For negative, replace **ще** with **няма да**)	(For negative, replace **щях/щеше/щяхме/щяхте/щяха** with **нямаше**)
аз	ще шия	щях да шия
ти	ще шиеш	щеше да шиеш
той	ще шие	щеше да шие
ние	ще шием	щяхме да шием
вие	ще шиете	щяхте да шиете
те	ще шият	щяха да шият

Past Active Participles

M	F	N	Pl
шил	шила	шило	шили

	Present Perfect	Past Perfect
аз	съм шил	бях шил
ти	си шил	беше шил
той	е шил	беше шил
ние	сме шили	бяхме шили
вие	сте шили	бяхте шили
те	са шили	бяха шили

	Conditional Mood	Imperative Mood	
аз	бих шил	**Positive**	**Negative**
ти	би шил	ший	не ший
той	би шил		
ние	бихме шили		
вие	бихте шили	шийте	не шийте
те	биха шили		

Past Passive Participles

M	F	N	Pl
шит	шита	шито	шити

248) **ядосвам/ядосам;** *make angry, annoy* **ядосвам/ядосам се;** *be angry*

	Present	Past Simple	Past Continuous
аз	ядосвам	ядосах	ядосвах
ти	ядосваш	ядоса	ядосваше
той	ядосва	ядоса	ядосваше
ние	ядосваме	ядосахме	ядосвахме
вие	ядосвате	ядосахте	ядосвахте
те	ядосват	ядосаха	ядосваха

	Future	Future in the Past
	(For negative, replace **ще** with **няма да**)	(For negative, replace **щях/щеше/щяхме/щяхте/щяха** with **нямаше**)
аз	ще ядосвам/ядосам	щях да ядосвам/ядосам
ти	ще ядосваш/ядосаш	щеше да ядосваш/ядосаш
той	ще ядосва/ядоса	щеше да ядосва/ядоса
ние	ще ядосваме/ядосаме	щяхме да ядосваме/ядосаме
вие	ще ядосвате/ядосате	щяхте да ядосвате/ядосате
те	ще ядосват/ядосат	щяха да ядосват/ядосат

Past Active Participles

M	F	N	Pl
ядосвал/ядосал	ядосвала/ядосала	ядосвало/ядосало	ядосвали/ядосали

	Present Perfect	Past Perfect
аз	съм ядосвал/ядосал	бях ядосвал/ядосал
ти	си ядосвал/ядосал	беше ядосвал/ядосал
той	е ядосвал/ядосал	беше ядосвал/ядосал
ние	сме ядосвали/ядосали	бяхме ядосвали/ядосали
вие	сте ядосвали/ядосали	бяхте ядосвали/ядосали
те	са ядосвали/ядосали	бяха ядосвали/ядосали

	Conditional Mood	Imperative Mood	
аз	бих ядосвал/ядосал	**Positive**	**Negative**
ти	би ядосвал/ядосал	ядосвай/ядосай	не ядосвай
той	би ядосвал/ядосал		
ние	бихме ядосвали/ядосали		
вие	бихте ядосвали/ядосали	ядосвайте/ядосайте	не ядосвайте
те	биха ядосвали/ядосали		

Past Passive Participles

M	F	N	Pl
ядосван/ядосан	ядосвана/ядосана	ядосвано/ядосано	ядосвани/ядосани

249) **яздя;** *ride*

	Present	**Past Simple**	**Past Continuous**
аз	яздя	яздих	яздех
ти	яздиш	язди	яздеше
той	язди	язди	яздеше
ние	яздим	яздихме	яздехме
вие	яздите	яздихте	яздехте
те	яздят	яздиха	яздеха

	Future	**Future in the Past**
	(For negative, replace **ще** with **няма да**)	(For negative, replace **щях/щеше/щяхме/щяхте/щяха** with **нямаше**)
аз	ще яздя	щях да яздя
ти	ще яздиш	щеше да яздиш
той	ще язди	щеше да язди
ние	ще яздим	щяхме да яздим
вие	ще яздите	щяхте да яздите
те	ще яздят	щяха да яздят

Past Active Participles

M	**F**	**N**	**Pl**
яздил	яздила	яздило	яздили

	Present Perfect	**Past Perfect**
аз	съм яздил	бях яздил
ти	си яздил	беше яздил
той	е яздил	беше яздил
ние	сме яздили	бяхме яздили
вие	сте яздили	бяхте яздили
те	са яздили	бяха яздили

	Conditional Mood	**Imperative Mood**	
аз	бих яздил	**Positive**	**Negative**
ти	би яздил	язди	не язди
той	би яздил		
ние	бихме яздили		
вие	бихте яздили	яздете	не яздете
те	биха яздили		

Past Passive Participles

M	**F**	**N**	**Pl**
язден	яздена	яздено	яздени

250) **ям;** *eat, consume*

	Present	Past Simple	Past Continuous
аз	ям	ядох	ядях
ти	ядеш	яде	ядеше
той	яде	яде	ядеше
ние	ядем	ядохме	ядяхме
вие	ядете	ядохте	ядяхте
те	ядат	ядоха	ядяха

	Future	Future in the Past
	(For negative, replace **ще** with **няма да**)	(For negative, replace **щях/щеше/щяхме/щяхте/щяха** with **нямаше**)
аз	ще ям	щях да ям
ти	ще ядеш	щеше да ядеш
той	ще яде	щеше да яде
ние	ще ядем	щяхме да ядем
вие	ще ядете	щяхте да ядете
те	ще ядат	щяха да ядат

Past Active Participles

M	F	N	Pl
ял	яла	яло	яли

	Present Perfect	Past Perfect
аз	съм ял	бях ял
ти	си ял	беше ял
той	е ял	беше ял
ние	сме яли	бяхме яли
вие	сте яли	бяхте яли
те	са яли	

	Conditional Mood	Imperative Mood	
аз	бих ял	**Positive**	**Negative**
ти	би ял	яж	не яж
той	би ял		
ние	бихме яли		
вие	бихте яли	яжте	не яжте
те	биха яли		

Past Passive Participles

M	F	N	Pl
яден	ядена	ядено	ядени

Index

Bulgarian Verbs — Index

Index of 500 Bulgarian Verbs

This index presents 500 less frequently used Bulgarian verbs that have the same conjugation pattern as the verbs in the book. The number next to the verb provides a reference to a conjugated verb which has the same paradigm. If the verb has a reflexive form with a different meaning, the reflexive particle **се** (in parentheses) follows the verb. The English translation is given on the right. If the verb has more than one meaning, non-synonymous meanings are separated by semicolons.

записвам/запиша 161	write down; record; enroll

The reflexive meaning (if any) is given last after a semicolon.

веселя (се) **11**	cheer, amuse; have a good time

* Forms past participle only for feminine.

** Past passive participle for both imperfective and perfective aspect ends in –н (завладяван/завладян, обосноваван/обоснован, основаван/основан, преживяван/преживян, преодоляван/преодолян).

*** No past passive particle.

Appendix

А

1	атакувам	attack

Б

2	балансирам	balance, equalize
3	безпокоя (се)	bother, disturb; worry, be concern
4	благодаря	thank, express gratitude
5	блестя	shine
6	боледувам	be ill, suffer
7	боря се	fight, battle
8	бръсна се	shave
9	бързам	rush, hurry
10	бягам	run, jog

В

11	варя	boil
12	вдигам/вдигна	lift, pick up, raise
13	вдишвам/вдишам	breath in, inhale
14	вечерям	dine, have dinner
15	вземам/взема	take, get, pick up
16	виждам/видя	see, observe, notice
17	викам/викна	call; shout, yell, scream
18	включвам/включа	include; turn on, plug in
19	влагам/вложа	put in, deposit, invest
20	влизам/вляза	enter, come in
21	влияя/повлияя	influence
22	влюбвам се/влюбя се	fall in love
23	внасям/внеса	carry in; import; deposit
24	воювам	be at war, fight
25	връщам/върна (се)	return, give back; go back, go home
26	въвеждам/въведа	bring into; introduce; initiate
27	възразявам/възразя	retort, object
28	вървя	walk, march, hike
29	вярвам/повярвам	trust, believe

Г

30	гледам	watch, look at, observe
31	глезя (се)	spoil, overindulge; behave badly
32	глобявам/глобя	fine, impose a fine
33	говоря	talk, speak
34	гордея се	be proud, take pride
35	горя	burn, burn up, be on fire
36	готвя	cook
37	греша/сгреша	make a mistake, be wrong
38	губя/изгубя	lose, drop, de defeated

Д

39	давам/дам	give, provide, offer
40	давя /удавя	drown, sink
41	движа (се)	move, set in motion; go, move
42	добавям/добавя	add, append, insert
43	довеждам/доведа	bring, take
44	доверявам/доверя (се)	confide, disclose; trust, believe
45	договарям/договоря	clear up, settle, resolve
46	донасям/донеса	bring, carry, take
47	дръпвам/дръпна	pull, draw, drag
48	държа (се)	hold, catch, keep; value; insist; behave

Ж

49	желая/пожелая	desire, wish
50	женя/оженя (се)	marry, wed; get married
51	жертвам	sacrifice, give up, surrender
52	живея	live, reside

З

53	забавлявам (се)	amuse, entertain; enjoy, have fun
54	забавям/забавя	delay, be delayed
55	забелязвам/забележа	notice, detect, spot
56	заблуждавам/заблудя	mislead, misinform; become disoriented

57	забогатявам/забогатея	grow rich, enrich, acquire wealth
58	забравям/забравя	forget, disregard
59	забранявам/забраня	ban, forbid, prohibit
60	завивам/завия	turn, take a turn, bend; cover
61	завися	depend
62	загивам/загина	perish, die
63	задушавам/задуша (се)	stew; stifle; suffocate
64	закусвам/закуся	have breakfast
65	закъснявам/закъснея	be late, be delayed, be overdue
66	заминавам/замина	depart, leave
67	запалвам/запаля (се)	light, fire up; kindle, inspire
68	запознавам/запозная	introduce, meet
69	запомням/запомня	remember, memorize, keep in mind
70	започвам/започна	begin, start, commence
71	заспивам/заспя	go to sleep, fall asleep
72	зная	know

И

73	играя	play, perform, participate
74	идвам/дойда	come, arrive
75	избирам/избера	choose, select
76	извинявам се/извиня се	excuse, apologize
77	изглеждам	look, appear, seem
78	излизам/изляза	go out, exit, leave
79	изненадвам/изненадам	surprise, shock, astonish
80	изобретявам/изобретя	invent, discover, create
81	използвам	use, employ, utilize
82	изпращам/изпратя	send, mail; accompany
83	изпълнявам/изпълня	execute, carry out, perform
84	изчезвам/изчезна	vanish, disappear
85	имам	have, possess, contain
86	интересувам се	to be interested
87	искам	want, desire, like

К

88	казвам/кажа	say, state, declare, tell
89	каня/поканя	invite
90	карам (се)	drive; quarrel, argue
91	качвам/кача (се)	carry up, take up; go up, climb; get on
92	кашлям	cough
93	колебая се	hesitate
94	крада	steal, pinch, rob
95	купувам/купя	buy, purchase
96	къпя (се)	bath, give a bath; take a shower/bath

Л

97	лежа	lie, recline, lie down
98	летя	fly
99	ловя	catch, seize
100	лъжа	lie, tell a lie
101	лягам/легна (си)	lie down; go to bed

М

102	меря	measure; try on
103	мечтая	dream, daydream
104	минавам/мина	pass, pass by, stop by
105	мириша	smell
106	мисля	think, reflect, contemplate
107	мия	wash, mop
108	мога	can, may, be able to
109	моля/помоля	ask, beg, request
110	мълча	be silent, keep silence, remain silent

Н

111	наближавам/наближа	approach, come close to
112	награждавам/наградя	reword, award
113	надявам се	hope, expect, trust
114	намалявам/намаля	decrease, reduce

115	намирам/намеря	find, discover; locate; think, consider
116	напомням/напомня	remind; resemble
117	нарушавам/наруша	break, violate; disturb
118	настоявам/настоя	insist, persist, persevere
119	научавам/науча	learn, find out, discover
120	нося	carry; wear
121	нуждая се	need, require
122	нямам	have not

О

123	обаждам се/обадя се	call, answer (a phone)
124	обещавам/обещая	promise
125	обичам	love
126	облекчавам/облекча	relieve
127	обличам/облека	dress, put on
128	обувам/обуя	put on (shoes, socks)
129	обядвам	have lunch
130	обяснявам/обясня	explain, describe
131	опитвам/опитам	try; taste
132	оплаквам се/оплача се	complain, grumble
133	оставам/остана	remain, stay
134	оставям/оставя	leave; abandon
135	осъждам/осъдя	convict, blame
136	осъзнавам/осъзная	realize, become aware
137	отварям/отворя	open
138	отговарям/отговоря	answer, reply; be responsible (only imperf)
139	отделям/отделя	separate; put aside
140	отивам/отида	go to, approach
141	отключвам/отключа	unlock
142	откривам/открия	discover; find out
143	отричам/отрека	refuse, decline, reject
144	отрязвам/отрежа	cut off, cut away, slice
145	отчайвам се/отчаям се	discourage, dispirit
146	оцелявам/оцелея	survive

	П	
147	падам/падна	fall, drop; reduce, decrease
148	пазарувам	go shopping
149	пазя	guard, protect, keep
150	пека	roast, bake
151	пера	wash, launder
152	печеля	earn, gain; win
153	пея	sing
154	питам/попитам	ask, inquire
155	пиша	write
156	пия	drink, drink up
157	плача	weep, cry
158	плащам/платя	pay, compensate, reimburse
159	плувам	swim
160	повтарям/повторя	repeat; recur
161	подписвам/подпиша	sign
162	подстригвам/подстрижа (се)	cut someone's hair; have a haircut
163	позволявам/позволя (си)	allow, let; dare
164	познавам/позная	know, be acquainted with
165	получавам/получа	receive, obtain; accept
166	помагам/помогна	help, assist, aid
167	помня/запомня	remember, memorize
168	поръчвам/поръчам	order, place an order; ask, tell
169	посещавам/посетя	visit, pay a visit; attend
170	потвърждавам/потвърдя	confirm, verify
171	почивам/почина	rest, relax; pass away (only perf.)
172	правя/направя	make, do
173	превеждам/преведа	translate, interpret
174	преглеждам/прегледам	look through; examine, check, inspect
175	предлагам/предложа	offer, propose, suggest
176	предпочитам/предпочета	prefer
177	представям/представя (си)	present, introduce; produce; imagine
178	прекарвам/прекарам	carry, transport; pass, drive; spend (time)
179	премествам/преместя	move, shift

180	пресичам/пресека	cut, cut off; cross, go across
181	преценявам/преценя	appraise, assess, estimate, judge
182	приготвям/приготвя (се)	prepare; cook; get ready
183	приемам/приема	accept, admit, acknowledge
184	пристигам/пристигна	arrive
185	притеснявам/притесня (се)	embarrass, make uneasy; rush; worry
186	проверявам/проверя	check, verify
187	продавам/продам	sell, vend
188	продължавам/продължа	continue, carry on; extend
189	пускам/пусна	release; drop
190	пуша	smoke
191	пътувам	travel, journey

Р

192	работя	work; operate
193	раждам/родя (се)	give birth; be born
194	разбирам/разбера (се)	understand; get along with; resolve
195	разболявам се/разболея се	get sick
196	развеждам/разведа (се)	guide, give a tour; get a divorce
197	разливам/разлея	spill, pour out, leak
198	разхождам/разходя (се)	take for a walk; walk, have a walk
199	ранявам/раня	hurt, injure
200	раста/порасна	grow up
201	решавам/реша	decide

С

202	свиря	play music
203	свързвам/свържа	bind, connect, relate, link, associate
204	свършвам/свърша	finish, terminate
205	слагам/сложа	put, place, set, position
206	следвам	follow, come after; study at a university
207	слушам	listen, pay attention
208	сменям/сменя	change, transform, convert
209	смея (се)	dare; laugh

210	спестявам/спестя	save, economize
211	спирам/спра	stop, discontinue
212	спомням си/спомня си	remember, recall
213	справям се/справя се	manage, handle, cope
214	спя	sleep
215	срещам/срещна	meet, get together, encounter
216	ставам/стана	get up, wake up; become; happen
217	стигам/стигна	reach, arrive at, get to
218	стоя	stay, wait; reside
219	събуждам/събудя (се)	wake, awaken, arouse; wake up, get up
220	съжалявам/съжаля	feel sorry, regret
221	съм	to be
222	съобщавам/съобщя	announce, declare
223	сядам/седна	sit, take a seat

Т

224	тръгвам/тръгна	leave, depart
225	търся	look for, search, seek

У

226	убивам/убия	kill, murder
227	увеличавам/увелича	increase, enlarge, raise
228	умирам/умра	die, pass away
229	употребявам/употребя	use, employ
230	уреждам/уредя	arrange, settle
231	усмихвам се/усмихна се	smile
232	успокоявам/успокоя	calm down, relax
233	успявам/успея	succeed, achieve, accomplish
234	уча	study, learn

Х

235	харесвам/харесам	like, love, adore
236	хващам/хвана	catch, grab, take
237	хвърлям/хвърля	throw, toss
238	ходя	go, walk, hike
239	храня (се)	feed, nurse; eat, consume, have meals

Ц

240	целувам/целуна	kiss

Ч

241	чакам	wait, stop
242	чета	read, study
243	чистя	clean, cleanse, dust
244	чувам/чуя	hear, listen
245	чупя/счупя	break, crack, fracture

Ш

246	шегувам се	joke, tease, mock
247	шия	sew, stitch

Я

248	ядосвам/ядосам (се)	make angry, annoy; be angry
249	яздя	ride
250	ям	eat, consume